The Asia–Europe Meeting

Focusing on economic, developmental, political and cultural issues in Asia–Europe relations, this book offers a critical assessment of the Asia–Europe Meeting (ASEM) process since its inception in 1996. ASEM now brings together all twenty-seven European Union (EU) members, the European Commission, sixteen Asian states and the ASEAN Secretariat. The underlying theme of the book is that the ASEM should be analyzed as an instance of international dialogue – in this case, dialogue between two groups of states from two different regions – rather than as a manifestation of two regions acting jointly to perform specific functions at an 'interregional' level. The conclusion is that with the exception of the discussion on the fight against international terrorism and the cultural dialogue, the Asia–Europe dialogue rarely meets the ideal conditions for international dialogue. The way forward proposed by this book in the conclusion involves a new approach combining the European practices of multilevel governance, variable geometry and several speeds.

Using a unique and an innovative theoretical framework synthesizing the work of Tzvetan Todorov and Jürgen Habermas and supported by extensive empirical research, this book will be of huge interest to students and scholars of Asian and European politics as well as comparative politics, international relations, EU external relations and EU–Asia relations.

Alfredo C. Robles, Jr. is Professor of International Studies at De La Salle University-Manila. The Philippines.

Routledge contemporary Asia series

The Asia–Europe Meeting

The theory and practice of interregionalism

Alfredo C. Robles, Jr.

Routledge
Taylor & Francis Group

LONDON AND NEW YORK

First published 2008
by Routledge
2 Park Square, Milton Park, Abingdon, Oxon OX14 4RN

Simultaneously published in the USA and Canada
by Routledge
711 Third Avenue, New York, NY 10017

Routledge is an imprint of the Taylor & Francis Group, an informa business

First issued in paperback 2012

© 2008 Alfredo C. Robles, Jr.

Typeset in Times by Wearset Ltd, Boldon, Tyne and Wear

British Library Cataloguing in Publication Data
A catalogue record for this book is available from the British Library

Library of Congress Cataloging in Publication Data
A catalog record for this book has been requested

ISBN13: 978-0-415-45223-6 (hbk)
ISBN13: 978-0-415-54091-9 (pbk)
ISBN13: 978-0-203-93326-8 (ebk)

Contents

Acknowledgments

It is my pleasure to acknowledge the many debts that I accumulated, in Asia and in Europe, in the course of the preparation of this book.

The Bancaja International Center for Peace and Development of the University of Castellon, Spain, and the University Institute for European Studies (IUEE) of the Autonomous University of Barcelona invited me to make presentations on ASEM in Spring 2001 that helped me to organize my thoughts at a time when I was still working on my book on ASEAN–EU relations.

Four grants from De La Salle University between 1999 and 2005 enabled me to carry out much of the research for Chapters 1 to 4. Comments on Chapter 1 from Dr. Benjamin Tolosa, Jr., of Ateneo de Manila University and on Chapter 2 from Gareth Richards encouraged me to persevere in my approach.

Dr. Sebastian Bersick of the European Institute of Asian Studies in Brussels, Dr. Julie Gilson of the University of Birmingham, Dr. Paul Lim of the Universiti Sains Malaysia and Professor Jürgen Rüland of the University of Freiburg provided me with copies of their writings or assisted me in obtaining materials that were difficult to obtain in the Philippines.

I am grateful to Maria Lourdes Rada, Charmaine Misalucha and Maria Thaemar Tana for the research assistance that they provided me at different times.

I was able to complete the manuscript while I was a visiting professor from October to December 2005 at the Department of International and Business Law of the International Graduate School of Social Sciences (IGSSS), Yokohama National University, Japan. Without access to the University's facilities, I would not have been able to finish my manuscript as rapidly as I did.

Comments from two anonymous reviewers provided guidance in the revision of the manuscript.

Last but not least, I wish to express my appreciation to Stephanie Rogers and to the staff of Routledge for their assistance in the preparation of the manuscript.

The usual caveats apply.

Abbreviations

ADB	Asian Development Bank
AEBF	Asia–Europe Business Forum
AECF	Asia–Europe Cooperation Framework
AEPF	Asia–Europe People's Forum
AEVG	Asia–Europe Vision Group
AFTA	ASEAN Free Trade Area
APEC	Asia–Pacific Economic Cooperation
ARF	ASEAN Regional Forum
ASEAN	Association of Southeast Asian Nations
ASEF	Asia–Europe Foundation
ASEM	Asia–Europe Meeting
ATF	ASEM Trust Fund
CAEC	Council for Asia–Europe Cooperation
CFSP	Common Foreign and Security Policy
EC	European Community
ECIP	European Community Investment Partners
EIB	European Investment Bank
EMM	ASEM Economic Ministers' Meeting
EP	European Parliament
EPC	European Political Cooperation
EPG	ASEAN–EU Eminent Persons Group
ESDP	European Security and Defence Policy
ETUC	European Trade Union Confederation
EU	European Union
FDI	Foreign Direct Investment
FIDH	Fédération Internationale des Ligues des Droits de l'Homme
FinMM	ASEM Finance Ministers' Meeting
FMM	ASEM Foreign Ministers' Meeting
FTA	Free Trade Area
GATS	WTO General Agreement on Trade in Services
GATT	General Agreement on Tariffs and Trade
GSP	Generalized System of Preferences
ICCPR	International Covenant on Civil and Political Rights

ICESCR	International Covenant on Economic, Social and Cultural Rights
ICFTU	International Confederation of Free Trade Unions
IEG	ASEM Investment Experts' Group
ILO	International Labour Organization
IPAP	ASEM Investment Promotion Action Plan
ITA	WTO Information Technology Agreement
JHTA	Japan Harbor Transportation Association
KEDO	Korean Peninsula Energy Development Organization
M & A	Mergers and Acquisitions
MEM	Most Effective Measures to Attract Foreign Direct Investment
MIA	Multilateral Agreement on Investment
NHMFC	National Home Mortgage Finance Corporation (The Philippines)
ODA	Official Development Assistance
OECD	Organisation for Economic Cooperation and Development
OSCE	Organization for Security and Cooperation in Europe
PAM/PDAM	Local government-owned water utilities (Indonesia)
RRD	Japan–EU Regulatory Reform Dialogue
SME	Small and medium enterprises
SOMTI	ASEM Senior Officials' Meeting on Trade and Investment
SPS	WTO Agreement on Sanitary and Phytosanitary Measures
TBR	EU Trade Barriers Regulation
TFAP	ASEM Trade Facilitation Action Plan
TRIMS	WTO Agreement on Trade-related Investment Measures
TRIPS	WTO Agreement on Trade-related Intellectual Property Rights
VER	Voluntary Export Restraints
WTO	World Trade Organization

Introduction

Contemporary relations between Asia and Europe deserve special attention, for they appear to have great potential for economic, political and cultural conflict. In economic terms, there is a perception in Asia that the European Union (EU) is tempted to embrace protectionism. In Europe, Asia is perceived not just as a rising competitor but in some senses as an unfair competitor. In political terms, many Europeans consider that the end of the Cold War heralded the triumph of democracy and capitalism and are less willing to tolerate authoritarian regimes. They now insist on the need to respect human rights, to promote democratization and to guarantee the rule of law. In contrast, some Asian countries have emerged as champions of the notion of "Asian" values in opposition to "Western" values. Frequently, these economic and political differences are attributed to inherent cultural differences. Thus, many Asians are tempted to attribute European economic problems to "Western" individualism. Conversely, the subordination of the individual to the collectivity tends to be perceived in Europe as the price to pay for Asian economic success.

A major step toward addressing these sources of conflict on a collective basis appeared to have been taken in 1996 when ten Asian countries [the seven members of the Association of Southeast Asian Nations (ASEAN), together with China, Japan and South Korea] met at Bangkok with the fifteen member states of the EU and the European Commission. The Asia–Europe Meeting (ASEM) had been proposed by the Prime Minister of Singapore, Goh Chok Tong, during a visit to Europe in 1994 and it received the support of the German Government, which had adopted its Asia Strategy in 1993, and the EU, which had also published a "New Asia Strategy" in 1994 (Goh Chok Tong 1993–94; European Commission COM (1994) 314; Bersick 1998; Pareira 2003). ASEM participants declared that they had forged a "new comprehensive Asia–Europe Partnership for Greater Growth," which would be implemented through "strengthened dialogue on an equal basis ... through the sharing of perceptions on a wide range of issues" (ASEM 1 1996: paras 3, 4). In September 2006, the sixth summit in Helsinki celebrated ASEM's tenth year, declaring ASEM to be "the prime point of convergence between Europe and Asia," supposedly enabling the two to "reap the benefits of globalization" and to "tackle the challenges of interdependence" (ASEM 6 2006b: paras 1, 2). Prior to the summit, the European Commission's tone had been even more triumphalist, for it claimed that ASEM had allowed states to "develop and test new ideas for future policy-making" (European Commission External Relations 2006: 19).

It is true that by 2006, it seemed that the first step had been taken toward meeting the demand of civil society groups for a social dimension in ASEM. Shortly before ASEM 6, ASEM ministers of Labor and Employment meeting in Germany had endorsed the proposal of regular dialogue and cooperation on employment and social policy, although the specific topics of mutual interest were as yet unidentified (Labour and Employment Ministers' Conference 2006: para. 16). By the sixth summit, the controversial issue of enlargement had been largely resolved. ASEM 4 in Hanoi (2004) had admitted thirteen states: the three new ASEAN members (Cambodia, Laos and Myanmar) and the ten new EU members. Myanmar, whose human rights record was justly criticized in Europe, had been an apple of discord between Asia and Europe. For years, the EU had refused to accept Myanmar's presence in ASEM, to which ASEAN countered that if its new members were not admitted, ASEAN would oppose the admission of new EU members. Disagreement over Myanmar had nearly provoked the cancellation of two summits (ASEM 2 in London, 1998 and ASEM 5 in Hanoi, 2004) and led to the cancellation of economic and finance ministers' meetings in 2004 and 2005. A compromise that downgraded the level of Myanmar's participation in the summit saved ASEM 5. In contrast, the decision of ASEM 6 to admit India, Pakistan, Mongolia and the ASEAN Secretariat was much less controversial, in spite of fears expressed by ASEAN in the past that the discussion of the India–Pakistani conflict in ASEM might weaken the unity of the Asian side.

While ASEM's enlargement may have given cause for satisfaction, it is difficult to avoid the impression that after six summits and innumerable meetings of economic, finance and foreign ministers, senior officials and investment experts, all is not well with ASEM. The sixth Summit's recommendations that ASEM focus on "issues within which ASEM can add value," "identify key priority clusters" and "implement action-oriented initiatives" (ASEM 6 2006b: paras 1, 2) echoed, almost word-for-word, similar recommendations made by ASEM foreign ministers in 2002, 2004 and 2005 and ASEM economics ministers in 2003 (FMM 5 2002; FMM 5 2003: 6; FMM 7 2005; EMM 5 2003: para. 15, Annex I). The areas identified by the summit – strengthening multilateralism and addressing global threats of common concern; globalization, competitiveness and structural changes in the global economy; sustainable development with a focus on the Millennium Development Goals; climate change, the environment and energy; intercultural and interfaith dialogue – are so broad that they inspire little confidence in ASEM's ability to chart out a coherent course for itself. Indeed, in a decade, ASEM had commissioned reports from no less than three groups [the Asia–Europe Vision Group, the ASEM Task Force on Closer Economic Relationship and the Council for Asia–Europe Cooperation (CAEC)], apparently to little effect.

Even more ominous for ASEM's future was the decision announced by the European Commission in October 2006 that it had decided to launch negotiations for free trade areas with ASEAN members and South Korea, all of them ASEM participants. They were identified as priorities because of their market potential, the level of protection against EU export interests and their Free Trade Area (FTA) negotiations with the EU's main competitors, the USA and Japan [European Commission SEC (2006) 1230: 14, 16]. In 1999, the Asia–Europe Vision Group had proposed a free trade area by 2025, but this would have included China and Japan on the Asian side. Apart from the limited geographic scope of the "new generation" of FTAs, the European Commission proposed that they cover not just trade in good in services but also investment, competition, protection of intellectual property rights, government procurement, trade facilitation and technical barriers of trade. All these issues are part of ASEM's Trade Facilitation Action Plan (TFAP) and Investment Promotion Action Plan (IPAP), suggesting that the FTA negotiations would be a mechanism alternative to ASEM for tackling them. The fact that the European Commission refrained from proposing FTA negotiations with China, described as "an opportunity, a challenge and a prospective partner" [European Commission SEC (2006) 1230: 20], strengthens the impression that treating Asia as a region will no longer be the hallmark of the EU approach to these countries. If so, the development of the putative "interregional" relationship that seemed to be embodied in ASEM may no longer remain a priority for Asian participants either.

This sobering prospect makes it imperative to undertake a critical assessment of the theoretical and practical significance of "interregionalism" after a decade of ASEM. In this endeavor, the small but growing body of literature on ASEM will not be of much use, since it has failed to assess properly ASEM's capacity to achieve its aims and to portray accurately the outcomes of ASEM activities. Much of the scholarly literature has confined itself to one or the other of the following tasks. One subset explains the attitudes of Asian and European participants toward dialogue. For instance, Japan's "embrace" of ASEM is ascribed to its desire to participate more actively in an emerging Asian community (Togo Kazuhiko 2004: 159). Germany's aims in ASEM were said to be a dialogue with Asia–Pacific Economic Cooperation (APEC), intensified relations with China and strengthened social and cultural relations with Asia (Bersick 2004d: 11). A second subset of studies speculates on ASEM's potential functions. For the CAEC, Asia–Europe cooperation should strengthen multilateralism; guarantee Asian, European and global energy security; contribute to stopping global warming; and assist in formulating development policies (Kaiser 2004; Wallace and Young Soogil 2004). Some of the claims put forward on behalf of ASEM are rather extravagant. ASEM's functions are alleged to be the prevention of conflict between states within Asia and within Europe, between individual Asian and individual European states and between the Asian and European regions; the prevention of the formation of regional blocks; the prevention of social conflicts within both regions or between Asia and Europe; the construction of multiregional or multilateral relationships in regional form as an alternative to state-centered multilateral relations; and increased and intensified participation of social actors in different fields in international relations (Pareira

2003). If these are truly ASEM's functions, one cannot but wonder if ASEM is doomed to failure. Finally, a third subset of the scholarly literature on ASEM makes unsubstantiated claims about ASEM's achievements. In the mythology of ASEM, projects have been launched that make possible an exchange of capital, resources, research and development and personnel in trade and investment; these are said to benefit primarily small and medium enterprises (SMEs) (Gilson 2002: 76–8, 97; cf. Yeo Lay Hwee 2004: 1).Careful perusal of documents reveals that no such projects have seen the light of day in the ASEM framework.

Many of these studies take for granted that a new level of international relations – the interregional level – is emerging and that at this level, states and regions would be able to perform a range of functions. ASEM's difficulties in defining its agenda, a decade after its inception, should make us more cautious about making such sweeping claims. This book adopts an alternative approach. Underlying it is the idea that ASEM should be analyzed as an instance of international dialogue – in this case, dialogue between two groups of states from two different regions – rather than as a manifestation of two regions acting jointly to perform specific functions at a putative interregional level. Thus, this book takes seriously the ASEM participants' claims that they are engaged in a dialogue. It offers a critical assessment of the ASEM process through an innovative theoretical framework, which is systematically used throughout the work in order to analyze different aspects of ASEM (economic and social development, politics and culture). The theoretical framework is a synthesis of the work of the Franco-Bulgarian semiologist, Tzvetan Todorov, who is unknown to many political scientists and international relations scholars, and of the work of German theorist Jürgen Habermas on communicative action and international relations. Unlike many authors inspired by Habermas, the framework takes into account structural contexts of action in order to determine the capacity and willingness of social actors to engage in dialogue and does so by relying on Habermas's empirical analyses of globalization and the EU. The theory that is rooted in and elaborated from the practice of social actors is then confronted with their practice. In other words, this book seeks to determine the extent to which dialogue among ASEM participants meets the ideal conditions for international dialogue identified by means of the framework.

The first chapter presents a critique of realist, liberal and constructivist conceptions of ASEM at an interregional level, identifies the conditions required for an international dialogue to take place with the help of the work of Todorov and Habermas and examines certain characteristics of ASEM as a forum for interregional dialogue, particularly the question of participation of civil society groups in the process. The other four chapters examine critically the attempts at dialogue undertaken in what are presumed to be Asia–Europe areas of common interest. The different components of ASEM's economic "pillar" are analyzed in three chapters, a focus that is amply justified by the large number of meetings held on economic issues. The second chapter begins by presenting the broad features of the structure of economic relations between Asia and Europe, which influences participants' capacity and willingness to engage in a dialogue. The

chapter then goes on to discuss dialogues that have not taken place: on poverty
alleviation and economic cooperation, as expected by the Asian developing
countries; on an infrastructure fund, as desired by the Asia–Europe Business
Forum (AEBF) and on social issues, as demanded by the Asia–Europe People's
Forum (AEPF). It took an unexpected shock, in the form of the Asian financial
crisis, for a fund to be set up that financed some small-scale projects for a
limited period. The ASEM Trust Fund could have compensated for the lack of
dialogue on poverty alleviation had it not been for the fact that its management
was left to the World Bank. This arrangement introduced a participant into the
Asia–Europe dialogue that pursues an agenda of its own in Asia and is not disposed to engage in dialogue on the substance of this agenda, as an examination
of projects in Indonesia, Malaysia and the Philippines demonstrates. Chapter 3
analyzes the claim that ASEM can provide stimulus to progress in other international organizations, using the debates on the reform of the international financial architecture and on World Trade Organization (WTO) issues as examples.
On the former, it is argued that following pressure from the weaker actors, the
Asian states affected by the Asian financial crisis, it initially appeared that Asia
and Europe had successfully identified an area of common interest, that of the
reform of the international financial architecture, and that after a dialogue, joint
action had been agreed upon through the ASEM Trust Fund. Yet, the small
window of opportunity opened by the Asian financial crisis has been closed
largely due to EU reluctance to engage in dialogue. On WTO issues, it is the
stronger actor, the EU, which insists that such a dialogue is an area of common
interest. In reality, the superficial consensus expressed in ASEM documents
masks genuine disagreement that has so far not been bridged through ASEM due
to two circumstances: the division of the Asian group into developed and developing countries and the EU's unwillingness to make concessions. Chapter 4
stresses that once more it is the EU, as the stronger actor, that urges an ASEM
dialogue on trade facilitation and investment promotion through which it exerts
pressure on Asian states to modify their domestic laws and thus ensure market
access for European firms. This argument is confirmed through a detailed examination of the reports submitted under the TFAP and the IPAP as well as through
an analysis of the Japan–EU regulatory reform dialogue. The latter serves as the
paradigm for EU action, which is backed by the implicit threat of sanctions
under the EU's Trade Barriers Regulation. Chapter 5 analyzes the dialogue
under ASEM's other two pillars, which appear not to have made as much
progress as economic dialogue. As in the economic areas, Asia and Europe have
made great efforts to identify areas of common interest and to engage in dialogue in a broad range of issues. In political dialogue, a distinction is made
between human rights and security issues, the latter being further subdivided
into regional and international security. It is pointed out that the EU is more
interested in Asian security than are the Asians in European security and that the
EU has in two instances been able to play a role in Asia without the need for
ASEM dialogue. In international security issues, ASEM dialogue has made little
progress. It is suggested that international cooperation against terrorism in the

wake of 9/11 may yet be capable of bridging the divide between regional and international security. Human rights issues have attracted less attention within ASEM. The chapter suggests that the experience of the China–EU dialogue on human rights may help us to understand this lack of progress: China is uninterested in dialogue; the EU is torn between the need to promote human rights and the pursuit of its economic interests and non-state actors [human rights non-governmental organizations (NGOs)] are marginalized. The last section of Chapter 5 takes up cultural dialogue that is not pursued as an end in itself within ASEM but as a complement to economic dialogue. Japan–EU cultural relations are suggested as a possible paradigm for dialogue among a larger group of Asian and European participants. The roles of the Asia–Europe Foundation, on the one hand, and leaders' retreats and culture ministers' conferences, on the other, are surveyed. The last chapter proposes ways forward for ASEM, which involve a new approach combining the European practices of multilevel governance, variable geometry and several speeds.

A few words about terminology are in order. In this book, "Europe" and "Europeans" are identified with the EU. Similarly, "Asia" and "Asians" refer to the Asian states that participate in ASEM. They comprised mainly East Asian states until 2004, but there is no implication in the text that they constituted, or should have constituted, anything other than a geographic region. Since 2006, the admission of India, Mongolia and Pakistan makes it abundantly clear that "Asia" in ASEM is not confined to a particular sub-region of Asia. ASEM is understood to be an "interregional" dialogue only to the extent that the participants are geographically situated in two different regions. The participants in ASEM meetings are not called "partners," the term used in official documents, because the term prejudges the existence of collaboration or cooperation within the ASEM framework. The more neutral term "participants" is preferred and should be understood to refer to Asian and European states and the European Commission. The term "participants" excludes non-state actors such as trade unions and NGOs.

1   In search of ASEM

It is easy to see how the Asia–Europe Meeting's (ASEM's) composition and organization can lead participants and observers alike to imagine that a new international level is emerging. One group of participants comprises European Union (EU) members and meets a group of states that has been moving towards closer regional cooperation in the last decade. In the search for theoretical explanations of "interregionalism," scholars have turned to realism, liberalism and constructivism. Yet, these theories suffer from fundamental epistemological weaknesses that undermine their claim to theorize ASEM as an interregional level with specific functions. Instead of presuming the latter's existence, we should start with the participants' own description of ASEM as a dialogue process and inquire into the conditions for successful dialogue. This chapter argues that the work of Tzvetan Todorov and Jürgen Habermas, while not directly addressing the problem of international dialogue, can nevertheless help us to identify the conditions that ASEM should fulfill if it is to be properly considered a dialogue process. After doing this, it will be possible to analyze some general features of ASEM as a forum for "interregional" dialogue.

An interregional level and its functions

Hypothesizing the existence of an interregional level and ascribing functions to it are complementary theoretical endeavors. Some authors simply take for granted that an interregional level exists. For instance, Gilson refers to an "interregional" framework, level, context or structure, "level of interregionalism," "interregionalism *per se*," an "explicitly interregional framework," a "region-to-region" format, a "nascent interregional dialogue" (Gilson 2002: xii, 2, 142, 158, 168, 63–4, 70, 104, 139, 153, 175). No definitions are provided that differentiate these notions from each other. Bersick, like Gilson, fails to define a "level" or an "institution" (e.g. Bersick 2004c: 15, 53, 63). It need hardly be said that the "interregional" character of ASEM cannot be taken for granted. Assuming that Europe is identical to the EU, Asia was not completely represented at the outset. Cambodia, Laos and Myanmar were not admitted until 2004; India, Pakistan and Mongolia were only accepted in 2006 and North Korea is still absent. Moreover, as Gilson realizes, Asia is not yet a fully fledged region, even if it is undergoing a regionalization process. If so, ASEM is a relationship between a "region" and a "region-in-the-making" and could, for this reason, not be fully "interregional."

This difficulty is obviated in Bersick's (1998: 99–105) earlier approach, which differentiated four different levels of cooperation in ASEM. The first level, cooperation between continents, is only an "ideal type" in the Weberian sense, since continents do not exist as social units. In the second, cooperation between subregions, Europe as a part of the European region meets one part of the Asian region. At this level, an institutional asymmetry exists: there is no organized East Asian partner comparable to the EU. At a third level, "higher-order cooperation," the EU as an institution cooperates with individual Asian states. At a fourth level, "lower-order cooperation," individual states cooperate with each other. Noting that ASEM 1 provided the opportunity for Asians and Europeans to hold numerous bilateral meetings, Bersick concluded that "lower order cooperation" predominates in the ASEM process.

A tripartite classification – interregional, biregional and transregional – based on the identity of the actors involved is presented by Andreas Pareira (2003). In the interregional form, the participants are governments and non-governmental organizations (NGOs) in regional formations: ASEAN+3 [seven Association of Southeast Asian Nations (ASEAN) members, China, Japan and South Korea], and the level of interaction is global. In the biregional form, the actors are governments organized in regional formations: ASEAN+3 and the EU, and the level of interaction is regional and biregional. In the transregional form, the actors are NGOs and economic and social actors organized in regional formations; the level of interaction is biregional and interregional.

The debate about the existence of an interregional level might appear to be an academic exercise, were it not for the very ambitious functions ascribed to ASEM. Bersick's interviews revealed that Singapore had official and unofficial motives for proposing the holding of ASEM (Bersick 1998: 50–61). Officially, the economic aims were to strengthen the multilateral trade system by promoting trade and investment liberalization; to strengthen cooperation in infrastructure development; and to promote scientific and technological cooperation, cooperation on the environment and on development issues and human resource development. The official political objectives were to deepen mutual understanding of the Asian and European security situations and to promote UN restructuring and democratization. Singapore's unofficial objectives included stronger European economic engagement in Asia in spite of EU enlargement; balancing US economic influence in Asia; stronger European cooperation in regional security; the development of a cooperation mechanism that could prevent future conflicts between Asia and Europe and sustain mutual interest in less favorable economic conditions; and Asian economic cooperation with China. In Bersick's account, the initial EU motivations were rather vague: to establish "a new partnership ... that (would) contribute to the global development of societies in both regions" (quoted in Bersick 1998: 59). The EU did insist on political dialogue that could lead to a better understanding of each others' values and needs.

The first scholar to link the notion of a new level to its unique functions was Jürgen Rüland, whose work has influenced subsequent scholarly discussions (the following is based on Rüland 1996, 1998b, 2001, 2002, unless otherwise indicated). These functions are as follows:

1 *Balancing and bandwagoning*: ASEM is a response to actual, perceived or anticipated shifts in the power of the three regions that allegedly constitute the triad of the world economy: North America, Europe and East Asia. ASEM is Europe's response to Asia-Pacific Economic Cooperation (APEC), which Europe feared would exclude it from access to Asia–Pacific markets. For Asia, ASEM could balance US power (Bersick 2004c: 58–9). Some believe that Asia–Europe cooperation could prevent or counteract US unilateralist tendencies (Maull and Tanaka 1997: 34, 37–8).

2 *Institution building*: If consolidated, ASEM would give rise to new institutions. It is said to have contributed to the debate on the Organization for Security and Cooperation in Europe (OSCE) in Asia (Gilson 2002: 122), though no evidence of this debate is available.

3, 4 and 5 *Agenda setting, controlling and rationalizing*: These functions arise as a result of the weaknesses of multilateralism. In negotiations that involve nearly 200 states, smaller groups of states, meeting in interregional fora like ASEM, can allegedly help to set the agenda (by introducing new themes) as well as to control it (by suppressing undesirable topics). Negotiations can be rationalized by interregional meetings that reduce the number of negotiating positions and partners and thus act as a sort of clearinghouse. For Yeo Lay Hwee (2003: 156), ASEM is itself a regime or metaregime – an overarching institution where norms and principles are guidelines for key areas of cooperation. Gilson (2002: 130, 101) speculates that ASEM can be a forum for renegotiating norms and can even provide a site of collective resistance to the WTO.

6 *Identity building*: Participation by Asia in ASEM would stimulate identity building (Gilson 2002). In Bersick's (2004c: 26) view, Asia emerged through ASEM 1 as an actor that the EU was willing to recognize as an equal partner. Higgott (2000: 42) believes that support for Asian monetary regionalism could be one ASEM function.

7 *Stabilization*: In Bersick's (2004c: 55–6) recent work, ASEM is defined as a regime addressing "the danger of instability of the international system after the end of bipolarity"; more specifically, ASEM contributes to management of Asia–Europe interdependence, in particular by minimizing relative gains.

8 *Development*: It is assumed – mistakenly, as we shall see – that ASEM can facilitate an "important exchange of capital, resources, Research and Development, ideas and personnel in trade and investment, and the exchange of know-how" (Gilson 2002: 97, 100).

In addition to these functions, it is claimed that ASEM provides a stimulus to relations between individual Asian countries and Europe as a whole. To take the example of Japan, ASEM allegedly provides an additional forum in which it can discuss its interests together with Asian states, and it can establish together with Europe an agenda that does not prioritize US concerns (Gilson 2000; Hook *et al.* 2001: 250–2; Bersick 2004c: 31). The implication is that ASEM's existence enhances the Japan–EU dialogue in some way, whether from the Japanese or the European perspective or the perspective of both. Similar arguments are implicitly presupposed in discussing ASEM's contribution to relations between the EU on the one hand, and China, South Korea, and Southeast Asia, on the other. Exactly how the existence of an additional forum could achieve this end is not explained by these authors. Does the increase in the number of participants improve the quality of dialogue? Or does the increase in the number of issues dealt with render possible an exchange of concessions?

In view of the very broad range of functions imputed to ASEM, it is not surprising that the assessment of ASEM's performance varies significantly. According to Bersick, ASEM has become the broadest cooperation mechanism between Asia and Europe. The politics of interregional relations is stimulating a reorganization of international relations by counteracting the danger of instability (Bersick 2004c: 15, 247 and *passim*). Other evaluations of ASEM are more cautious. Rüland (2002: 3–4) is of the view that ASEM has best performed the balancing and bandwagoning function; its inability to perform the other seven functions is said to be the result of weak institutionalization. Yeo Lay Hwee (2003: 148) doubts that ASEM provided the greater impetus to identity building in Asia than the Asian financial crisis. For Dent (2003: 231), ASEM has not added anything new or significant to the work of multilateral institutions.

These divergent assessments should prompt a critical examination of the contending theoretical explanations of ASEM.

Toward a critique of theories of the interregional level

A brief explanation of the notion of level is in order before we undertake a critique of the way in which realism, liberalism and constructivism have been brought to bear on the analysis of ASEM. The existence of an interregional level cannot be presumed lightly. The disagreement on the number of levels, which has been unresolved since J. David Singer identified two levels (the national and the international) in 1961, reflects an absence of consensus on the rules or criteria for designating a particular level. For constructivists like Onuf (1995), the ontological status of levels is uncertain, for conventions or rules establish the boundaries between fields. In the 1990s, the debate centered around whether the level of analysis problem is one of explanation – what is the relative importance of causal factors at different levels of behavior of a unit of analysis (foreign policy) – or one of ontology – whether a level really exists and whether it can behave. Wendt (1991) takes the first position, and Hollis and Smith (1991) adopt the second. Barry Buzan's (1995: 202–3) proposed synthesis differentiates ontology and epistemology. In terms of ontology, levels are units of analysis organized on a spatial scale, of which at least five exist (system, sub-system or region, unit, bureaucracy and individual). From the point of view of epistemology, however, levels are simply different types or sources of explanation for observed phenomena.

In an earlier work (Robles 2004: 8), I argued that an interregional level may emerge if actors from different regions forge relatively enduring relationships that enable and constrain them, providing opportunities and setting constraints on their actions that are different from opportunities and constraints at other levels. Actors' strategies should be deployed, and the consequences of their actions perceptible, in the regions as defined by the actors and not merely in one country in each region. The existence of an interregional level presupposes the presence of certain material conditions, particularly resources and technology, and is accompanied by the formulation of intersubjective conceptions and ideologies as well as the development of specific interregional institutions. The nature of such a level will be conditioned by structures of production and of international order (defined as the configuration of forces that defines the problem of war and peace) at both global and regional levels (Cox 1987). This structural approach to levels will be attentive to tensions and contradictions within and between levels and within relationships between actors from different regions. While it is to be expected that actors in a relationship often act in ways that perpetuate their respective positions, actors are capable of realizing the constraints and discovering the opportunities inherent in their relationship. Consequently, they can devise strategies that seek to free themselves from these constraints and to exploit the opportunities offered to them in different spheres of the relationship. The degree of success achieved by each actor in a particular sphere of activity will be determined not only by the strategies of the other actor but also by the impact of structural conditions at the global and regional levels.

So far, no one has attempted to determine whether ASEM has established new types of relatively enduring social relations among the participants. Realist, liberal and constructivist approaches have been mobilized to explain ASEM, but these explanations commit one or more of the following errors: they contradict the basic assumptions of the theory; they fail to address fundamental objections to these theories or they fail to provide convincing empirical evidence that supports their theoretical claims.

A realist approach

Yeo Lay Hwee (2003: 14) contends that realism sheds light on the nature of ASEM as a framework for diplomacy. Realism allegedly points to a shift in the relative power position of Asia vis-à-vis Europe, creating the need for a confidence-building multilateral diplomatic forum. ASEM supposedly enables leaders to get to know each other, be educated, break down mutual suspicion and raise profile of issues (Yeo Lay Hwee 2003: 72–9).

This application of realism contradicts basic assumptions of realism. First, most realists do not accept regions as important international actors. This being the case, it is hardly possible to draw a parallel between the balance of power behavior of states and that of regions, whether as "hegemons" or as "challengers." Second, diplomacy is hardly the preferred realist strategy for coping with the rise of a hegemonic challenger. As Robert Gilpin explains, the hegemonic state has various alternatives: it can increase resources devoted to maintaining its commitments and position; it can reduce the costs of its commitments by weakening or destroying the challenger through preventive war, further expansion, unilaterally abandoning certain commitments or entering into alliances or seeking a rapprochement with less threatening powers; or it can make concessions to the rising power. Gilpin (1981: 187–98) predicts that most often the disequilibrium between the dominant and the rising powers persists, but that the stalemate seldom persists. The most frequent means of resolving the disequilibrium is hegemonic war. Finally, the idea of socialization is absent in realism. The balance of power and anarchy persists precisely because states are unable to learn (Ashley 1986; Wendt 1998). Consequently, realism cannot serve as a framework for analyzing confidence-building measures.

A liberal approach

Bersick (2004c: 41) accepts Krasner's classic definition of international regimes as "principles, norms, rules and decision-making procedures around which actor expectations converge in a given issue-area" (Krasner 1983: 1). The issue-area in which the ASEM regime supposedly applies is the danger of instability in the international system after the end of bipolarity. ASEM is said to be an instrument of interregional interdependence management. ASEM norms are the voluntary character of cooperation and equality; its rules are informality and openness of agenda; its principle is non-institutionalization and its decision-making procedures are consensus and non-negotiation (Bersick 2004c: 40, 74–94).

Yeo Lay Hwee, for reasons that are not entirely clear, prefers to Krasner's definition – a simpler definition of regime as "facilitators of information exchange and creation." ASEM appears to her to be a regime or metaregime – "overarching institutions where norms and principles are laid as guidelines for governing key areas of cooperation." ASEM can supposedly be considered a regime on two grounds. First, there was sufficient "recognition of mutual interest and convergent goals between the EU and East Asia to contemplate establishing a framework for cooperation." Second, ASEM supposedly embodies certain features of a regime. ASEM upholds certain principles (stress on equal partnership, multilateralism, recognition of the benefits of open market economies, an open multilateral trading system, open regionalization, non-discrimination and transparency). Multilateralism is said to be embodied in a norm calling for the support of multilateral organizations. Furthermore, Yeo Lay Hwee points out that within the ASEM framework there are central tenets concerning appropriate decision-making procedures. ASEM has created institutions such as the Asia–Europe Foundation (ASEF) and the Asia–Europe Environmental Technology Centre (AEETC). Finally, a set of elites manages the process, which is characterized by intense bargaining and use of issue-linkage strategies. ASEM encompasses a network of governmental as well as non-governmental ties and has a large number of action programs in various fields (Hwee 2003: 157, 191–3).

Both attempts to portray ASEM as a regime or a metaregime are less than convincing, for they appear to be unaware of the theoretical difficulties that beset regime theory and are unresolved to this day (Fritz 1997). The theoretical imprecision of regime theory was already evident many years ago to critics. Haggard and Simmons pointed out that in Krasner's definition, the conceptual boundaries demarcating principles from norms and norms from rules are quite blurred:

> "principles" (which include not only "beliefs of fact and causation but also of rectitude") shade off into norms, "standards of behavior defined in terms of rights and obligations." Norms, in turn, are difficult to distinguish from rules, "specific prescriptions or proscriptions for action."
>
> (Haggard and Simmons 1987: 493)

An exponent of regime theory, Robert Keohane (1984: 57–9) admits that the concept of norms is ambiguous. If norms are morally binding regardless of considerations of narrowly defined self-interest, then the conception of regimes based on self-interest would be a contradiction in terms. Moreover, rules are difficult to distinguish from norms; at the margin, they merge into one another.

Perhaps because of this ambiguity, the demonstration of the so-called ASEM regime's elements is unconvincing. A few examples should suffice. For something to be called a norm, it must be a standard of behavior defined in terms of rights and obligations (Krasner 1983: 2). Unfortunately, Bersick's "norm" of "voluntary character of cooperation" implies precisely the absence of rights and obligations. The norm of (legal) equality identified by Bersick and Yeo Lay Hwee is undoubtedly a norm, but it has been part of general international law since the Peace of Westphalia in 1648 and can in no way be considered specific to ASEM. A decision-making procedure is a prevailing practice for making and implementing collective choice (Krasner 1983: 2). Bersick's alleged decision-making procedure of "non-negotiation" means exactly the opposite: a practice for not making and implementing collective choice. The voluntary character of cooperation, informality, non-institutionalization and non-negotiation all signify the absence of constraint, an idea that is incompatible with Krasner's (1983: 5–8) formulation that regimes can in certain conditions act as intervening variables and thus influence outcomes.

Yeo Lay Hwee's portrayal of ASEM as a regime also relies on the existence of mechanisms of consultation and cooperation, including the appointment of ASEM contact officers within states and ASEM coordinators for each side. However, consultation mechanisms cannot automatically be equated with the existence of regimes. The rather awkward attempt to glorify bureaucratic procedures as constitutive elements of a regime points to a lack of understanding of the concept of regime. If the elements of a regime are principles, norms, rules and procedures, the reverse is not necessarily true: the existence of principles or norms or rules or procedures or any combination thereof does not logically entail the existence of a regime. Otherwise, the entire body of international law would be a regime. This is the position held by Grotian scholars, such as Puchala and Hopkins (1983), but this is apparently not Yeo Lay Hwee's or Bersick's position. Once more, the conceptual specificity of a regime vanishes.

As Keohane (1984: 85–97) explained over twenty years ago, states establish international regimes because of two institutional deficiencies that characterize world politics and inhibit mutually advantageous cooperation. First, there exist externalities, such that states do not bear the full costs or receive the full benefits of their actions. Second, states can, through a regime, create conditions that ensure that externalities do not prevent coordination among themselves. The regime facilitates agreements by raising anticipated costs of violating others' property rights, altering transaction costs through the clustering of issues and providing reliable information to members. Regrettably, neither Bersick nor Yeo Lay Hwee demonstrates that all these conditions are met by ASEM. No indication is given of the externalities that are supposed to prompt cooperation between Asia and Europe. Without this first condition, it is impossible to estimate the cost of violating others' property rights and transaction costs, and there is no need to provide reliable information to members. Yeo Lay Hwee's statement that ASEM provides information indicates that in her view, the supply of any information to states is sufficient to constitute a regime. Keohane's conception clearly rules out this interpretation.

The distinction that Yeo Lay Hwee makes between a regime and a metaregime is untenable when applied to ASEM. She readily admits that ASEM's principles and norms are all nested upward in the larger multilateral order, that is, they relate to universal norms and principles embodied in universal declarations or international agreements.

> The aim is not only to reiterate these norms and principles but is (*sic*) implicit hope that cooperation between Asia and Europe would ensure better compliance with wider global regimes.
>
> (Yeo Lay Hwee 2003: 191)

If the purpose of ASEM is to ensure better compliance with wider global regimes, then it cannot be a metaregime. It is the global regimes that are the metaregimes, with ASEM being something else (not necessarily a regime).

Portraying ASEM as a (meta)regime flies in the face of the position repeatedly expressed by participants themselves that ASEM is not a negotiating forum. Of course, a regime can emerge in spite of the actors' intentions. But as Haggard and Simmons (1987: 493) warn us, "the existence of patterned behavior alone should not lead one to suspect that a regime lurks below the surface." If a regime can emerge in spite of actors' conceptions, Bersick and Yeo Lay Hwee must describe the process whereby the principles, norms, procedures and rules emerge. In this case, concepts like expectations will have to assume center stage.

This brings us to the most serious theoretical objection to conventional regime theory that was raised by Kratochwil and Ruggie (1986) two decades ago: the contradiction between the positivist methodology employed by its adherents and the meaning-centered (reflectivist) definition offered by Krasner (1983: 1): "principles, norms, rules and decision-making procedures around which actor *expectations* (my italics) converge in a given issue-area." A norm does not "cause" behavior in the same way that dropping a ball from a tower "causes" the ball to fall. Therefore, the positivist methodology is inappropriate when determining the constraints that norms impose on social action. The contradiction identified by Kratochwil and Ruggie is a near-fatal theoretical shortcoming of regime theory for the simple reason that positivism and meaning-centered approaches are incommensurable. For Kratochwil (1988), speech act theory and a jurisprudential approach are more helpful in understanding the functions of norms in social life. Until this contradiction is resolved, one should be wary of any recourse to regime theory for the analysis of ASEM.

A constructivist approach

A meaning-centered approach to ASEM, strongly influenced by Alexander Wendt (1992, 1998), is defended by Julie Gilson. Following Wendt, Gilson assumes that interaction is a level of analysis distinct from structure and agency. A region may feel its "region-ness" in large part through interaction with other regions. ASEM allows Asia and Europe to perceive a "like region." Asia acts as Asia for the purpose of engaging with Europe, and Europe responds as if it were responding to Asia, thus reinforcing Asia's sense of identity. In turn, the EU will (re)define its own sense of we-ness in the context of interregional dialogue. As the interaction continues, ideas and understandings of the self and other are constantly formed and reformed, to the extent that without the other self would be incomprehensible. In addition, the identities (re)created in the interaction in the ASEM framework may spill over into other forms of activity. ASEM itself may participate in international institutions. Echoing Wendt's famous statement "Anarchy is what stakes make of it," Gilson (2002: 4, 11, 13, 15–16, 21–4, 27, 29, 84) asserts that "a region is what a region thinks itself to be."

How are identities and interests generated through interaction? Following Wendt, Gilson argues that through interaction, norms can be established and sometimes renegotiated; intersubjective structures may then be formed; embedding practices also play a role. Institutions, defined as regularized channels of communication, are the most obvious means of channeling communication among participants and their behavior at the interregional level. The second means operates through perceptions of the self and the other: interaction shapes and reshapes the structure of the self and the other (ibid.: 15–17, 20–1, 130).

A number of grave theoretical weaknesses undermine Gilson's sweeping claims on behalf of a constructivist theory of ASEM. In addition to the theoretical imprecision already mentioned, institutions are defined in a circular manner. One means of channeling communication among the participants of a region or is said to be institution(s); simultaneously, institutions are defined "as regularised channels of communication among state representatives" (ibid.: 16–17). No effort is made to distinguish institutions from rules, norms or structures or to explain the way in which institutions shape and constrain the behavior of agents.

Two other equally serious conceptual weaknesses are individualism and idealism, both of them imported from Wendt's constructivism. Notwithstanding Wendt's (1987) claim to have satisfactorily resolved the agent-structure problem that he delineated, Wendt's, and therefore Gilson's, brand of constructivism, is individualist (Palan 2000). Indeed, there is no conception of social structure in the sense of relatively enduring social relations, as opposed to structures of intersubjective knowledge. It is therefore not surprising that while Gilson sees all sorts of opportunities for successful interaction in ASEM, she is unable to identify, theoretically and empirically, the structural constraints that can prevent fulfillment of the array of functions and/or goals that she attributes to ASEM.

Wendt's idealism reflects a category mistake that Ronen Palan uncovered, thanks to a distinction made by the French anthropologist Claude Lévi-Strauss. The latter observed that the characteristics of material entities such as "raw," "cooked" or "rotten" are categories of mythic thought. This observation entails the claim that the object of knowledge can be defined only through the medium of a particular logical and conceptual structure; but it only justifies the statement that the "raw" and the "cooked" are linguistic and hence "cultural" categories. It most certainly does not justify the assertion that "ideas" constitute the "raw" and the "cooked." The notion that ideas constitute material force is an extreme idealist view, which contradicts the philosophical realism that Wendt claims to subscribe to (Palan 2000: 589–90). By extension, Gilson's argument that intersubjective structures, knowledge and norms resulting from interaction constitute a region is an extreme idealist position. Gilson, consistent with idealism's neglect of material conditions, fails to investigate the sources of knowledge and norms, that is, the factors or conditions that shape their emergence, persistence, modification or eventual disappearance. Not surprisingly, Gilson is unable to provide evidence for the claim that ASEM can be a site for collective resistance to the World Trade Organization (WTO). The idealist conception of structure as comprising purely intersubjective knowledge and norms offers few, if any, conceptual tools for analyzing resistance, domination, contestation, contradictions and struggles.

One last objection to Gilson's constructivist approach is that it would explain only one goal of ASEM assigned to it by Singapore, which was to strengthen regionalism in Asia (including the socialization of China). This goal may be well achieved through economic cooperation or political dialogue, or even civil society participation. That said Gilson's approach cannot provide a coherent theoretical account of the process of dialogue and/or cooperation in specific fields that the actors have identified – economic cooperation, international and regional security or human rights. Doing so would require investigation of the material resources at their disposal and the structures of opportunities and constraints existing in each area, a task that constructivism is ill-equipped to undertake.

Before proceeding to examine the notion of international dialogue, we should mention one epistemological tendency common to these: the propensity to resort to incommensurable theories. In Rüland's work, this manifests itself in an enumeration of interregionalism's functions based on incommensurable theories. The balancing and bandwagoning function is derived from realist theory; the agenda setting, controlling and rationalizing functions, from liberal institutionalism; identity building, from constructivism; and stabilization and development functions, from theories of the EU as a security and international actor. In Yeo Lay Hwee's and Bersick's work, this propensity underlies the attempt to use different theories to explain different aspects of ASEM: realism for diplomacy (Yeo Lay Hwee) or for ASEM's power-balancing function (Bersick); regime theory for functional cooperation (Yeo Lay Hwee) or for interdependence management (Bersick); and constructivism for identity building (Bersick).

It goes without saying that these theories have contradictory, if not incommensurable, assumptions. It follows that if under one set of assumptions, it is anticipated that ASEM can fulfill a certain function, by the same token, the fulfillment of another function will be excluded. For example, realism, which predicts balancing behavior, assumes fixed identities of states, as constructivists have never tired of reminding us. As a result, the formation and transformation of states' identity cannot be conceptualized under realist assumptions. The claim that ASEM can generate both balancing behavior and identity (trans)formation must explain how it is possible that the actors behave in ways that produce contradictory outcomes (balancing and identity transformation). To take another example: the claim that ASEM is capable of playing agenda setting, controlling and rationalizing functions assumes that cooperation among states is the rule rather than the exception, as realism postulates. Balancing behavior presupposes a willingness to change sides when the balance of power changes, behavior that is the very antithesis of cooperation. Unless it is assumed that actors or institutions are schizophrenic, incommensurability of the theories and of the predictions derived from each practically ensures that ASEM will not be able to fulfill all functions attributed to it. This notion of incommensurability is implicitly rejected by Yeo Lay Hwee who asserts that "using a combination of frameworks of analysis rather than relying on a single theory to discuss ASEM is a better approach" (Yeo Lay Hwee 2003: 12). Similarly, Bersick (2004c: 54) contends that each one of the three paradigms contains explanatory power. Both authors then proceed to apply different theories to different dimensions of ASEM. Regrettably, neither author explains the way in which the incommensurable elements in these theories can be reconciled, or even the philosophy of science that could justify this curious epistemological attitude, which runs the risk of producing an academic patchwork.

The next section outlines an approach to ASEM conceptualized as an international dialogue.

The concept of dialogue

Our approach to ASEM starts from the assumption that social agents can supply reasons for their behavior, reflexively monitor and potentially adapt it and make decisions (Wendt 1987: 359). We can therefore take as starting points for analysis the descriptions given by the actors – leaders, ministers, senior officials and experts – in the ASEM process. In this regard, the chairman's statement of ASEM 2 (1998a) is particularly clear. The ASEM process, which is to be conducted on the basis of an equal partnership, mutual respect and mutual benefit, should enhance mutual understanding and awareness through dialogue and lead to cooperation in the identification of priorities for concerted action. It should seek to stimulate and facilitate progress in other fora and go beyond governments in order to promote dialogue between business and the private sector, think tanks and research groups and the peoples of the two regions (ASEM 2 1998a: para. 3). These statements of purposes do not, of course, guarantee that the dialogue is truly conducted on the basis of an equal partnership, mutual respect and mutual benefit, or that it has led to understanding and cooperation in identification of priorities or stimulated progress in other international organizations.

A first step in assessing the capacity of dialogue to achieve ASEM's lofty aims requires that we distinguish dialogue from negotiation. A manual for practitioners defines negotiation as a "process in which explicit proposals are put forward ostensibly for the purpose of reaching agreement on an exchange or on the realization of a common interest where conflicting interests are present" (Iklé 1964: 4).

Notwithstanding the participants' denial that ASEM is a negotiating forum, negotiation has clearly taken place. At ASEM 2 (1998b), leaders decided to establish an ASEM Trust Fund in response to Asian demands for European assistance during the Asian financial crisis (see Chapter 2). If we stretched the definition of negotiation somewhat by considering declarations issued at the end of summits and ministerial as a "common interest," then discussions of their text could also be construed as negotiations. Dialogue and negotiation are not polar opposites; rather they are situated along a continuum, with a simple exchange of views at one end, and coercive diplomacy at the other, and diplomacy somewhere in between. A simple exchange of views could be a preliminary to negotiation. Japanese diplomacy is said to be characterized by lengthy and cautious efforts to gather information about the negotiating partner's needs and perceptions through informal means. Informal contacts are also used in order to extract prenegotiation assurances, commitments or other forms of guarantee against the failure of impending negotiations (Cohen 1991: 7, 57–8). This said, we must take seriously the ASEM actors' account of their behavior as dialogue rather than negotiation and thus set aside the voluminous literature on negotiating techniques designed for practitioners.

How does dialogue operate? One could legitimately ask whether dialogue has taken place if glossy brochures are exchanged; if there is a restatement of views between participants who already shared them before the meeting; if there is a restatement of opposing views, with the participants failing to reconcile their differences; if an academic gives a lecture to an audience that is already convinced; or if an academic gives a lecture to a hostile audience that remains unconvinced after the lecture. Perhaps dialogue embraces all these modalities? The enumeration suggests, at the very least, that if the notion of dialogue is to serve a purpose, we must specify not just the issues of common interest that are the object of the dialogue but also the conditions of interaction. In this section, the conditions essential for dialogue to take place will be identified with the help of the work of Todorov and Habermas.

Tzvetan Todorov and the problematic of "the Other"

In his book, *La Conquête de l'Amérique* (The Conquest of America), Todorov (1982) explores the problematic of the encounter between the self (represented by Europe) and the distant other (the New World). Todorov identifies the different dimensions along which a relationship with "the Other" can be constructed, as well as the positions, represented by historical figures, that are emblematic of the ideal along each dimension.

Three axes constitute a typology of relations to the other. Along the axiological axis, which is that of value judgments, the self decides that the other is good or evil, or is equal or inferior to the self. Along the praxeological axis, which entails coming closer (*rapprochement*) or distancing (*éloignement*), the self may adopt the values of the other, reduce the other to submission or remain indifferent to or neutral vis-à-vis the other. Along the epistemic axis, the self may come to know the identity of the other or remain ignorant of it. Three historical figures came close to achieving the goal of reconciling difference and equality. Along the axiological axis, the missionary Las Casas confronted each individual with his/her own values rather than with a single ideal. Through this higher form of egalitarianism, Las Casas was able to evaluate human sacrifice in the context of Aztec civilization and conclude unexpectedly that human sacrifice was acceptable for factual and legal reasons. Along the praxeological axis, the paradigmatic figure is Álvar Núñez Cabeza de Vaca, a survivor of a Spanish expedition who lived for eight years with Indians. His accounts differentiated three groups of people: Christians, Indians and "us," with the last comprising a group, including Cabeza de Vaca, which was external to both worlds precisely because it had lived in both. Along the epistemic axis, the contemporary dialogue of cultures was prefigured in the work of Diego Durán, a Dominican priest, and that of Bernardino de Sahagún, a Franciscan priest. Durán, who was born in Spain but went to live in Mexico at the age of five or six, identified himself with the Aztec point of view, while refusing to question his Christian faith and the goal of converting the Indians. In his effort to reconcile the Indians' religion and Christianity, Durán found resemblances between the two that were sometimes improbable. Sahagún's aim was to preserve Nahuatl culture; his accounts avoided value judgments, for example, by using alternately the terms "god" and "devil" to designate the Aztec gods (Todorov 1982: 233–4, 236–8, 249–51, 254–73, 310).

The conquistadores who destroyed the empires of the Aztecs and the Incas had very different attitudes. Along the axiological axis, Columbus oscillated between the two views of the Indians. He considered them his equals, and there-fore identical to him, in an assimilation of the self to the other that made him suppose that the Indians wished to be converted. A refusal of conversion would make the Indians different from him, giving rise to a feeling of his superiority and a judgment of Indian inferiority. Hence, the Indians would have to be com-pelled to convert. Along the epistemic axis, Columbus had very little knowledge of the Indians; and along the praxeological axis, Columbus, in his search for gold, reduced them to slavery. Unlike Columbus, Hernando Cortés sought to gain knowledge about the Indians, yet he manipulated this knowledge and ended up destroying the Aztec empire. The reason for this paradox can be found in the refusal of Cortés to recognize the Indians as his equals, with inequality justify-ing exploitation. The lessons for the contemporary era are that dialogue should seek equality without identity and difference without superiority or inferiority (Todorov 1982: 48–67, 128–85, 310).

Two critical issues raised by the specific nature of international dialogue cannot be addressed through Todorov's work. A first question concerns the iden-tity of participants in international dialogue: who should participate? An even more crucial question is how to act systematically and consciously with a view to achieving the ideals embodied by Las Casas, Cabeza de Vaca, Durán and Sahagún and avoiding the perils represented by Columbus and Cortés. Todorov admits that in Sahagún's work, the dialogue of cultures is fortuitous and uncon-scious (Todorov 1982: 302). The challenge is therefore to identify the conditions in which an ideal international dialogue – a dialogue between peoples, classes, cultures, states, regions and other organizations claiming to represent any or all of the others – can be organized. For this purpose, we now turn to Habermas's theory of communicative action.

Jürgen Habermas and communicative action in the context of globalization

Habermas's (1987a: 160) starting point is the contrast between strategic action, also known as purposive, rational or instrumental action, and communicative action, described as a cooperative process of interpretation. The fundamental difference lies in the orientation to success of the first and the orientation to reaching understanding of the second (Habermas 1984: 156). The instrumental actor is primarily oriented to obtaining his/her goal and selects the appropriate means for achieving the goal in the given situation. The communicative actor is also goal-directed, but the goal is a reasoned consensus. Communicative actors seek to reach understanding about a situation and their plans of action in order to coordinate their actions by way of agreement. A particular action situation pre-sents itself not only as a "field of actual needs for mutual understanding" but also as a field of "actual options for action." The understanding reached then serves as the basis for the subsequent action. In this theory, dialogue is different from bargaining, which is a form of strategic action that involves the exchange of concessions.

Habermas points out that although social actors share a lifeworld, or a background of culturally ingrained preunderstanding, they have to negotiate common definitions of particular situations in which they interact. They try to convince each other to change their beliefs in order to reach a reasoned consensus about validity claims. In order to define a situation, actors simultaneously refer to the three worlds of strategic, normative and dramaturgical action – the objective, social and subjective worlds. In a given situation, actors oriented to understanding will raise at least three validity claims, all of which are in principle criticizable. They will ask whether a statement made by another actor is true in relation to the objective world; whether it is right in relation to the normative context or the social world and whether it is truthful or sincere in relation to the subjective world. Each participant in an interaction accepts or contests a validity claim raised by other participants on the basis of grounds or reasons. If there is a divergence in actors' definitions of the situation, the task for them consists in incorporating each other's interpretations of the situation into one's own so that the divergent definitions of the situation can coincide sufficiently. Habermas clarifies that communicatively achieved agreement is not diffuse; rather its contents can be expressed in differentiated propositions. It has a rational basis, which means that it cannot be imposed by either party. It rests on common convictions and cannot be objectively obtained by force (Habermas 1984: 156–8). In the communicative practice of everyday life, though, stability and absence of ambiguity are the exceptions rather than the rule A more realistic picture is that of "diffuse, fragile, continuously revised and only momentarily successful communication in which participants rely on problematic and unclarified presuppositions and feel their way from one occasionally commonality to the next" (Habermas 1984: 155).

What are the presuppositions of communicative rationality? First of all, it presupposes an ideal speech situation that is free of inequality of oppression. In this situation, which is not empirical but counterfactual (Haacke 1996: 259), actors try to persuade each other and are themselves open to being convinced. Nothing but the better arguments count. In an idealized and formalized version of communicative action, conditions are established aimed at ensuring that only argumentative convincing is allowed to take place and at reducing the impact of repression and inequality on discourse. Chambers (1995: 238–9) summarizes these conditions as follows: No one with the competency to speak and act may be excluded; everyone is allowed to question and/or introduce any assertion whatever as well as express his/her attitudes, needs and desires; no one may be prevented by internal or external coercion from exercising these rights; the participants must treat each other as equal partners; they should listen and respond to one another and justify their positions to one another; and they should put themselves in the position of other participants and try to see the situation from their perspective.

As can be expected, Habermas's theory of communicative action has not gone unchallenged. One set of criticisms questions Habermas's emphasis on the centrality of rationality in the evolution of society. Modes of interaction that are not subsumable under argumentative reason, such as modes of greeting or salutation, topical allusion and story-telling, are said to be marginalized (Dallmayr 2001: 343). Habermas's alleged devaluation of creativity and of openness to the world renders it inapt to understand alternative forms of interpretation and life (Arnason 1991: 183). His theory of communicative action is said to presuppose the specific values of European modernity (Outhwaite 1995: 54).

More important for us are the doubts regarding the feasibility of reproducing the "ideal speech situation" and of achieving consensus. It is not enough for defenders of Habermas to say that he did not intend to transform the world into a gigantic seminar (Outhwaite 1995: 44). The first and fundamental question is the following: what induces or compels social actors to engage in communicative action? "If actors refuse to take this first step, the whole game cannot begin" (Outhwaite 1995: 111). Even if this first step is taken successfully, the pluralism and complexity of modern societies diminish considerably the likelihood of arriving at consensus on many issues (Cochran 2002: 535). In addition, persistent economic, political and social inequalities mean that it would not be fair to treat different people by the same standard. Justice would require applying different standards to different people (Love 1995: 55, 62). In developing countries, such inequalities are even greater, so that many public debates center on distributional questions. In such contexts, powerful elites may manipulate deliberation and impose consensus. If consensus is not imposed, it may simply not be achieved. Given these circumstances, the (unattainable) consensus as a goal of public deliberation should perhaps be replaced by compromise (Kapoor 2004: 479). Taking into account the existence of inequalities inevitably leads to the recognition that in modern societies, capitalism competes with communicative rationality as a principle of integration (Love 1995: 54). Critics accuse Habermas of failing to grasp contradictions and considering that class conflict is settled (Arnason 1991: 176–8).

The weight of these objections would be magnified in any attempt to transpose or adapt Habermas's theory to international dialogue. The cultural and religious diversity that is even greater across societies than within societies would seem to rule out hopes for practical agreement, calling instead for mere damage control (Haacke 1996: 262). Rustin goes further and claims that it would be misguiding to rely on Habermas's theory to analyze international society, to the extent that many governments participating (or wishing to do so) in any such debate are not truly representative of their people (Rustin 1999: 12). Thomas Risse (2000: 14) readily admits that there is no common lifeworld – no common language, history or culture – and that power relationships are never absent in international relations.

Despite these objections, it is still possible to accept that strategic action and communicative action, based on deliberation, dialogue and persuasion, coexist in international relations (Lynch 1999: 12). In Sandholtz's (1999: 87–9) account (which apparently owes little to Habermas's theory), dialogue among international actors about rules is generated by behavior; the dialogue then modifies the rules; the latter in turn provide reasons for subsequent behavior and discourses, and so on. In Thomas Risse's approach, the opportunities for dialogue – or arguing, as he prefers to call it – arise in various situations. In the context of a negotiation, arguing facilitates agenda setting by convincing actors that there is a problem to solve in a cooperative process. It would also establish common knowledge about the situation and the principles for the negotiation. In the negotiation, arguing might be necessary when searching for an optimal instead of a "lowest common denominator" solution to a collective action problem. More generally, argumentative behavior is likely if actors are uncertain about their own identities, interests and views of the world and/or if rhetorical arguments are subject to scrutiny and counterchallenge (Risse 2000: 20–1, 23).

Marc Lynch believes that deliberation is episodic rather than ongoing, occurring mainly during periods where existing arrangements break down and are motivated by the search for new foundations for relations between states. Most of the time, politics presupposes an underlying consensus on procedures, norms and expectations. Where relations between two states are characterized by hostility, a dialogue could enable them to identify common higher interests that transcend lower level conflicts and reduce doubts and suspicions about long-contested issues. Dialogue takes place in an international public sphere; it thematizes issues, frames and interprets their significance and identifies alternative solutions. Lynch (2000: 319–20, 323) warns against assuming that consensus or cooperation will inevitably follow from dialogue. Whether or not dialogue is episodic or frequent, argumentation oriented towards a reasoned consensus precedes the articulation of common identities and interests and may in this manner facilitate problem-solving.

The ideal conditions for international deliberation or dialogue are similar to those required for successful dialogue in a national context. All interested and affected parties must participate in the deliberation and treat each other as equals. Each actor must persuade others to adopt his/her view by offering reasoned arguments for his/her positions. No coercion or power may be used to prevent actors from participating in the deliberation or to convince actors to accept an argument. While presenting reasoned arguments for one's position, each actor must be ready to be convinced by the arguments of others and consequently to change his/her positions. The resulting consensus, according to Habermas, should be propositionally differentiated.

The requirements that participants must treat each other as equals and refrain from the use of power are similar to conditions identified by Todorov. Other requirements set by Todorov's ideal seem to be more stringent. On the axiological dimension of dialogue, treating the other participant as an equal may lead to acceptance of the other's view, even if this view is totally alien to the first participant. Along the praxeological axis, it is not only that each participant should be willing to change his/her preferences in the course of dialogue and accept that the outcome of dialogue can be open-ended, as Lynch puts it. Todorov's ideal figure, Álvar Núñez Cabeza de Vaca, developed an entirely new identity, one that was a synthesis of two identities. Along the epistemic axis, Lynch explains that the purpose of exchange of information should be to provide reliable knowledge about the actors' preferences. It cannot be limited to improving each side's understanding of consequences of a particular agreement; otherwise, each actor will have an incentive to reveal information selectively (Lynch 2000: 313). Todorov's ideal figures, Durán and Sahagún, went further. In the process of acquiring knowledge, they also sought commonalities while avoiding value judgments of superiority or inferiority. In the process, they not only preserved knowledge; they also generated new knowledge.

As in the case of dialogue in the domestic public sphere, the question must be raised regarding actors' willingness to participate in dialogue. Inequalities of power might make weaker actors refuse to enter into dialogue, for fear of finding themselves under pressure from stronger actors to compromise their vital interests. For their part, powerful actors might be unwilling to change their preferences in favor of the preferences of weaker actors (Lynch 2000: 323–9). The references to power remind us to be cautious about concluding that a theoretical approach to (international) dialogue is necessarily, if not exclusively, agent-centered and/or constructivist (e.g. Payne and Samhat 2002: 2). An approach to international dialogue that neglects material conditions would make it theoretically and practically impossible to evaluate the impact of power and inequality among (potential) participants in a dialogue and thus to ascertain the prospects of achieving the "ideal speech situation" and of arriving at a consensus among international actors. In other words, an approach to international dialogue is compatible with a structural approach, which is required if the willingness of actors to engage in dialogue, the interests and preferences that they bring to the dialogue, and their behavior in the course of (and even after) the dialogue are to be properly grasped.

An attempt to analyze dialogue in light of (material) structural conditions does not do violence to Habermas's approach to communicative action. To begin with, Habermas himself has criticized the idealism of George H. Mead, whose work on discourse ethics has strongly influenced that of Wendt and by extension, Gilson. "Idealism ignores the material reproduction of society – securing its physical maintenance both externally and internally." It neglects economics, warfare and the struggle for political power. As a result, "the constraints of reproducing the social system ... remain closed off to an analysis restricted to structures of interaction" (Habermas 1987b: 110–11). It is an open question whether the same shortcoming is not replicated in Habermas's work (Outhwaite 1995: 86), but the point cannot be denied. Next, we should not forget that in Habermas's own analysis of contemporary Western society, the scope of the lifeworld, in which communicative action is the means of coordinating social action, is progressively diminished by the expansion of the economic and political systems, causing pathologies among actors in the lifeworld. For this reason, analysis of social interaction cannot be isolated from the operation of economic and political mechanisms. Finally, we cannot ignore Habermas's attempts to delineate the crises specific to contemporary capitalist societies. It follows that even at the national level, dialogue must be set in a broader, structural context constituted by the economic and political systems and their evolution over time.

International issues have figured more prominently in Habermas's recent work. His empirical analyses of globalization and its impact on international relations give us an idea of the way(s) in which his theory of communicative action is combined with a structural perspective. It is significant that before speculating on the possibility of establishing procedures for the coordination and generalization of interests at the international level, Habermas always takes pains to outline the changing structural context in which individuals, classes, organizations and states find themselves and the extent to which they shape and constrain the behavior of these actors (the following is based on Habermas 1998, 2000 and 2001). Habermas is of the view that national economies have become dependencies of the world economy, characterized by the expansion and increased density of trade; the global networking of financial markets; the growing power of multinational corporations, acting in competition with nation states and the mounting competitive pressures exerted on developed economies by the rapid rise in industrial exports of newly industrializing countries. Habermas stresses that globalized locational competition increases unemployment in developed countries, overburdens social security systems, shrinks the tax bases and undermines the welfare state, the key compromise that reconciled capitalism and democracy. Globalization splits the world into two and stratifies world society: increasing productivity and economic development, on the one hand, and impoverishment and underdevelopment, on the other.

Habermas's international problematic is the following: how should (supranational) politics "catch up" with (globalized) economics? More specifically, how can the welfare state's functions be transferred from the nation state to a larger political grouping such as supranational agencies? Only such a transfer can ensure the maintenance of these functions. The EU immediately comes to mind as a possible communicative space characterized by an interplay between institutionalized processes of public opinion and will formation and informal networks of public communication (Schlesinger and Kevin 2000: 210). Habermas does not assume that the EU's economic and monetary union will automatically alter the pattern of international relations if it merely creates free market conditions at the transnational level. The task facing political actors is twofold: to establish the conditions for the worldwide development of informed political opinion and will formation and to guarantee binding decisions; and to bring global economic networks under political control. To this end, political alliances among states may be a necessary condition. Interestingly enough, Habermas believes that the "global powers" have to be willing to broaden their perspectives on what counts as "national" interest from the viewpoint of global governance (Habermas 1998: 112). This condition seems to imply that developed countries bear a special responsibility for global governance and that to discharge these responsibilities, they should be willing to transcend narrow national interests, and perhaps even make concessions to developing countries. If this were an appropriate interpretation, one of the conditions for engaging in dia-logue – that participants should consider each other as equals – would be relaxed somewhat to the extent that the more powerful actors would have to bear a greater burden of ensuring the success of dialogue and of the joint action carried out after the dialogue. The "ideal speech situation" would be modified, in a sense favorable to the weaker participants.

This rather lengthy excursion into Habermas's international problematic drives home the point that any attempt to bring to bear Habermas's theory of communicative action on the analysis of international issues must take into account structural conditions, which include both material and ideological ele-ments. If ASEM is to be analyzed as a forum for dialogue between a group of states in Asia and a group of states in Europe, it is not enough to declare that the dialogue must take place in conditions that approximate those of the ideal speech situation (each participant must consider the other as an equal, must give reasons for his/her arguments, must be willing to listen to the other participants and to change his/her views in the course of the dialogue). Habermas's injunc-tion to the great powers to adopt a broader conception of their national interest must also be kept in mind. Finally, it is imperative to inquire into the particip-ants' willingness and the capacity to engage in a dialogue; and to do this, one must examine the economic and political conditions at the national, regional or international levels that shape this willingness and capacity in each area of common interest where dialogue is to take place.

We shall discuss the areas of common interest taken up in the ASEM dia-logue in the following chapters. Only then will it be possible to ascertain whether ASEM is an appropriate forum for dialogue in each area; whether the actions of ASEM participants provide reasoned arguments for their positions; whether they refrain from using power to back up their arguments and whether they exhibit a willingness to change their positions. In the following section, we shall briefly discuss some fundamental features of ASEM as a forum for interre-gional dialogue.

ASEM as a forum for interregional dialogue

ASEM's uniqueness as a dialogue is said to lie in three features: it is a dialogue between Asia and Europe; it is a dialogue among equals; and it follows (or seeks to follow) the "Asian" way. ASEM is much less innovative in the way it treats demands by non-state actors for participation in the official process.

ASEM as a dialogue between Asia and Europe

ASEM 1 set the tone for the process when it characterized ASEM as a dialogue between Asia and Europe, each of which was assumed to constitute a region (e.g. ASEM 1 1996: paras 4–6, 9, 10, 14, 15, 17, 18). These statements begged the question of which Asian states and which European states had the right to participate in the dialogue. In the next decade, disagreement over enlargement of participation in ASEM was such that it occasionally threatened to paralyze the dialogue. Underlying the divergences between Asian and European states was the desire of each group to ensure the representation of certain economic and political interests in the dialogue.

Shortly before or immediately after ASEM 1, a very large number of Asian and European states made known their desire to participate in ASEM: India, Pakistan, Australia and New Zealand on the Asian side; and European Free Trade Association (EFTA) states, Bulgaria, the Czech Republic, Hungary, Poland, Russia, Romania, Switzerland, Slovakia, Turkey and Ukraine (Pou Saradell 1996: 208; Bersick 1998: 45). ASEAN and the EU decided that each group would decide which states from its respective region would be invited to the summit, supposedly to facilitate the summit's launching and to make it more manageable (Ton Sinh Thanh 1998). ASEAN's decision to invite only China, Japan and South Korea did not deter India that sought to join the European group (Bersick 1998: 46). ASEM 1 gave no guidelines on the criteria or the procedure for enlargement of participation; it confined itself to affirming that the ASEM process was "open and evolutionary" (ASEM 1 1996: para. 18).

Following ASEM 1, enlargement became a controversial issue not only in view of the prospect of enlargement of ASEAN and the EU, but also because each side believed that admission of one or the other state would reaffirm economic and political principles or interests that it wished to safeguard during the dialogue.

The accession of Laos and Myanmar to ASEAN in 1997, followed by Cambodia in 1999, made ASEM enlargement a pressing issue. ASEAN defended the view, based on the principles of equality and non-interference in internal affairs, that the three states should automatically be allowed to participate in ASEM. The EU strongly objected to the membership of Myanmar, on which the EU had imposed a series of sanctions for the widespread human rights abuses committed in that country and the military junta's refusal to proceed with democratic reform. ASEAN threatened to prevent the EU's new members from participating in ASEM if the EU vetoed Myanmar's participation. For the EU, its efforts to formulate a common foreign and security policy made it imperative that all EU members be represented at all international meetings that the EU attended; hence, it was impossible to exclude the new members, admitted in 2004, from ASEM.

Of concern to ASEAN was the fact that the EU advocated the admission of other states that would have joined the Asian side, not the European side. These were India, Pakistan, Australia and New Zealand, all of which had strong economic ties with Europe. In the EU's 1994 New Asia Strategy, South Asia had already been identified as a priority together with East Asia. After ASEM 3, the Commission went one step further by incorporating Australia and New Zealand in Asia. Most ASEAN states were reluctant to consider enlargement of ASEM to the four states for economic and political reasons. As regards South Asia, India had been mentioned in the Singapore prime minister's proposal for ASEM. Subsequently, ASEAN's attitude changed, out of a concern that treating the problems of a "dynamic" East Asian region and a slow-growing South Asian region in the same forum would reduce ASEM's effectiveness. ASEAN also feared that membership of the two traditional adversaries India and Pakistan would weaken the Asian group's unity and that ASEM itself would become another forum in which the India–Pakistan conflict would be played out (Pareira 2003: 128; Ton Sinh Thanh 1998: 101). With respect to Australia and New Zealand, ASEAN and China objected that they were not Asian. In Malaysian Prime Minister Mahathir's view, admitting them to ASEM was as incongruous as admitting Arab states to the EU (Pareira 2003: 129). At ASEM 3, Malaysia declared that if the EU insisted on their participation in ASEM, the two states would have to join the European group (Bersick 2004c: 124). The objection to the two states' participation was obviously less geographic than political. If Australia and New Zealand, both Western-style democracies, had joined the Asian group, their presence would have posed formidable obstacles to reaching a consensus on political issues within the group.

Between ASEM 1 and ASEM 2, support for Australia and New Zealand declined perceptibly, and the admission of India and Pakistan receded into the background. Until 2004, disagreement centered on Myanmar's participation. In June 1997, the EU's General Affairs and External Relations Council announced that Myanmar's accession to ASEAN did not automatically mean membership of ASEM. In December 1997, the EU informed ASEAN that EU sanctions restricting granting of visas to Myanmar officials would prevent Myanmar's participation in ASEM 2 in London in 1998. Malaysia countered with a threat of an ASEAN boycott of the summit, which did not make any progress in identifying rules and procedures for enlargement (Ton Sinh Thanh 1998: 101). The Asia–Europe Cooperation Framework (AECF) adopted at ASEM 3 (2000) proposed a two-step procedure for enlargement that the EU Commission had proposed in 1997. First, the applicant state would have to obtain the agreement of the states in its region; in the second phase, a consensus between the two groups of states was required for admission.

Successive foreign ministers' meetings failed to resolve the deadlock (FMM 3 2001: para. 19; FMM 4 2002: para. 11; FMM 5 2003: para. 8), resulting in a de facto moratorium on enlargement. Prior to EU enlargement and ASEM 5 in 2004, the evolution of ASEAN attitudes toward Myanmar gave out hope of a resolution of the issue. The military junta's arrest in May 2003 of Aung San Suu Kyi and other leaders of the National League for Democracy had prompted unprecedented criticism from other ASEAN members, which urged the immediate release of Aung San Suu Kyi and a transition toward democratic reform. In response, the military junta launched a constitutional convention and agreed to explain its roadmap for reform to Asian and European states at the Bangkok Forum in December 2003. However, the April 2004 forum meeting was cancelled. It is likely that the ASEAN states' increasing frustration with Myanmar made it possible for the ASEM foreign ministers to issue a public statement on Myanmar for the first time (FMM 5 2004: 6). In other circumstances, ASEAN would have considered the statement an unacceptable interference in internal affairs. In the absence of further progress in Myanmar, economic ministers' and finance ministers' meetings (EMM and FMM) scheduled to be held in 2004 were cancelled. A last-minute compromise suggested by the EU, whereby Myanmar would be admitted but represented at a low level, saved ASEM 5 in Hanoi in October 2004. Thus, it became possible to admit the three new ASEAN members and the ten new ASEAN members at Hanoi. Surprisingly, the summit did not call for Aung San Suu Kyi's' release, notwithstanding the fact that her fate was discussed behind closed doors [according to the European Commission (EC) president] and the summit issued a statement on the political situation in her country (Fogarty 2004). Once the deadlock over Myanmar had been resolved, the decision of ASEM 6 (2006a) to allow India, Pakistan, Mongolia and the ASEAN Secretariat, on the Asian side, and the new EU members, Bulgaria and Romania, to participate in the next summit no longer aroused controversy.

Enlargement may be a source of satisfaction for advocates of Asia–Europe dialogue, but we should not overestimate the impact of the controversy on dialogue at other levels. It is noteworthy that the controversy never led to the cancellation of any meetings of the Senior Officials on Trade and Investment, the Investment Experts' Group or of the Working Groups under the Trade Facilitation Action Plan (TFAP) and the Investment Promotion Action Plan (IPAP). This is an unambiguous sign that the aims pursued by the EU through these groups, as will be indicated in the following chapters, were far too important work to be sacrificed on the altar of Myanmar's human rights record.

Some observers are concerned that since there is no more room for ASEAN expansion, the continuing enlargement of the EU will aggravate the disparity in numbers between Asia and Europe. This would make it difficult to maintain ASEM's character as a dialogue among equals, to which we now turn.

ASEM as a dialogue among equals

The rhetoric of ASEM never fails to emphasize that it is a dialogue "conducted on the basis of equal partnership" (e.g. AECF 2000: 8). Much is made of the willingness of the former (European) colonial powers to meet with their erstwhile colonies. As one Chinese scholar put it, because of the history of European imperialism in Asia, establishing cooperation on an equal footing is a historic event (quoted in Bersick 2004c: 140). As mentioned above, Bersick and Yeo Lay Hwee both believe that equality is a constitutive norm of a putative ASEM regime.

On the European side, the stress on equality is no mere rhetorical flourish. Equality means that the dialogue is no longer dominated by the donor–recipient relationship of the past (European Commission 2001c: 2). Concretely, equality rules out any discussion (much less provision), of official development assistance (ODA) in ASEM, which would be tantamount to recognition of an unequal relationship. An official of the EC put it explicitly: "The granting of ODA is excluded from ASEM in order to clearly pass the political message: the former colonial great powers recognize the Asian states as equals" (Reiterer

2004: 258). Not that the EU or its member states are unwilling to provide ODA; discussions of ODA are confined to bilateral (individual EU member state–individual Asian state; or EU–individual Asian state) relations.

Attempts to introduce a development dimension into discussions have not met with any success. In 2002, the Philippines, reporting on its fight against terrorism, explained that military success had to be supported by social–economic measures. With this in mind, the Philippines sought from the EU (1) a reduction, if not an abolition, of the tariffs on Philippine tuna, production of which employed 15,000 Filipino Muslims and (2) provision of ODA for projects in the south of the country, where most Muslims lived (Bersick 2004c: 235–6). Given the EU's view of the "equality" of the participants, it was not surprising that no response to these requests was forthcoming in ASEM. This was also the fate of an indirect proposal made by a Senior Officials' Meeting on Trade and Investment (SOMTI) to fund the participation of the poorest ASEM participants in ASEM meetings (SOMTI 9 2003: Annex 1). The cautious suggestion probably reflected a genuine sentiment of frustration among the poorer Asian states, which was probably not alleviated by the fact that the Senior Officials themselves failed to make any recommendations to remedy the problem. Again, the observation did not elicit any reaction from the EMM to which it was submitted (EMM 5 2003: Annex 1).

ASEM as an interregional dialogue in the "Asian way"

The character of ASEM as an "informal process" has impressed many observers, particularly the Europeans, to the point that a number of them believe that informality is one principle of a putative ASEM regime. The absence of a predetermined agenda for ASEM 1, the refusal to undertake negotiations and the refusal to institutionalize ASEM are said to reflect very strongly Asian preferences, particularly the "ASEAN way" (e.g. Rüland 1996; Ton Sinh Thanh 1998: 80; Yeo Lay Hwee 2003: 40). The ASEAN way has spawned a voluminous literature that cannot possibly be reviewed here (for recent restatements, see e.g. Acharya 1998, 2003). We will simply assume that it refers to the habit of consultation and accommodation fostered by frequent interaction that is multi-level and multi-dimensional, based on informality; a preference for process; a non-legalistic approach; a non-binding approach; and provisions for flexibility; consultation, accommodation and consensus (Snitwongse 1998: 184). The ASEAN way was sustained by frequent consultation and meetings of heads of state, ministers and senior officials, giving rise to a process of elite socialization. The ASEAN way is sometimes made to appear as the product of personal dispositions; low-key diplomacy was supposedly made possible by the fact that "ASEAN leaders respected one another" (Solidum 1997: 354). More often, cultural dispositions are cited. The preference for informal ways is said to be a cultural trait, leading to an avoidance of formal mechanisms and procedures of conflict, in contrast to the highly institutionalized and binding commitments typical of European organizations. Negotiation takes place between friends and brothers rather than between opponents (Acharya 1998: 211–12), and decision-making in (Southeast) Asia is by consensus. The European way of majority voting is widely believed to create, if not isolate, minorities. The existence of authoritarian governments in many ASEAN members was a permissive condition for this process, as presidents, prime ministers and foreign ministers stayed in office for years and even decades.

There is some evidence that when Singapore proposed ASEM, it envisioned a similar process of socialization occurring among Asian and European leaders. According to the Singaporean scholar Yeo Lay Hwee, ASEM's overarching objective was to open channels of dialogue between Asia and Europe so as to promote greater understanding. Summits are said to have educational value for leaders, forcing them to focus on international issues that would have escaped their attention and providing them with additional information and insight. During face-to-face meetings, leaders may be able to build up personal relationships. The exchange of information and communication is said to create a conducive atmosphere for long-term cooperation "as opposed to measures aimed at reaping instant benefits or solving immediate economic problems" (Yeo Lay Hwee 2002: 62, 95). The arguments presumably are valid for foreign, economic, finance ministers and other state actors as well.

The most common explanation put forward for the supposed European willingness to follow the "ASEAN way" is Asia's enhanced bargaining power, deriving from rapid economic growth and increased self-confidence. A European refusal to adapt to Asian preferences would have jeopardized ASEM. If the EU adapted to the (Southeast) Asian way, the beneficial consequences of the latter would be replicated in the ASEM process. Soesastro and Nuttall (1997: 76, 81) predicted that the existence of a dense network would generate habits of behavior that can be as binding as formal commitments.

From this perspective, ASEM is vulnerable to criticism for not sufficiently stimulating informal dialogue. In 2001, the EC observed:

> The initial ideas of an informal and candid dialogue have … vanished on the way: The more we see each other, the more formality and preparation seem to take place…. Our ministers and Leaders seem sometimes to be caught in a routine approach to international conferences: they read out prepared statements, sometimes without even realising that their intervention does not fit
>
> (European Commission 2001c: 2)

At ASEM 3, the lack of informal and interactive discussions was blamed on the Korean president's inability to steer the discussions (Bersick 2004c: 81–3). To promote dialogue, informal intervals and informal retreat sessions, for which there would be no indicative list of topics and no minutes would be taken, were suggested by the EC. The first such retreat was held on the topic "Dialogue on cultures and civilizations" at ASEM 4

The hope or expectation that meetings between leaders and ministers would lead to socialization neglects the structural context in which the "ASEAN way" developed. During ASEAN's first decade (1967–77), it was major changes in the external environment – the UK withdrawal from Southeast Asia in 1968, the US announcement of the Guam doctrine in 1969, the USSR's proposal for an Asian collective security system, the loss of Commonwealth privileges for Singapore and Malaysia following EC enlargement, and the reunification of Vietnam in 1975 – that compelled ASEAN members to deepen political and economic cooperation. Needless to say, analogous external stimuli are absent in the ASEM process, though 9/11 may change this. There is no obvious third party toward or against which Asia and Europe can formulate a common political and/or economic interest and direct their common action. Another condition that contributed to socialization of Southeast Asian officials – very frequent annual meetings – cannot be reproduced to the same extent in the ASEM process. One wonders if biennial summits or ministerial meetings are sufficient to trigger a socialization process among Asian and European elites. Yeo Lay Hwee (2002: 50, 64–5, 108) fears that ASEM's continuity might be affected by changes of government, which in her opinion are frequent in Europe. Of course, such changes are normal in democratic political systems; Asia–Europe cooperation could hardly be promoted at the expense of democracy in Europe.

The EC experience with European political cooperation (EPC) gives us an idea of the conditions in which informal dialogue among states might give rise to a socialization process. Although EPC took place outside the EC framework, member states shared the same overall objectives and participated in the same intergovernmental and supranational processes. The EPC consultation process was regular and intensive, and coordination was made possible by the existence of a telex network. Thanks to this socialization process, early consultation among EC members became natural; unilateral initiatives became less frequent and it became more difficult for a member state to present other members with a *fait accompli* or to change positions after a common position had been agreed on (Øhrgaard 1997: 1–29). In other words, where states already share overall objectives and are already engaged in cooperation in other fields, there will be a disposition to engage in dialogue. In the absence of these shared overall objectives, the dialogue process will be more arduous and its results uncertain. If these premises are accepted, the implication for ASEM is that it might be facing a vicious circle: socialization requires agreement on objectives and cooperation in a number of areas, but without agreement and cooperation in these or other areas, socialization cannot take place. More informal intervals and retreat sessions may fail to compensate for the absence of these structural conditions and bring about genuine socialization, even if dialogue continues.

ASEM and non-state actors

While it is one requirement of an ideal dialogue that all affected actors participate in it, this requirement cannot be taken literally in the case of international dialogue if we refer to actors who will have to bear the consequences of dialogue. The requirement can be reformulated to read that representatives of those who will have to bear the consequences of dialogue participate in it. The question that arises is whether only states or international organizations (like the EU) can represent such groups in the ASEM process or whether non-state actors should be allowed to participate in the interstate process.

Business has been the non-state sector that Asian and European states have encouraged to participate in ASEM (ASEM 1 1996: 14) since the first summit, which established an Asia–Europe Business Forum (AEBF). Young people, students and tourists would also be drawn into the process, under the heading of people-to-people cooperation. The sole reasons for including them in the dialogue would be to promote greater awareness and understanding and to overcome misperceptions between the two regions (ASEM 1 1996: 17). To these three groups, ASEM 2 and the AECF added the public, think tanks, research groups, universities and "all sectors of society generally," but their participation would be restricted to social and cultural cooperation (ASEM 2 1998a: paras 19–20; AECF 2000: para. 11). In addition to the AEBF, a Council for Asia–Europe Cooperation (CAEC) was set up, bringing together think tanks from Asia, Europe and Australia. In the first few years, CAEC acted as the unofficial Track II of ASEM, providing a rationale and supplying expert comment. For the Asia–Europe Vision Group (AEVG 1999: 26; Richards 1999a: 152–5), a forum for societal exchanges involved primarily the strengthening of ASEF. It was only at ASEM 3 that there was a timid recognition of the need for a dialogue on socioeconomic issues that would include globalization (ASEM 3 2000: para. 16). Even then, the dialogue was to be limited to the ASEM partners; that is, the dialogue would be an interstate dialogue.

This is all the more ironic, because one of the most potentially far-reaching, but unintended, consequences of ASEM is that it has stimulated the mobilization of NGOs, within the Asia–Europe People's Forum (AEPF), to a much greater extent than in the context of the ASEAN–EU dialogue. From the very first summit, the restricted conception of non-state actors and their forms of participation has been challenged by the AEPF, which holds parallel summits. The AEPF 1 (1996) demanded representation of organizations of workers, women, indigenous and tribal communities, popular organizations and NGOs. AEPF 2 (1998a, 1998b, 1998c) reiterated the call for mechanisms to be put in place to enable civil society groups, 150 of which participated in the AEPF, to have a say in all aspects of the ASEM process, including the Summit itself. By the time of ASEM 3 (2000), the demand for popular participation had crystallized into a proposal for a Social Forum, an independent body that would act as the channel of communication and interaction between civil society organizations and ASEM. The Social Forum would organize the civil society's participation in ASEM meetings and programs and present its opinions to the official ASEM process. AEPF 4 (2002) demanded once more the creation of a "Social Forum," which could act as an interface between the official ASEM process and civil society, including trade unions (AEPF 4 2002). Between ASEM 4 and ASEM 5, the EU Commission organized a consultative seminar with civil society, which recommended, among others, efforts to involve labor ministers and social partners in ASEM dialogue; strengthen relations between Asian and European trade unions; promote core labor standards, workers' participation as well as corporate social responsibility; and promote exchanges between civil society leaders (European Institute of Asian Studies 2003: 17–20). In the run-up to ASEM 5 (2004a), an informal consultation with civil society was sponsored by the ASEF held in Barcelona; among its suggestions was ASEF support for civil society capacity building and for NGO participation in the AEPF (ASEF *et al.* 2004: 6).

To explain the AEPF's failure to convince Asian and European states to give them a voice in the interstate process, Gilson (2002: 170) cites the alleged lack of a coherent and targeted agenda and the inability to present a united front. In the same vein, an EC official asserts that the AEPF lacks focus (Reiterer 2004: 270). That the AEPF agenda resembles a very long wish list can hardly be denied, but this mirrors the "laundry-list" approach of ASEM. In particular, the topics touched on in leaders' and ministerial meetings are identical to those on the UN General Assembly's agenda. The AEPF would surely be criticized if it did not express any views on most, if not all, of the issues that leaders and ministers have touched upon.

As an organization comprising liberal–democratic states, the EU officially has an open disposition towards civil society organizations. In 1998, the AEPF received verbal support from the EC president, and its representatives were able to meet with Commission officials in the presence of the UK Secretary of State for International Development, Clare Short, at the AEPF. However, the British prime minister and the foreign secretary refused to receive an AEPF delegation. In the run-up to the Seoul Summit, the EC also met with the Asian NGOs that were organizing AEPF in May and October 2000, though it was emphasized that the Commission officials were attending in their personal, and not in their official, capacities. In May 2000, Asian NGOs met with their French counterparts with a view to lobbying the Ministry of Foreign Affairs of France, which was to occupy the EU presidency at the time of ASEM 3. Perhaps as a result of these meetings, the Commission declared in its Communication on ASEM 3 that "the output of civil society must be heard in the official process" and that "the scope and intensity of civil society dialogue can be strengthened in a wide range of areas" [European Commission COM (2000) 241: 5].

One reason often put forward by the Europeans for the failure to integrate NGOs into the ASEM process is the resistance of Asian states, particularly China. At Seoul, the only Asian countries that agreed to meet with the NGOs were Japan and South Korea (Fouquet 2001: 3). There is certainly more than a grain of truth in this. The Chinese reject the concept of civil society for its European origin and its distinction between state and society, which is said to be inexistent in China (European Institute of Asian Studies 2003: 9).

The difficulties of reconciling authoritarian governments' positions and those of civil society were highlighted when AEPF 5 was held in Hanoi in 2004. The Vietnamese participants, all of whom were members of state-sponsored mass organizations, were carefully selected. Under pressure from Cambodia, Vietnam refused entry to a critic of the Cambodian regime. Above all, a statement condemning the Myanmar military junta and calling for its exclusion from ASEM was resisted by the Vietnamese organizers (Schmidt and Herberg 2004).

Without denying the weight of this obstacle, it must be recognized that the authoritarian states' opposition serves as a convenient excuse to EU members and the EC, which are in reality reluctant to envisage civil society participation in the official ASEM process. The European reluctance stems from the existence of two sets of contradictions inherent in such participation: the first between the EU's economic agenda and that of the AEPF; and the second between the political agenda of the Asian countries and that of the AEPF. As we shall see in Chapters 3 and 4, the ASEM economic agenda advocated by the EU is little more than the program it pursues at the WTO. This program is challenged by the AEPF's radical reform proposals such as reform of the global financial system, the cancellation of Third World debt and the imposition of a tax on foreign exchange transactions. On the other hand, the AEPF political agenda theoretically coincides to a large extent with the EU's agenda for political dialogue – human rights, democratization and the rule of law. It comes as no surprise that political dialogue of this type is being resisted by Asia. At the WTO, it is possible for developing (Asian) countries and NGOs to set aside for the moment human rights issues and to form a tactical alliance that aims to resist the US and EU alliance there.

Owing to these contradictions, neither Asian nor European participants can consider accepting civil society participation, even if the refusal entails abandoning the possibility of forming tactical alliances with NGOs in the dialogue with the other group. The EU fears that ASEM would become a platform for NGO critique of the EU's economic agenda and thus prefers to do without support from Asian and European civil societies in the political dialogue. Authoritarian Asian states that may be receptive to NGO critiques of the EU agenda would nevertheless object to the AEPF's political agenda. The tendency of each group of states to present a common position in the dialogue also prevents individual Asian or European states from entering into partnerships and alliances with like-minded NGOs. There can be little doubt that the workings of the EU's Common Foreign and Security Policy (CFSP) will prevent individual EU members from making unilateral changes of policy or contradicting a common position adopted by all other EU members.

Now that the conditions for interregional dialogue have been elucidated, we can turn to the substantive areas of dialogue within ASEM. The next three chapters will take up the issues under ASEM's economic pillar, on which most efforts at dialogue have been concentrated since 1996.

Summary

It is important to specify the conditions of existence of an international level, failing which it will be impossible to determine whether an interregional level, supposedly embodied in ASEM, is truly emerging and if so, whether ASEM is performing the functions attributed to it. Realist, liberal and constructivist approaches to ASEM are unpersuasive. The realist approach fails to realize that for realists, regions and international organizations are not important actors and that even assuming there could be such a thing as shifts in the balance of power between regions, diplomacy is not the preferred means of adjusting to changes in the balance of power. Liberal approaches, which conceptualize ASEM as a regime, are unable to distinguish elements of a regime or identify elements that are incompatible with the definitions of these elements given by regime theorists. The constructivist approach is undermined by its reliance on idealism and individualism, rendering it incapable of analyzing the material forces that can determine whether ASEM fulfills the functions attributed to it.

An alternative approach takes as its starting point the ASEM participants' claim that they are engaged in dialogue and goes on to identify the ideal conditions for dialogue on the basis of the work of Todorov and Habermas. For Todorov, a dialogue with the other takes place along three dimensions: axiological (involving value judgments on the other), praxeological (involving rapprochement with the other) and epistemic (generating knowledge of the other). Since Todorov provided no guidelines as to how to act consciously in a dialogue, we turned to Habermas's theory of communicative action. According to Habermas, a consensus can be generated among participants to a dialogue and can serve as a basis for joint action in an area of common interest if all interested parties participate in the dialogue and treat each other as equals; if each party persuades the others to adopt its views by offering reasoned arguments and refrains from using force in the process; and if each is willing to change its views or positions. Dialogue is to be differentiated from bargaining. Habermas's theory leaves unanswered the question of how to convince social actors to engage in dialogue in the first place.

This difficulty is magnified if dialogue is undertaken at the international level, as weaker actors might fear that dialogue with powerful actors will compromise their interests, while the latter refuse to change their views. Nevertheless, dialogue is still possible in international relations, either prior to or during bargaining in the course of negotiations or as a means of identifying common interests among hostile states. The conditions for ideal dialogue at the international level are largely similar to those identified for dialogue in the domestic sphere, except that an analysis of international dialogue must take into account the structural conditions in which the actors find themselves, which include both material and ideological elements.

Having identified the conditions for dialogue, the chapter then briefly analyzed some features of ASEM as a forum for interregional dialogue. First, it is a dialogue between Asia and Europe, but between 1996 and 2004, the participants' disagreement over economic and political interests prevented them from enlarging the circle of participants to Asian and European states that represented challenges to these interests (Myanmar for the EU, India, Pakistan, Australia, New Zealand and the new EU members for ASEAN). Second, ASEM is said to be a dialogue between equals, which the EU interprets to mean that development assistance cannot be discussed in ASEM, even if some Asian participants wish to do so. Third, ASEM was said to be a dialogue in the Asian way – informal, non-binding and non-institutionalized. It is unlikely, though, that ASEM could promote an informal process of socialization of Asian and European leaders similar to that which occurred among ASEAN leaders, because ASEM participants do not already share overall objectives and are not already engaged in cooperation in other fields. Finally, while ASEM has stimulated the mobilization of non-state actors grouped in the AEPF, the latter has not been integrated into the process because of the contradictions between its economic aims and those of the EU, on the one hand, and between its political aims and those of the Asians, on the other. The AEPF's critique of the EU's economic agenda, based on the EU's agenda at the WTO, makes the EU reluctant to accept it as a participant. Similarly, the AEPF's agenda of democratization and human rights makes it unacceptable as a participant to the Asian states. The following chapters examine the areas of common interest in which Asia–Europe dialogue has been attempted since 1996.

2 ASEM dialogue for poverty alleviation, economic cooperation and social development

In this first of three chapters on the Asia–Europe Meeting's (ASEM) role in economic cooperation between Asia and Europe, the structure of relations between the two groups at the time of ASEM 1 (1996) will be broadly outlined. As argued in the previous chapter, knowledge of this structure, no matter now approximative, and of its evolution is essential to assess the willingness and capacity of participants to engage in a dialogue that fulfills the ideal conditions enumerated earlier. For the moment, our analysis will demonstrate that although Europe is a powerful economic actor at the international level, in its relations with Asia, it is in significant respects weaker as compared to the USA and Japan. Given this weakness, its overall objective is market access for European goods and capital, which it wishes to obtain – and indeed can only obtain – through dialogue. On the Asian side, it goes without saying that most of the Asian participants are heavily dependent on access to the European market for trade, but rapid economic growth in some Asian countries increased their attractiveness to Europe and potentially enhanced their bargaining power.

After this initial presentation, the chapter will raise the question whether ASEM dialogue has contributed to poverty alleviation and social development in Asia and stimulated Asia–Europe economic cooperation. The argument here is that at the outset, each side had a distinct view of the area of common interest of Asia and Europe. Neither side was very receptive to the other's view of the common interest. The Asians anticipated concrete development and economic cooperation projects, which the Europeans were reluctant to undertake. On the other hand, the European states and firms' eagerness to increase European investment in Asian infrastructure did not meet with an enthusiastic response from the Asians. ASEM's response to the Asian financial crisis marked a turning point in the dialogue. The creation of the ASEM Trust Fund (ATF) apparently enabled implementation of projects of the type envisaged by the Asians. Unfortunately, the decision to allow the World Bank to administer the ATF introduced into the Asia–Europe dialogue a powerful new actor that is neither Asian nor European, has a well-known agenda of promoting structural adjustment, and is not well disposed to dialogue with borrowing states or civil society on this agenda. The European Union's (EU's) agreement to this arrangement lends credence to the critique by the Asia–Europe People's Forum (AEPF) of ASEM as an instrument for deregulation, privatization and liberalization and compares unfavorably with the EU's resistance to the proposal for a Social Forum that Asian and European civil society groups have long advocated. Perhaps, the initiation by states of a dialogue on the quality of labor is a sign that they are finally beginning to heed the AEPF and to focus attention on a new area of common interest.

Asian–European relations: from the rhetoric of equality to the reality of inequality

Protestations of equality cannot obscure the reality of inequality between Asia and Europe in ASEM. But this is not a straightforward situation in which the power of one "region" is to be contrasted with the weakness of the other "region." Rather the positions of each in relation to the other are a combination of strength and weakness.

We need little reminder of the European countries' strengths at the international level in general and vis-à-vis developing countries in particular. EU members constitute the world's largest trading bloc (accounting for over one-fifth of world exports in 1999); they are the headquarters of some of the world's largest transnational corporations and banks; and they are the largest source of humanitarian aid and Official Development Assistance (ODA). For these reasons, the EU will usually be in a position of strength whenever it wishes or refuses to enter into a dialogue. As we shall see, the Asians' inability to convince the EU to include poverty alleviation on the ASEM agenda and the initial difficulties in persuading it to provide assistance during the Asian financial crisis are manifestations of the structural power of European states.

A slightly different picture emerges if we examine the EU's relations with Asia, which in several respects appear unsatisfactory from the European perspective. In 1993, a year before the EU's New Asia Strategy was adopted, the European trade deficit with Asia amounted to $38.15 billion, of which $27.25 billion was the deficit with Japan (Ton Sinh Thanh 1998: 22). The rise in imports from Asia was described by Sir Leon Brittan, the then EU Commission vice president, as dramatic (Brittan 1994: 1). In investment, there were clear signs in the 1990s that European firms in Asia were lagging behind their American and Japanese competitors. In 1993, only 3 percent of EU outward foreign direct investment (FDI) was in the Asian developing countries; the comparable figures for Japan and the United States were 12 percent and 7 percent, respectively. Asia accounted for only 4 percent of total outward EU FDI and actually declined by 2 percent in the period 1980–92. This state of affairs was reflected in low relative shares of Asia in FDI from individual member states, ranging from 1.9 percent in France to 7.2 percent in the UK, with Germany (5 percent) and the Netherlands (4.3 percent) in between. The EU share in total FDI in Asia was only 14 percent, a decrease of 5 percent between 1980 and 1992 (Thanh 1998: 23). In China, the EU share of FDI, which rose from $1.551 billion in 1985 to $22.634 billion in 1996, represented a decline from 6.7 percent of the total to 4.8 percent; the respective shares of the USA and Japan in 1996 were 5.6 percent and 7.5 percent. In South Korea, European investment increased from $241 million in 1986 (6.6 percent of total FDI) to $4.021 billion in 1996 (22.8 percent of the total). In contrast, the Japanese share in the same year was 30.5 percent, and the US share was 28.8 percent. In Japan itself, EU FDI totaled $5.972 billion, which was equivalent to only 5 percent of Japanese FDI in the EU. Between 1989 and 1996, the EU share of FDI in Japan rose from 16.6 percent to 27.6 percent, but the US share more than doubled, from 23.5 percent to 60.4 percent (Dent 1999: 113, 137, 204). From 1990 to 1993, FDI from the EU into Association of Southeast Asian Nations (ASEAN) totaled $2.324 billion, a figure that already represented a substantial increase from the figure of $336 million recorded for the period 1985–87. In 1993, total stock of FDI from EU in ASEAN was estimated to be $18.04 billion (IPAP 1997: Annex 2, pp. 12, 14, 15; Robles 2001: 8).

According to the EU's New Asia Strategy, the European approach to bilateral questions stressed "a non-confrontational dialogue of equals." Closer consultation and dialogue could generate a greater understanding of the viewpoints and problems of dialogue participants and facilitate the search for consensus solutions, which could in turn help to avert disputes and provide an environment conducive to business [European Commission COM (94) 314 final: Part IV, para. 2.1]. The strategy's implications for each area of economic cooperation will be discussed in the appropriate section. For now, it should suffice to point out that engaging in a dialogue on economic questions would be complicated by the EU's desire to engage at the same time in political dialogue, encompassing not only security issues (e.g. arms control and non-proliferation) but also democratization, human rights and the rule of law.

Compared to the Europeans, the Asian participants in ASEM formed – and still form – a heterogeneous group, comprising developed (Japan), newly industrializing (Malaysia, Singapore, South Korea, Thailand), developing (China, Indonesia, the Philippines) and least developed (Vietnam since 1996, Cambodia, Laos, Burma/Myanmar and Vietnam since 2004 and Pakistan and Mongolia from 2008) countries. The last two groups received substantial amounts of ODA either from individual EU member states or from the EU or both. Even if their main markets were the United States and Japan, access to European markets was vital for them. Their vulnerability was highlighted by the reform of the EU's Generalized System of Preferences (GSP) for ASEAN (Robles 2004: 69–76) and China, which decreased tariff preferences for them, and the increasing number of antidumping complaints brought against their exports to the EU by European companies, usually ending with the imposition of duties that raised the prices of Southeast Asian exports to Europe. In fact, at the launching of the EU's New Asia Strategy, Singapore accused the EU of closing European doors to Asian exports with antidumping actions (Seet-Cheng 1994: 2, 4). ASEAN suggestions that an early warning system on dumping complaints be established did not meet with success in the ASEAN–EC Joint Cooperation Committee (Robles 2004: 76–95).

It has become a truism that the EU became interested in dialogue with Asia because of the latter's growing strength in the world economy. In the words of the European Commission:

> The Union stands to lose out on the economic miracle taking place (in Asia) ... because of the strong competition from Japan and the United States and also increasingly from companies within the region's newly industrialised and capital rich countries such as Korea or Taiwan.
>
> [European Commission COM (94) 314 final: 13]

The Commission was convinced that Europe needed to maintain a strong presence in Asia if it was to maintain its position in the world economy.

On the other hand, the Singaporean proposal for ASEM recognized East Asia's structural vulnerability vis-à-vis the EU. The Singaporean proposal for ASEM declared that Asia's goal was to ensure that European integration took place in the broader context of liberalization (Goh Chok Tong 1994/95: 1100, 1104–5), an oblique reference to Asian fears that the Single European Market would transform the EU into a "protectionist fortress." Enhancing trade meant, in Asian eyes, that ASEM should discuss and alleviate what Asians perceived to be European protectionist practices (Jung and Lehmann 1997: 55; AEVG 1999: 9; Yeo Lay Hwee 2003: 40). In such discussions, the pressure of China, Japan and South Korea could be added to that of ASEAN (Ton Sinh Thanh 1998: 82). Singapore hoped that the Asians could bring to bear their collective pressure on the Europeans by circumventing the EU's institutions, particularly the Commission. In this manner, the Asians could avoid being faced with a Europe that spoke with one voice and instead deal directly with individual EU member states. The aim, confirmed by a Thai diplomat, was to undermine the EU's bargaining power. This explains why initially Singapore was unwilling to allow the European Commission to participate in ASEM (Bersick 2004c: 181–2). Moreover, the Asians were suspicious of the European desire to engage in a comprehensive dialogue, which implied a discussion of political issues that were sensitive for authoritarian governments; hence the Asian insistence at ASEM 1 that the phrase "for greater growth" be added to the European formulation "a new comprehensive Asia-Europe partnership" (Bersick 2004c: 99–100).

With the overall structure of relations between East Asia and Europe in mind, we can now turn to the issue of whether in ASEM the dialogue has advanced economic and development cooperation between East Asia and Europe.

ASEM, poverty alleviation and economic cooperation

To some Asian participants, ASEM 1 seemed to herald a new phase in cooperation for the purpose of poverty alleviation. That no such dialogue has taken place is largely attributable to the EU reluctance to initiate one. Similarly, the expectation of some European states and the Asia–Europe Business Forum (AEBF) that cooperation in infrastructure would be stimulated has been stymied by Asian indifference.

Asian hopes may have been boosted by the Chairman's Statement of ASEM 1, which

> stressed the need to improve development cooperation between the two regions, giving priority to poverty alleviation, promoting the role of women and cooperating in the public health sector, including the strengthening of global efforts to combat AIDS and to promote AIDS prevention.
>
> (ASEM 1 1996: para. 15)

In addition, the two regions were to promote a dialogue on development cooperation with other regions. Apparently, economic cooperation would also be reinforced, as senior officials were requested to look into "how training programmes, economic cooperation and technical assistance could be further intensified in order to facilitate trade and investment" (ASEM 1 1996: para. 15).

The fact that several Asian countries proposed concrete projects at ASEM 1 gave the impression that, for them, dialogue was not to be limited to a mere exchange of views and was to be the starting point for new opportunities for cooperation. A Vietnamese diplomat confirmed that some Asian states, especially the ASEAN members, expected concrete results from ASEM, in the form of projects (Ton Sinh Thanh 1998: 106). Malaysia proposed a Trans-Asian Railway Network and an Asia–Europe University Program, while Thailand supported the establishment of an Asia–Europe Environmental Technology Centre (AEETC). Singapore went further and offered seed funding of $1 million for an Asia–Europe Foundation (ASEF). A Mekong River Basin Development Program was also mentioned in the chairman's statement. The number of projects put by the Asians on the table surprised many observers (e.g. Rüland 1996). In contrast, the only follow-up measure that any EU member offered to undertake in 1996 was the hosting of the AEBF in France (ASEM 1 1996: para. 19). The European Commission took pains to stress that ASEF and AEETC were the exceptions rather than the rule (Ton Sinh Thanh 1998). In our view, it was no coincidence that the projects were proposed primarily by ASEAN, whose behavior was undoubtedly a reflection of the ASEAN experience of cooperation with the EU, involving (European) funding for development projects, regional cooperation and trade and investment promotion.

A careful reading of the EU's New Asia Strategy would have disabused the Asians in this respect. Cooperation to alleviate poverty was indeed a European priority, but this European support was to take the form of "economic cooperation." In the EU jargon, economic cooperation, which is not to be confused with development assistance, refers to activities that are of mutual benefit (i.e. to the recipient and to the EU). These generally encompass the promotion of business cooperation through business councils or joint investment committees; provision of information; and the creation of a favorable framework for industrial cooperation, notably for small and medium enterprises (SMEs). As regards Asia, the Commission cautioned that the EU would have to "ensure that the balance between poverty alleviation and economic co-operation fits the changing conditions in Asia" [European Commission COM (94) 314 final: Part IV, para. 2.2.8]. In other words, in the new European approach, poverty would be reduced through economic cooperation, not development assistance, which would decrease as the Asian countries developed. ASEM's understanding of economic cooperation was even more limited. According to ASEM 1, cooperation would be restricted to ensuring that ASEM participants fully implemented the Uruguay Round agreements, pursued further negotiations at the World Trade Organization (WTO) and undertook facilitation and liberalization involving simplification and improvement of customs procedures and standards conformance (ASEM 1 1996: paras 11–12).

Europe's conception of economic cooperation explains why there have been practically no discussions about development cooperation (not to mention development cooperation with other regions) after ASEM 1. Occasionally, Asian developing countries may have attempted to introduce development issues behind closed doors, prompting a European Commission official to chide them gently for forgetting that ASEM's character as a dialogue among equals serves as a reason for excluding development cooperation from ASEM (Reiterer 2004: 264). Discussions around economic cooperation have not yielded any concrete results either. The Asia–Europe Cooperation Framework (AECF 2000) sought to give an impetus to economic cooperation that would go beyond a dialogue by identifying priority industrial sectors (agrotechnology, food processing, biotechnology, high technology, information technology, energy and environmental engineering) (AECF 2000: para. 16). Vietnam, which hosted the third Economic Ministers' Meeting (EMM) in 2001, gave the impression that it understood the AECF provision to be a proposal for cooperation in industrial areas and submitted proposals in the same areas to the EMM (EMM 3 2001: para. 7). It is not clear whether the Vietnamese proposals were circulated after the meeting for appraisal or feasibility studies. By 2006, it could safely be said that no proposal for industrial cooperation has ever been seriously considered within ASEM.

Official communiqués do not identify the states that were not very enthusiastic about industrial cooperation in ASEM. It is quite likely, though, that European states were in this group, for two reasons. First, in its bilateral relations with Asia, various EU facilities have already been made available to Asian and European firms for joint ventures and other investment projects. Among these are the European Community Investment Partners (ECIP), Asia-Invest, Asia-Partenariat, ASEAN-Partenariat and European Business Information Centres and access to the European Investment Bank (EIB) (Robles 2004: 96–127). Consequently, any ASEM joint action would amount to duplication of efforts, which would have to be financed by the EU. Equally important, if not more so, the European concern was market access, which could be achieved through modification of the legislation of Asian countries, as we shall see in Chapter 4.

In the areas of poverty alleviation and economic cooperation, the relationship between the EU and most Asian participants is obviously one of inequality. Bearing in mind that funding of such activities is a unilateral act and not an obligation for the EU states, we realize that Asian participants dispose of few means with which to persuade the EU to undertake them. One wonders whether participation by the civil society groups would have persuaded or compelled ASEM to allocate resources to poverty alleviation or economic cooperation. The AEPF's recommendations have tended to be general rather than specific. For example, during the Asian financial crisis, they called upon Asia and Europe to "ensure the poor's participation in the definition of policies and programs that affect their lives and livelihoods" and to "learn from successful development projects (community banks, sustainable resource management, etc.) and alternatives that emanate from poor communities, and support, replicate and adopt from these people-led initiatives." (AEPF 2 1998a) For AEPF 3 (2000), Asia–Europe relations should also reduce gender-based inequalities and eliminate the most intolerable forms of child labor. It is conceivable that the capacity to make arguments of this type could have increased Asian states' interest in AEPF participation in ASEM, had it not been for the fact that in the same statements, Asian values were equated with Suharto-style "family values" (AEPF 2 1998a) and ASEM participants were urged to respect workers' rights to join a trade union of one's choice and to organize and bargain collectively (AEPF 3 2000). Needless to say, the summits failed to heed any AEPF recommendations. The EU's unwillingness to consider the AEPF's demands as a basis for discussion of development cooperation probably arises from the fact that these issues are already tackled in the bilateral dialogue between the EU and the individual ASEM participants, while the purpose of ASEM is to secure market access.

The European refusal of dialogue on poverty alleviation and economic cooperation appears to be matched by the Asian reluctance to undertake a dialogue on infrastructure development in Asia. For European states and firms, it was the development of Asian infrastructure in electricity, gas, transportation, telecommunication and water that offered significant opportunities, at least prior to the Asian financial crisis. Energy, transportation, telecommunication, aviation and aerospace were identified by the European Commission [COM (94) 314 final: Part V; COM 2000 (241): 8] as the priority areas in which Europeans had a comparative advantage. A number of EU programs already offered lending facilities to EU firms interested in Asia, but their disadvantage was that they involved competition with proposals from other regions of the developing world outside the African, Caribbean and Pacific (ACP) group, particularly South Asia and Latin America. Even if specific programs were reserved for Asia, the amount of funding they could provide for actual project implementation was limited (Robles 2004: 113–17).

The Asia–Europe Vision Group (AEVG) called for the adoption of an improved ASEM infrastructure framework for energy, telecommunications, transport and water. Asia–Europe cooperation would have consisted mainly in benchmarking the current status of and the large gaps in public–private infrastructure financing needs, legal forms of partnerships, guarantee instruments and anti-corruption measures taken by the World Bank, the Asian Development Bank (ADB) and the Organization for Economic Cooperation and Development (OECD); and systematic cost–benefit analysis of the most viable infrastructure projects (AEVG 1999: 13–14).

The AEBF, relying on the World Bank estimate that investment needs in Asian infrastructure over a decade would amount to $1.5 trillion (AEBF 1 1996: 4), has been the most consistent advocate of cooperation in the area of infrastructure. Asian needs were to be met through a Europe–Asia infrastructure fund, cooperation among export credit agencies and training in project management and risk assessment. The idea of a fund met with a lukewarm reaction from the first EMM, for whom risks could be mitigated and transaction costs reduced through a regulatory framework and the launching of appropriate tools: model contracts, standard bidding and contractual guidelines, with possible instruments for encouraging contract observance (EMM 1 1997: Part V). In view of the economic ministers' attitude, the AEBF shifted gears, admitting that the establishment of an infrastructure fund was no longer central and recommended instead that an infrastructure round table be set up in each state. A legal task force would be convened to survey procurement methods, the role of the public partner in the venture, adaptation and renegotiation clauses, dispute avoidance and appropriate regulatory framework (AEBF 2 1997: 3–4). Subsequently, the AEBF emphasized the need for improved public–private partnerships (PPPs) and advocated the establishment of e-commerce and SME-related databases, training of human resources and alleviation of difficulties for entry into telecommunications markets (AEBF 4 1999: 3). Probably, the most extraordinary AEBF proposal originated in its working group on water, which requested that ASEM 2 establish a public awareness program "to educate consumers in the real cost of water services and thus (to increase) their willingness to pay for such services" (AEBF 3 1998: para. 10). The background of this bold proposal will be examined in the following section. In response, the EMM (EMM 2 1999: para. 17) simply requested that the AEBF draw up an analysis of best-practice conditions governing private-sector involvement in projects of this type. AEBF 6 (October 2001) recommended that a task force examine PPP development in the provision of public utility services in the ASEM participants (AEBF 6 2001: 6). States were urged to create the conditions for the implementation of PPP contracts and launch PPP pilot projects in infrastructure sectors (ABEF 7 2002: 4).

There is no evidence that the discussions in the AEBF and the EMM had a catalytic effect on European investments in Asian infrastructure. It is difficult to avoid the conclusion that Asian states were reluctant to cooperate in infrastructure projects. As in the case of poverty alleviation and economic cooperation, there is no evidence in the public domain regarding the arguments that may have been raised by participants in the dialogue, forcing us to speculate on the reasons for lack of progress in dialogue. For the European Commission and/or member states, an infrastructure fund might have been a duplication of the facilities offered by other programs to Asian countries, e.g. the EIB, ECIP and Asia-Invest. The Asian attitude may have been motivated by the desire to maintain control over the awarding of contracts to local and foreign firms, as suggested by the experience of Indonesia's water privatization, to be examined in the following section. In this case, it is Asian states that are in a structurally stronger position, controlling as they do a key asset – access to the market for infrastructure projects.

Awareness of this constraint may have convinced the ASEM Task Force for Closer Economic Partnership between Asia and Europe, created by ASEM 4 (2002), to shift the focus of infrastructure cooperation from infrastructure investment in Asian countries to facilitation of the long-term development of transportation, communications, water and energy infrastructure in the "societies forming the land bridge linking Europe with Asia." A long-term ASEM cooperation strategy with regard to these countries, which are energy producers or exporters, would contribute to stabilizing the ASEM participants' future energy supply (ASEM Task Force 2004: Annex IV). These "societies," which are not named in the report, presumably range from Western China to the former Soviet republics of Central Asia. The energy resources of several of the latter are the object of intense competition among China, Russia, the United States, Japan and other US allies (e.g. Turkey). Perhaps, the European members of the Task Force see a partnership with one or the other of the Asian states possessing financial and technological capabilities to invest in Central Asia as a way of enhancing a European presence in that region. It is too early to say how the Central Asian states themselves will react to any such initiative. It is not even sure if they were consulted during the preparation of the task force report, which should have been the case if they were considered equal partners. As regards the initiative itself, at this point, we can only say that it resembles the declaration of intention at ASEM 1 that development cooperation of Asia and Europe with other regions would also be on the agenda of Asia–Europe dialogue and may go the same way as that declaration.

The abortive attempts to discuss poverty alleviation, economic cooperation and infrastructure development highlight one of the unresolved questions in Todorov's and Habermas's approaches to dialogue: how can an actor that does not wish to engage in dialogue be persuaded to do so? The ASEM debate on the Asian financial crisis, which indirectly reintroduced poverty alleviation into the ASEM agenda, provides us with one possible answer: an unexpected shock may jolt actors out of their indifference, passivity or complacency and spur a dialogue.

The ASEM trust fund: a pyrrhic victory for Asians?

The Asian financial crisis, arguably the first crisis of globalization, became something of a crisis for ASEM as well (Brittan 1999; on the Asian crisis, see Bello 1998; Bevacqua 1998; Freeman 1998; Jomo 1998; Mitchie and Smith 1999). European agreement at ASEM 2 (1998) to set up an ATF, widely seen in Asia as an evidence of European willingness to listen to Asian requests for European assistance, may yet turn out to be a Pyrrhic victory, in view of the decision to lodge the ATF at the World Bank.

From European indifference to European assistance

The initial European analysis of the causes of the crisis and the proposed solutions, expressed within ASEM as well as in the International Monetary Fund

(IMF), hewed very closely to the orthodoxy represented by the United States and the IMF and took little account of Asian views. Although ASEM was not conceived as a negotiating forum, the Asian states affected by the crisis sought support and assistance from Europe through ASEM 2 (1998b), compelling the Europeans to listen to their views. The decision to establish a Trust Fund by ASEM 2 appears to bear witness to the success of the Asian strategy.

The outbreak of the Asian financial crisis was as much a shock for Europeans who had confidently predicted that "East Asian economic growth and social development (would) be sustained" (Lehmann 1998: 74), as for Asians who had asserted that "Asia must now be courted" (Seet-Cheng 1994: 4). Meeting in Bangkok in September 1997, barely a month after the collapse of the host country's currency, the ASEM finance ministers referred only to what they called "the recent currency turbulence in some Asian economies" (FinMM 1 1997). Asian and European common interests were defined in very broad terms: the need for international cooperation that could "reduce risk and enhance stability," and the need for "exchange of information and sharing of best practices in such areas as financial supervision and regulation, operation of financial markets and management of payments systems." The only concrete measures proposed were the holding of regular consultations of financial supervisors on international financial issues and examination of the possibility of establishing a computerized communication network among the finance ministers (FinMM 1 1997: paras 4, 9, 16) to facilitate information sharing. Neither measure was subsequently implemented, leaving us to doubt the effectiveness of the dialogue that had taken place. Meeting in Japan later in that same month, economic ministers confidently expressed the view, based on

> sound economic fundamentals, abundant investment opportunities and high savings ratios, and the consistent application of sound, market-oriented and outward-looking policies, [that] transient economic difficulties, export slowdown and exchange rate fluctuations observed in some ASEM partners would not harm the significant long-term potential of these economies.
>
> (EMM 1 1997: 2)

Again, no specific measures to address the "transient economic difficulties" were envisaged (Robles 2001: 19–20). At the ASEF inaugural lecture in January 1998, the European Commission President Jacques Santer downplayed market panic, contagion or speculation as causes of the crisis. He repeated the mantra that liberalization of trade and services was the long-term global solution and denied that the EU, which was already contributing to the international rescue packages coordinated by the IMF, had any additional role to play.

At the IMF, Asians and Europeans were unable to reach a consensus as regards either the causes of the crisis or the solutions to it. At the annual meeting, held in Hong Kong at almost the same time as the Finance Ministers' Meeting (FMM), European analyses referred primarily to domestic causes, and in so doing, placed the blame squarely and exclusively on the Asian countries.

For Germany, the "currency turbulence" was due to "delayed implementation of exchange rate policy adjustments in combination with other risk factors, such as excessive and short-term foreign currency debt and a high and potentially rising current account deficit" (IMF 1997: 117). France blamed Thailand for ignoring warnings that the IMF is alleged to have given:

> (T)he IMF anticipated the crisis in Thailand, pointing out to anyone willing to listen that certain external deficits had become unsustainable and that obstinate defense of exchange rates no longer based on sound economic policies was dangerous and bound to fail.
>
> (IMF 1997: 114; see also the statement by Austria: 50)

This extraordinary statement flew in the face of evidence to the contrary available from many other sources. To take one example among many: the 1997 IMF *Annual Report* actually praised Thailand's "remarkable economic performance" and the Thai authorities' "consistent record of sound macroeconomic policies." Nor was this an accidental lapse. The IMF also "welcomed Korea's continued impressive macroeconomic performance (and) praised the authorities for their enviable fiscal record" (quoted in Sachs 1997).

In contrast to the EU positions, the Philippines pointed to the possibility of panic among market players as an aggravating factor in the spread of the crisis – "contagious and self-fulfilling prophecies of doom that start from one country and spread like a virus" (IMF 1997: 204). Malaysia went further, charging that the intensity of the contagion effect was "to no small extent aggravated by the workings of unscrupulous speculators" (IMF 1997: 167).

The European approach to the crisis followed closely the U.S. approach that stressed the key role of multilateral, as opposed to regional, institutions and the significance of conditionality. As France put it at the IMF meeting,

> (O)nly an institution with universal scope, such as the IMF is capable of fulfilling all of the conditions necessary for handling crisis …. The needed financing can be mobilized only on the basis of member countries' confidence in the firm and objective IMF conditionality. Nothing could be more dangerous than organizing financial support without backing it with the discipline provided by the IMF.
>
> (IMF 1997: 114)

Among the developed countries, only Japan ventured the view that close regional cooperation was essential for the prevention and control of crisis, in view of the possibility of contagion (IMF 1997: 150). Consistent with the stress on the domestic causes of the crisis, European states strenuously denied that "capital transactions should be more strongly regulated or controlled" (Germany, in IMF 1997: 118). France warned that the developing countries could not have their cake and eat it too: "A government cannot applaud inflows that enable it to finance accelerated growth and then denounce outflows when an

excessive external deficit or economic policy blunders drive investors away."
(IMF 1997: 114) Surprisingly, Germany expressed the belief that the IMF
should be given a new, extended mandate to include promoting the liberalization
of capital transactions (IMF 1997: 118; cf. also Austria in IMF 1997: 50).

Probably fearing that such a move might be the monetary equivalent of
jumping from the frying pan into the fire, Thailand put forward the view that as
regards capital account convertibility, his country "would be more comfortable
if the Fund would proceed in a more cautious and gradual manner." If the IMF
were given jurisdiction over the capital account, this "should not be construed as
an obligation for members to liberalize, but rather for the Fund to ensure the
orderly and smooth operation of international flows" (IMF 1997: 237). For the
Malaysian governor, who alluded to "unscrupulous speculators" twice in his
statement, a future international framework "to cope with market excesses associated with destabilizing capital flows" should contain rules that must be binding
on capital market participants, and not just on states (ibid.).

European concerns in the early stages of the crisis lay primarily in two areas.
Within the EU, "European concerns," as Payoyo so aptly puts it, "were focused
less on what Europe could do to help solve the crisis than on what impact the
crisis was having or would have on Europe." Europeans worried about the
impact of the crisis on the launching of the euro in 1999. The consensus in
Europe was that the crisis would not derail the euro's introduction (Payoyo
1999: 400–1). The second European concern was to ensure that the Asian countries made commitments to improved access to their financial markets by the
December 1997 deadline set by the WTO. The ASEAN member states were on
the WTO list of twenty priority countries that were to make concessions on
financial liberalization. At the height of the crisis, on 26 September 1997,
Brittan, the European Commission vice president, called on the Asian states to
make added commitments that would improve access to their financial markets
before the deadline. To the satisfaction of the EU, five Asian states did submit
improved offers for market access and national treatment to foreign providers of
services (Payoyo 1999: 391–3; Robles 2001: 20–2).

Asia's crisis-affected countries hoped that an ASEM contribution would
complement unsatisfactory multilateral solutions and failed regional initiatives
(the following draws heavily on Rüland 1998a; Wesley 1999; Chang and Rajan
1999; Bowles 1999). The Asian Monetary Fund had been withdrawn by its proponent, Japan, under US and EU pressure. Other regional solutions floated (e.g.
a common market with a common currency from Malaysia or the acceleration of
ASEAN Free Trade Area's (AFTA's) implementation from Singapore) were "ill
conceived and not backed up by in-depth studies" (Rüland 1998a: 10), while a
Manila Framework adopted for cooperative financing arrangements and an early
warning system would have taken time to implement. Given the dissatisfaction
with the IMF and the World Bank packages and uncertainty over the outcomes
of the regional approach, an ASEM contribution was worth trying.

Asian frustration with European indifference was palpably expressed in the
run-up to ASEM 2 in 1998 (Payoyo 1999: 400–02). Europe was warned by

Singapore's Senior Minister Lee Kuan Yew that it had missed earlier opportunities to show concern for Indonesia and Thailand. He argued that because European banks faced substantial losses, it was in Europe's interest to contain the crisis of confidence. On the same day, Brittan declared in Hong Kong that the EU was ready and willing to share expertise in financial market opening and prudential supervision. Whether or not this was a coincidence, it did not clear the air. Some Asian officials were apprehensive lest Europe insist on the pursuit of trade liberalization at ASEM 2: "Europe must be realist and not expect too much from us.... ASEM cannot have too high expectations until we are on the way to full recovery. Asia will not close its markets but its markets will be smaller" (Coloma 1998). A comparison of the contributions of Japan ($19 billion), the United States ($8 billion) and Europe ($6.2 billion) to the IMF rescue packages prompted a Japanese diplomat to describe Europeans as "free riders on Asia's economic success but unwilling to share the responsibility for helping it out" (Cornwell 1998). The reasons for the perceived European indifference were not too difficult to fathom: "Saving Asia is costly, complicated, and diplomatically tricky, and there are few votes in it back home" (Parry 1998).

Asian specific demands for EU assistance challenged the concept of ASEM as a forum for dialogue that excluded negotiation. A Thai non-paper prepared for the summit listed the options that could be negotiated with the EU: extending EU loans to restructure industrial and agricultural production in the medium or long term; provision by the EU of ODA; provision by the EU of technical assistance in finance and banking; an increase in EU funding under the ECIP and encouraging top executives of large European companies to expand their investments in Asia. Although the European Commission admitted that Europe would be forced to respond, it stated flatly that the response "would not be a financial one, and no one expected that the Summit would come up with some billion-dollar package" (Bersick 2004c: 216–18).

The ASEM 2 statement on the Asian economic and financial situation represents, in many observers' view, a convergence of interests based on European acknowledgment that the financial crisis was a matter of vital concern to all ASEM participants. European receptiveness to Asian concerns was justified by the German Chancellor Helmut Kohl in terms of enlightened self-interest: "If Asia is doing badly today, Europe will do badly tomorrow." As a major exporter, Germany had good reason to maintain close cooperation with Asia ("If Asia suffers, so do we, says Kohl" 1998). Payoyo points out that by mid-1996, European banks had claims of $76.5 billion in Indonesia, South Korea, Malaysia, the Philippines and Thailand. By the end of 1996, the total had risen to $89.5 billion. By mid-1997, banks from the EU had combined claims on five Asian countries totaling $98.1 billion; Japanese banks had total claims of $97.2 billion and American banks, $23.8 billion (Payoyo 1999: 415).

The ASEM 2 Financial Statement departed in significant respects from the positions taken by several European states at the IMF meeting held six months earlier, suggesting that the European states were reformulating their interests as a result of dialogue with the Asians. ASEM appeared to have offered a congenial forum for generating an analysis of the crisis distinct from earlier European analyses, on the one hand, and the United States and IMF analyses, on the other. The generation of such new knowledge is precisely one of the outcomes of dialogue, as Todorov reminds us (see Chapter 1). First, ASEM participants conceptualized the reform of the international financial system as one that went beyond strengthening IMF capacity to respond to financial crises and one that included "enhanced and more transparent global IMF surveillance." Europe recognized that the global mechanism had to be complemented in Asia by a new regional surveillance mechanism. ASEM leaders also called for strengthened cooperation, regulation and supervision in financial sectors. However, the willingness to consider monitoring of short-term capital flows did not extend to approval of controls on capitals (ASEM 2 1998b: para. 4). The Europeans reportedly feared that reference to improved transparency in international financial and capital markets would shift blame for the crisis to international factors ("Europe must match words with deeds," 1998) and implicitly contradict the IMF and U.S. view that the crisis was one of corrupt and inefficient "Asian capitalism." Without Kohl's strong support for the Asian position, the Asian view might not have been reflected in the statement. Perhaps as a response to the widespread criticism that the burden of adjustment had fallen only on the Asian states and populations, the ASEM participants stressed the importance of securing private sector involvement in the concluding debtor/creditor fora and providing financial assistance such as trade credit. Finally, reference was made to the need to consider the social impact of the crisis: reform should be accompanied by efforts "to protect social expenditure" and to "develop well-designed and affordable social safety nets ..." (ASEM 2 1998b: paras 5, 10). According to a Singaporean correspondent, who cannot be accused of a pro-European bias, it was the European leaders who persuaded their Asian counterparts to express concern over the social consequences of the crisis (Chua Min Hoong 1998b; Robles 2001: 26–9).

How was this new-found consensus translated into joint action? First of all, the commitment to implementing initiatives that were already underway was reaffirmed. This "commitment" may have been somewhat disappointing to the Asians, for these initiatives referred to cooperation in human resource development, the promotion of SMEs and implementation of the ASEM Trade Facilitation Action Plan (TFAP) and Investment Promotion Action Plan (IPAP). It was also proposed to send a high-level business mission to Asia as part of an effort "to enlarge understanding of the consequences of the crisis" (this mission appears never to have taken place). The participants promised "to resist any protectionist measures and at least to maintain the current level of market access while pursuing further liberalisation ..." (ASEM 2 1998b: paras 9, 14, 14 bis, 16).

The nature of EU "assistance" to Asia during the financial crisis deserves careful examination. In the first place, since tariffs have been bound for many years now following a series of General Agreement on Tariffs and Trade (GATT) rounds, they cannot be unilaterally changed in times of crisis and even under strong domestic pressure to take protective measures. Under GATT and

WTO rules, states do have at their disposal a number of legal instruments, such as antidumping and safeguard clauses, that would enable them to take measures in the face of "market disruption." It was probably these measures that the European participants were referring to when they undertook "not to take any restrictive measures in the legitimate exercise of their WTO rights that would go beyond that which is necessary to remedy specific situations, as provided for in WTO rules" (ASEM 2 1998b: para. 14). To get a sense of the extent of this commitment, it should be pointed out that the power to institute measures of this type is shared by states with non-state actors. In the case of antidumping, complaints are brought by firms that claim to have suffered from dumping and not by governments or by the European Commission. This being the case, the pledge simply meant that in case complaints were brought to the Commission, it would not abuse the powers granted to it by the WTO. The pledge implied that such abuse was possible in other circumstances. It would have been more convincing if it had implied that the European governments and/or the European Commission would actively seek to prevent antidumping complaints from being presented, refrain from imposing antidumping penalties and/or undertake media campaigns to urge European consumers to continue purchasing goods and services from the Asian countries affected by the crisis. The investment side of the pledge, which was added upon German suggestion (Bersick 2004c: 219), was even less specific. At the very least, it was a tacit commitment that the EU and its member states would not hinder implementation of existing programs, such as Asia-Invest (Robles 2001: 26–7).

In another respect, the actions of the EU, as a group composed of powerful (creditor) states, tacitly indicated that it was taking a broader view of its self-interest, as Habermas urged powerful states to do. The little information at our disposal points to a dialogue having taken place, followed by the negotiation of a compromise. The Asians' goal was financial assistance, which the Europeans were initially unwilling to provide. The compromise came in the form of a trust fund, which met the Asian demand, but the fund had a relatively small endowment, in conformity with the EU position that the package would not be a multibillion dollar one. The fund would be financed by the EU and was thus distinct from IMF–World Bank packages that had been severely criticized in Asia. On the other hand, the fact that the fund's administration was left to the World Bank was probably upon the insistence of the Europeans, who did not wish to break ranks with the IMF and the United States in the approach to the crisis.

An ATF, initially amounting to $25 million, for two years and lodged at the World Bank would provide technical assistance in support of restructuring of the financial sector and on "finding effective ways to redress poverty" (ASEM 2 1998b: para. 7) The World Bank would be responsible for implementation to donors, whose views would be sought for activities above $1 million or having particular policy significance. All Asian countries would be eligible, except for Japan, Singapore and Brunei. It was also proposed to create a European network "for increasing the quality and quantity of technical advice in reforming the financial sector" (ASEM 2 1998b: para. 8). This European Financial Expertise

Network (EFEX) would serve as a clearinghouse to identify European expertise that would meet demand for financial sector advice in Asia.

The two measures implied recognition that Asia and Europe were not equal partners. That said, few would probably have refused some sort of European assistance even at the cost of admitting the de facto inequality among the participants. What was significant for many Asian leaders and observers was that the ASEM consensus appeared to constitute a vindication of the Asian position and of the ASEM process itself. The Thai Prime Minister Chuan Leekpai declared that the outcome had exceeded his expectations ("Europe Must Match Words with Deeds," 1998). The Singaporean Prime Minister Goh Chok Tong, confessing that up to the meeting "we were not sure if Europe understood the gravity of the nature of the problem in Asia," interpreted the outcome "as a strong signal that Europe has sent to Asia" that "Europe cares." If we are to believe Goh Chok Tong, the meeting strengthened the ASEM process (Hoong 1998a; "Europe 'doing more now' for Asia," 1998). Payoyo (1999: 408–9) asserts that "it was the ASEM process that supplied the indispensable mechanism to address and to resolve Europe's Asia crisis. In effect, the Asian leaders used ASEM as a grievance machinery that compelled the Europeans to respond." That said, the Trust Fund's mandate may not have lived up to the expectations of the Asians. To begin with, Singapore's expectation was already quite modest: the Fund's main purpose was "to assist in assessing the poverty impact of the crisis" (Koh 1998) and not to alleviate the suffering caused by the crisis. The amount set aside for the already modest goal was further reduced by a decision to reserve half of the total funds to the financial sector. Surprisingly, the country that was reported to have been very receptive to Asian complaints, Germany, did not contribute to the Fund, reflecting a preference for a bilateral approach ("Europe must match words with deeds," 1998).

It goes without saying that the AEPF had a radically different analysis of the causes of the crisis. For the AEPF, rapid trade and financial liberalization, growing dependence on foreign capital, the lack of responsible government regulation and monitoring, and speculation were the main causes of the crisis. Consequently, the AEPF advocated more radical solutions to the crisis. The ATF was denounced as a "smokescreen": if the purpose was to study impact of the crisis on the poor, the AEPF claimed that detailed information on this impact had already been obtained by non-governmental organizations (NGOs). In the AEPF's view, the professed concern for the social impact of the crisis was contradicted by the ASEM's tribute to the IMF whose rescue packages had only intensified the poverty caused by the crisis. The AEPF advocated two components of ASEM action: the European policies that directly tackled poverty; and fundamental reform of the IMF and other international financial institutions. The AEPF called on the EU members to use their 29 percent share of IMF voting power to reverse IMF's stabilization programs and to review IMF's objectives, decision-making processes, transparency and accountability. At the same time, ASEM participants were urged to adopt measures to monitor and regulate international financial flows and to control speculation, such as the

Tobin tax (see Chapter 3). Opposing the EU insistence on further trade and financial liberalization, the AEPF demanded that legally enforceable codes of conducts for transnational corporations be developed. Finally, EU was urged to withdraw its support of the Multilateral Agreement on Investment (MIA) then negotiated at the OECD (AEPF 2 1998b).

As we shall see in Chapter 3, at subsequent ASEM meetings, expressions of deep dissatisfaction with the international monetary system were heard from the Asian countries, suggesting that they were more receptive to consider radical proposals for reform. The AEPF's views with respect to the reform of the IMF highlight once more the contradictory position in which the AEPF finds itself: if the support that the AEPF could lend to some Asian positions may tempt a handful of Asian governments to consider AEPF participation in ASEM, the very nature of the AEPF's views would ensure EU opposition to any such participation.

The attempted ASEM dialogue on the reform of the international financial architecture will be taken up in the following chapter. In the following section, we will undertake a rapid analysis of the World Bank's administration of the ATF, which may lead us to a less optimistic assessment of the decisions taken at ASEM 2.

The World Bank as a participant in ASEM dialogue

During the first phase of ATF 1, which ended on 31 December 2002, seventy-seven projects worth $47.5 million were approved. Six projects, with a total disbursement of $39.5 million, were implemented. As anticipated in 1998, approximately 50 percent of the total supported social sector programs, while the other 50 percent funded financial and corporate sector programs. The allocation between the two sectors varied significantly from country to country. China, Malaysia, the Philippines and Vietnam emphasized financial and corporate sector programs (82 percent, 67 percent, 62 percent and 90 percent, respectively, of the total grants to these countries), whereas the social sector received the bulk of funds granted to Indonesia (84 percent of the total awarded to it), Korea (67 percent) and Thailand (68 percent). The largest recipient of funds was Indonesia (17 percent), followed by the Philippines (16 percent), China (14 percent), Vietnam and Thailand (13 percent each), Korea and multicountry projects (11 percent each) and Malaysia (5 percent) (World Bank 2003: 29).

Evaluation of the impact of these projects, particularly in the long term, is not easy, in part because of the relatively small amounts involved. The sum of $39 million disbursed is a pittance compared to the billion dollar packages prepared by the IMF for Indonesia, South Korea and Thailand, not to mention the billions of dollars that fled Asia during the crisis. At their 2005 meeting in Tianjin, China, the finance ministers identified the following impacts:

> (T)he ATF has provided timely support to the Asian countries concerned in responding to the crisis and contributed to the (*sic*) social development and poverty reduction. ATF has also served as an effective platform for enhanc-

ing mutual understanding and complementing comparative advantages between Asia and Europe.

(FinMM 6 2005: Annex, para. 3)

With all due respect to the ministers, these conclusions should be taken with a grain of salt.

As regards the alleged first impact, the fact that three out of the six countries allocated the bulk of their grants to the financial sector suggests that the impact on social development and poverty reduction could be at best indirect and long term. In the three countries, the amounts involved were relatively small and permitted the implementation of full-scale, independent social projects in only a very small number of cases. The best example of this was probably the Philippine Out-of-School Children and Youth Development (POSCYD) projects, which received $980,000 in 2000 and 2001. Of the sixteen sub-projects funded, five provided out-of-school children and youth with formal education and combined formal and technical education (566 beneficiaries in three projects); an alternative learning system was offered through two projects (300 beneficiaries); and eleven sub-projects provided integrated technical education (1,290 beneficiaries). The beneficiaries received funding for school needs, such as uniforms, shoes, bags and notebooks. A system of formal accreditation and equivalency was also offered to 753 out-of-school youth. It was reported that the total number of beneficiaries reached 4,119 (37 percent above the target of 3,000) and that the employment rate among the participants in the technical education projects was 70 percent (the national average was 44 percent) (ATF No. 02513, 023514). Far be it from us to deny the substantial improvement in the beneficiaries' chances of finding gainful employment, this cannot prevent us from pointing out that, first, these beneficiaries had not been directly affected by the financial crisis, and second, their number was very low – almost infinitesimal – in a country with a population of eighty million at the time.

As pointed out earlier, the amounts allocated to most social projects were very small. As a result, the funds were allocated to components of larger World Bank projects. This circumstance cannot but prompt us to raise questions regarding the projects' capacity to contribute to social development and poverty reduction. One such World Bank program was the Indonesian Water Utility Rescue Program. A rather lengthy explanation is essential if we are to understand the context in which an ATF grant was awarded to Indonesia (the following relies heavily on Hadad 2003 and Wermasubun 2003).

In Indonesia, local government-owned water utilities (PAM/PDAM) were the most reliable providers of safe water. In the early 1990s, their services reached only a fraction of the urban population, and rural populations, not at all. In 1993–94, Indonesia began to privatize the water sector under a World Bank policy emphasizing promotion of the private sector's role in that sector. Privatization gained momentum after the Asian financial crisis, which raised the PDAMs' operating costs and prevented them from servicing World Bank and the Asian Development Bank loans. In 1998, the World Bank initiated the Water

Utilities Rescue Program, under which the PDAMs were to raise rates and encourage the private sector as partners of local governments. The latter would cease to be service providers, refrain from intervention in PDAM management (particularly rate-setting) and act instead as facilitators and regulators. For its part, the World Bank would facilitate bids by domestic and international companies for the design and development of water companies.

The ATF grant of $396,000 (of which $300,593.13 were disbursed) was intended to assist the PDAMs to survive the crisis and to improve their operational and financial efficiency, consistent with the World Bank's Indonesia Urban Water Supply Policy Framework and the Indonesian government's Water Supply and Sanitation Policy Framework for Urban and Rural Areas (ATF, Nos. 022671, 022672). According to the World Bank, the first objective was not achieved because of an eighteen-month delay in program start-up. The second objective was achieved, in that ten pilot PDAMS and local governments were made more aware of the PDAM's problems and possible solutions to them. One local government paid off its PDAM's loan; others approved rate increases.

Regrettably, neither the World Bank nor the ATF grant were able to draw the lessons from the problems encountered by privatization of water services in the mid-1990s, which involved two major European companies (this relies heavily on Hadad 2003). Following receipt of a World Bank loan to improve the infrastructure of Jakarta's water company, Thames Water Overseas Ltd, in partnership with one of Suharto's sons and Suez Lyonnaise, in collaboration with a Suharto crony, competed to run Jakarta's water system. In the end, the rivalry was resolved by dividing Jakarta water management into two equal parts for the two companies, without any competitive bidding. After Suharto's fall in 1998, mass demonstrations forced the government to consider renegotiating the contracts; only the threat of lawsuits prevented it from continuing with its plans. As was to be expected, privatization was followed by two large increases in water rates in six years. Critics charge that neither company has fulfilled its contractual obligations of reducing water leakage from 50 percent to 35 percent and providing service to 50 percent of the urban population in five years. In their defense, the companies blamed the crisis and the refusal of Indonesian employees to cooperate with their foreign employers. The AEBF's extraordinary request to the ASEM 2 in 1998 that a program be established "to educate consumers in the real cost of water services and thus (to increase) their willingness to pay for such services" (AEBF 3 1998: para. 10) was probably another component in the European companies' self-defense strategy. At least, ASEM 2 had the good sense not to take note of this request. To return to the ASEM finance ministers' conclusion, if an ATF grant contributes to privatization of water carried out in these conditions, then the assertion that the ATF promotes social development and poverty reduction becomes less self-evident.

Did ATF grants serve as a "platform for enhancing mutual understanding" on development issues between Asia and Europe? One would hesitate to respond to this question in the affirmative. The size of the grants and their integration into the World Bank's program entailed two consequences. First, in practice, the

World Bank became the interlocutor of the Asian country; and second, the World Bank's instinct was to push its agenda of privatization, deregulation and liberalization. In other words, what took place between the World Bank and the Asian recipients was hardly dialogue. The experience of three ATF grants will illustrate these arguments.

Indonesia received a grant for monitoring the regional implementation of structural reforms and deregulation (ATF 020611). For the World Bank, the financial crisis offered an opportunity to abolish obstacles to internal trade – such as commodity taxes within and between provinces, prohibitions on trade in certain commodities and provincial monopolies. The ATF grant's purpose was to monitor progress in Indonesia's commitment to the World Bank to implement liberalization and to demonstrate benefits of deregulation to regional governments. It comes as no surprise that the studies commissioned by the grant clearly demonstrated that deregulation resulted in increased competition and payment of a higher portion of a commodity's value to the farmer and that the decrease in local government revenues was not due to a loss of trade taxes and levies but rather due to the loss of significant revenue sources, such as vehicles transfer taxes. The World Bank's well-known commitment to deregulation makes one wonder if genuine efforts at dialogue were undertaken between the ATF-funded consultants and the Indonesian authorities concerned.

The Philippines received an ATF grant for social protection and social housing in support of the World Bank's strategy for the country on non-bank financial sector reforms related to social protection and social housing. The ATF grant's aims were to review the entire retirement income system; to provide technical assistance to design a home-ownership assistance program that would combine budgeted subsidies with loans at market rates; to explore alternative beneficiary-led housing delivery mechanisms for families that cannot afford to purchase individual homes; and to assist in designing a strategy for disposition (i.e. abolition) of the functions, assets and the liabilities of the National Home Mortgage Finance Corporation (NHMFC), one of the government's major agencies providing loans for low-cost housing (the following is based on Navarro-Martin and Olalia 2001). The World Bank pointed out that the Philippines relied heavily on public pension agencies, the Government Service Insurance System (GSIS) and the Social Security System (SSS) to finance low-income housing programs at low interest rates. Both faced high risks due to poor collection rates on low-income housing loans. The ATF program was not able to review the Philippine retirement income system; under the social housing component, only the study on the NHMFC and initial work on a Homeowner assistance program were pursued. The World Bank rated implementation of the ATF grant as unsatisfactory for its failure to assist the Philippine government in designing reforms.

An initial reaction might be to deplore the fact that the funds were paid to the consultants for studies that were never utilized and recommendations that were never implemented. Upon closer inspection, the program's failure may not be so unfortunate after all. Sources within the NHMFC claim that it was the World Bank and not the Philippine government, that proposed the study on the abolition of the NHMFC. The claim is not as implausible as it sounds: after all, the ATF grant was integrated into the World Bank's Country Assistance Strategy for the Philippines. These same sources criticized the choice of the Philippine consultant, a well-known accounting firm with no particular expertise in housing. The reversal of the Philippine government policy to which the World Bank attributes the failure to implement the study's recommendations may have been partly a response to opposition within the agency and sectors of the public to liquidation of the NHMFC. The Philippine government may not be able to escape the blame for requesting the ATF grant in the first place. On the other hand, it is not too far-fetched to assume that the World Bank's ideological commitment to privatization prevented it from anticipating adverse reactions to the proposed liquidation of the NHMFC in the Philippines.

The World Bank is already well entrenched in the Philippines, one of its best clients, with which it is engaged in a constant "dialogue." In Malaysia, the World Bank wished to use the ASEM Grant for Financial Sector Strengthening in an effort "to become re-engaged" in that country (Xiaofeng 2003). One of the grant's aims was to assist the Bank Negara Malaysia (BNM) (the Central Bank) in developing an early warning system to better monitor the banking system. The early warning system was designed, tested and adopted by the BNM between July 1998 and July 2001. What is remarkable about the grant implementation is the very low rate of utilization – only $57,679 out of a total grant of $675,000 were disbursed. The World Bank admitted candidly that the original allocation was evidence of hasty project preparation, which in turn was motivated by the World Bank's desire to "become re-engaged" in Malaysia, a country that is well known for keeping at arm's length the international financial institutions, even at the height of the Asian financial crisis, and for advocating measures (e.g. the imposition of capital controls) that the World Bank and the IMF disapprove of. In other words, the World Bank wished to use the ATF grant in order to secure a foothold in Malaysia once more.

Having cast doubt on the ASEM finance ministers' first two claims for the ATF impact, we now turn to the third – that the ATF served as a platform for "complementing (the) respective comparative advantages between (sic) Asia and Europe" (FinMM 6 2005: Annex, §3). As far as we can tell, only one ATF grant could conceivably claim to focus on comparative advantage. Through a grant for enhancing industrial and export competitiveness (May 1999–May 2001), Malaysia requested technical assistance in reviewing policies that it had initiated prior to the crisis and recommending new policies to promote as well as to diversify exports (Tan Hong 2002). Studies were conducted that sought to identify the downstream products for rubber, palm oil and timber and wood; to review fiscal incentives, including level of technological capabilities, infrastructure and investment needs and marketing arrangements in the domestic industry; and to assess the potential for exports through marketing studies. Technical assistance was also provided for the purpose of developing an information system to monitor industrial and export performance. The project was deemed successful, even if it spent only $76,435 out of a total of $161,000. Since Europe does not produce rubber, palm oil and tropical timber, we can agree that this grant "served as a platform for complementing comparative advantage." On the other hand, the project did not recommend or require European involvement (e.g. in the form of investment) in the development of that comparative advantage.

That only one out of seventy-seven ATF projects examined the potential comparative advantage of one Asian country can hardly bolster the claim that the ATF served as an "effective platform for ... complementing (the) respective comparative advantages" of Asia and Europe. As for the World Bank, it was hardly in a position to refuse the Malaysian request. A refusal would have jeopardized its effort to regain a foothold in Malaysia. It is probable that the World Bank did not recommend to any other ASEM Asian country a similar project, which probably reminded it too much of industrial planning and government intervention in the economy.

The adverse impact of the World Bank's dominant role vis-à-vis grant beneficiaries in the ATF administration may well have accounted for the implementation problems that the World Bank euphemistically referred to as "ownership issues": "The most significant issues in implementation arose around country ownership issues – the degree to which the beneficiaries were convinced that their views and priorities were reflected in project selection and design (World Bank 2003: 37)." To respond to the Asian states' request that they exercise clear ownership of programming and monitoring of ATF activities, it was decided, following an EU review in March 2002, to set up an "In-County Steering Committee" (ICSC) in each recipient country, comprising representatives from the recipient, the donors and the World Bank. Under the new arrangement that would last until the end of the ATF second phase in 2006, the ICSC would prepare the country strategy notes, set priorities and monitor progress, though the World Bank would continue to review proposals for "consistency, quality enhancement and cross-fertilization purposes" (World Bank 2003: 35), the last probably referring to integration into existing World Bank programs.

An indicator of the Asian wish to make the ATF play a role in an Asia–Europe dialogue, rather than in a troika (with the World Bank as the third member), may be found in proposals made by China and Thailand in April 2005. For China, additional support was needed in new areas, and a new partnership had to be based on a new set of objectives. Thailand agreed that the reform and development agenda remained unfinished and that further support was needed. It advocated a new facility that would be delinked from the crisis nature of ATF 1 and ATF2 and would be based on emerging needs among ASEM participants (ATF 2005a: para. 21). Even if China's support added weight to the proposal, the chances of fresh funding being made available by the EU for development purposes remain uncertain. Some European states immediately declared that they were in no position to support the idea.

Assuming that the EU eventually agreed, it cannot be excluded that the World Bank would continue to play a role in this "dialogue," since it is the Bank that is undertaking consultations with Asian and European states on a possible new facility to allow a continued "cooperative dialogue" between Asia and Europe initiated under ATF1 and ATF2 (ATF 2005b: para. 4). In that case, "ownership issues" might emerge once more in the selection and design of projects. On the other hand, if in the best-case scenario, the ATF were transformed in the way that China and Thailand are proposing, a new fund might compete with the idea of a Social Forum that Asian and European civil society groups have long been urging ASEM participants to establish.

Towards a social forum?

That poverty alleviation and social development are inextricably intertwined is a truism. The linkage might explain why in the EU's New Asia Strategy, no particular attention was devoted to social issues that presumably could be subsumed under the heading of poverty alleviation through economic cooperation [European Commission COM (94) 314final: Part IV, para. 2.2.8]. ASEM 1 mentioned poverty alleviation, the role of women and cooperation in the health sector in passing (ASEM 1 1996: para. 15). ASEM 2, preoccupied with the Asian financial crisis, collapsed social and cultural cooperation into one category but put forward no proposals for action in the social field (ASEM 2 1998a: paras 19–20). This silence was maintained in the AECF, which identified no priority in the social field (AECF 2000: para. 17). At ASEM 3 (2000: para. 16), which was held in one of the countries worst affected by the Asian financial crisis, the chairman's statement for the first time mentioned the leaders' agreement on "the need to ensure that the benefits of globalization are widely shared while reducing its adverse effects" and their commitment to strengthen ASEM dialogue on socioeconomic issues. Between ASEM 3 and ASEM 4, trade unions and NGOs lobbied intensively for the creation of a social pillar, so that ASEM 4 felt compelled to make a gesture in their direction. It endorsed the holding of an ASEM Workshop on the future of employment and the quality of labor, "in view of the interplay between economic growth and progress in the social sphere, and in order to ensure long-term social cohesion" (ASEM 4 2002). At ASEM 5 (2004: para. 3.5), no particular initiative was approved.

The social issues that could be addressed in an Asia–Europe dialogue are not only numerous but quite diverse. For dialogue to be possible and effective, it is essential to define its scope before creating the appropriate mechanisms for dialogue. The following sections will contrast the long-standing demands of the AEPF and trade unions for a social pillar with the nebulous official agenda.

The civil society agenda

In the conception of NGOs and trade unions, dialogue within a social forum is only a precondition for concrete action on the ground. For opponents of a social forum, the very large number of issues proposed implies a lack of focus (Reiterer 2004: 260) and casts doubt on the viability of dialogue in the first place. AEPF and Trade Union (TU) demands do converge on the importance of enforcing core labor standards, which may thus constitute a starting point for dialogue in a social forum.

The AEPF has campaigned to put on ASEM's agenda issues concerning women, children, ethnic minorities, migrants and workers. ASEM should aim to reduce gender-based inequalities in politics and in the economy (AEPF 3 2000: paras 2.2, 2.3) and work to end the sexual exploitation of children and the most intolerable forms of child labor (Caillaux 1997) and to this end, evolve transparent mechanisms for participation in the monitoring and reporting progress on the UN Convention on the Rights of the Child (AEPF 3 2000: paras 3.2, 3.3, 4.1; see also AEPF 2 1998a); protect the lives and livelihoods of ethnic minorities (AEPF 5 2004); stop the forced repatriation of migrant workers (AEPF 2 1998a) and ratify the UN Convention on the Protection of All Migrant Workers and Their Families (AEPF 5 2004).

Trade unions have put forward a number of specific demands: the OECD Guidelines on Multinational Enterprises, which are voluntary, should be incorporated into the ASEM IPAP; an ASEM mechanism to monitor multinational corporations should be created (ASEF *et al.* 2004); the ASEF should be restructured to promote the inclusion of social policy work programs (ICFTU 2004: para. 6); the ATF should be restructured in order to alleviate poverty and address other social concerns [ASEM Trade Union Conference, 2002: paras d), f) and k)] and a dialogue on corporate social responsibility should be initiated (European Institute of Asian Studies 2003: 19; ASEF *et al.* 2004: 7). As if this agenda were not ambitious enough, European academics have suggested that ASEM deal tackle the contribution of "differentiated social protection systems" to the steady development of unequally developed economies" and discuss the creation of effective social mechanisms" (Hauff 2002: 15; Bergé 2002: 13).

The AEPF and trade unions agree that ASEM governments should respect the fundamental rights of all workers, known as core labor standards. These are the right to join a trade union of one's choice and to organize and bargain collectively the following: freedom from slavery and bonded labor; freedom from discrimination on the basis of gender, race, color, religion, political views or national or ethnic origin; and an end to exploitative and hazardous forms of child labor [AEPF 3 2000: para. 1.1; ASEM Trade Union Conference, 2002: paras g), h)]. The dialogue on core labor standards should not be confined to ASEM but should also take place at the International Labor Organization (ILO), the IMF, the World Bank and the WTO, "with a view to removing misunderstandings and overcoming disagreements" (ASEM Trade Union Conference 2002, h; see also ICFTU 2004: 2).

The AEPF and trade unions proposed two types of mechanisms for dialogue and cooperation on social issues. First, labor and social ministers would meet regularly, as the economic and finance ministers do. Second, a trade union consultative mechanism, inspired by the ILO and OECD models, would be set up having formal consultative status comparable with that enjoyed by the Asia–Europe Business Forum" (ICFTU 2004: para. 2). In the run-up to ASEM 4 (2002) and ASEM 5 (2004), NGOs and trade unions campaigned in favor of a social pillar. In 2003, the ICFTU requested its affiliates in ASEM countries to discuss its recommendations with their governments, their country's representative on the ASEF Board of governors, and their country's executive director for the World Bank. The European Trade Union Confederation transmitted the trade unions' recommendations to the European Commission, which replied that it would not be feasible to create a new body within the official structure. The Commission promised instead that it would try, together with ASEF, to organize consultative meetings with civil society organizations and trade unions as often as possible. One such meeting was held in Barcelona in 2004. The Commission also indicated that social issues could be discussed within the framework of the TFAP and the IPAP, although it did not explain how this could be done, and in fact, this has not been done. The European Commission also held out the possibility that a new project would be established by the Seminar on Employment in 2004 (see the next section). Since then there has been little progress (ICFTU 2004: 13)

It is not possible to undertake here a detailed examination of all social issues put forward by the AEPF and trade unions, nor of the potential contribution of Asia–Europe dialogue to addressing these issues. Agreement between the AEPF and trade unions constitutes a sufficient basis for a dialogue centered on the implementation of core labor standards and the associated idea of a social clause. The "social clause" refers to proposals to link respect for core labor standards and enjoyment of international trade liberalization measures (Maupain 1996; Robles 2003b; Scherrer and Greven 1999; Siroën 1996; Stückelberger 1996). In the most radical proposals, a clause would be inserted in the WTO agreements whereby goods exported from countries that fail to respect workers' rights would be sanctioned with the imposition of tariffs by importing countries. Support for a social clause is very strong in Europe and in the United States, where governments, trade unions and NGOs argue that the social clause will protect human rights and ensure that the benefits of trade liberalization are properly distributed. U.S. efforts to include a version of the clause in the Uruguay Round failed (Dufour 1995). At the Singapore Ministerial Meeting in 1996, WTO member states agreed that the competent organization to deal with the issue was the ILO (Leary 1997; on the ILO, see Ghebali 1987; Adam 1993). Despite further strenuous lobbying by the United States and Europe, core labor standards were thus excluded from the agenda of a future WTO round.

Governments and even trade unions in developing countries stress that their opposition is not directed at the idea of core labor standards but at the idea of enforcing them through trade sanctions, for a number of reasons. First, the worst conditions can be found in plantations, construction and small services, sectors that would not be affected by trade sanctions (Edgren 1979: 525). Trade sanctions might even worsen the plight of some groups. For example, if the importation of goods produced by child labor is prohibited, child workers might be dismissed and, in the absence of alternative employment, end up in prostitution. Second, trade sanctions in support of core labor standards are more likely to hinder economic development. A tariff imposed on imports produced in conditions that violate a core labor standard will lower demand for labor in the export sector (Brown 2000: 56). Finally, it is feared that trade sanctions could be very easily manipulated for protectionist purposes. The danger arises from the widespread perception in developed countries that wages kept at artificially low levels by repressive governments are the key to the competitiveness of developing countries' products. The temptation would therefore be great to advocate trade sanctions on developing countries that violate core labor standards, in order to preserve employment in the developed countries. Developing countries argue that attempts to enforce these labor standards would raise their labor costs and undermine their competitive advantage in international trade.

There are also political reasons for developing countries' opposition to discussion of respect for core labor standards. For authoritarian governments, these political reasons might even outweigh the economic arguments. Among the core labor standards are freedom of association and collective bargaining. According to ILO Convention 87, workers and employers have the right to establish organizations of their own choosing without previous authorization, and the organizations should enjoy guarantees to carry on their activities without interference from state authorities. ILO Convention 98 protects workers against acts of anti-union discrimination, safeguards workers' and employers' organizations from mutual interference and promotes voluntary negotiation between labor and management. Full respect of these rights will obviously strengthen the bargaining position of trade unions vis-à-vis authoritarian governments.

A few years ago, some ASEM observers contended that ASEM could be useful if it engaged in an "objective discussion of the causes and merits" of the expansion of the WTO agenda to cover labor standards (Nuttall 2000: 160). Indeed, what could be a more ideal issue to discuss for the EU if it was determined to promote democracy and human rights in Asia? After all, core labor standards are simultaneously economic and political in nature, and the EU could hope to obtain the support of many civil society organizations, particularly trade unions, in both Asia and Europe, in exerting pressure on Asian states. Contrary to expectations, the EU has been unwilling to join forces with civil society organizations in their calls for a social pillar. The tendency in Europe is to cite the opposition of authoritarian Asian governments as an obstacle to engage in a dialogue with civil society organizations on what they deem to be sensitive issues (Fritsche 2002: 4).

This reason is not implausible, but it is only part of the explanation for the EU's lack of enthusiasm for discussion of core labor standards in any social pillar. Another, and more basic, reason for the EU attitude has to do with the EU's main goal of market access. If the EU were to push for a social pillar, practically all Asian states would be antagonized, and EU efforts to obtain their consensus in trade and investment would be jeopardized. As we shall see in the next chapter, in practically all of the "new" WTO issues, it is the EU seeking concessions from the developing countries, so that it is in no position to provide a quid pro quo to the latter. For their part, the Asian developing countries would have little interest, if any, in a discussion in a limited forum, in which, by definition, the possibility of forming tactical alliances with sympathetic European states or with developing countries from other regions would be excluded. It might be possible to allay the Asian countries' fears that core labor standards would serve as a pretext for protectionism by providing them with assistance in implementing these core labor standards. Such a program would inevitably create pressures on the EU not just to adopt new policies but also to allocate financial resources for their implementation. As we have seen, the EU is unwilling to do so for poverty alleviation and industrial cooperation projects. The same logic would arguably dictate its attitude to social policy projects.

For many years now, the AEPF and trade unions have faced the problem encountered by Asian states that sought European assistance during the Asian financial crisis – that of persuading actors uninterested in dialogue to initiate one with them. In the absence of an unexpected shock comparable to the crisis, it can be plausibly argued that the perseverance of AEPF and the trade unions may be at least partly responsible for prodding a number of Asian and European states to define an official agenda in social policy. It is to this question that we must now turn.

The search for an official agenda

At ASEM 4 (2002), Germany, China, Ireland and Spain submitted a concept paper on the future of employment and the quality of labor (Germany *et al.* 2002). Its declared long-term aim of integrating labor and social affairs ministers into the ASEM process was similar to a core element in civil society demands for a social pillar. The seminar's rationale was to demonstrate that globalization could lead to clear improvement in the living and working conditions of populations in developed and developing countries. It would address the nature of future jobs; the shaping and guaranteeing of employment protection; the form of corporate social responsibility; international mobility and management of work migration. It was claimed that "unlike virtually any other Forum, the ASEM-process offers outstanding potential for the discussion of ways to solve the problems now being faced."

This sweeping claim must be taken with a healthy dose of skepticism. ASEM's potential would have been truly outstanding had it not taken six years (1996–2002) before governments actually made a show of responding to concerns repeatedly expressed by NGOs and trade unions from one AEPF to the next. The agenda of the seminar would have inspired greater confidence in governments' ability to define a problematic if it had been more focused. As it is, this agenda was equally vulnerable to the charge made against AEPF demands that the goals were not attainable – how could one seminar conceivably hope to discuss all these issues, let alone do something about them?

At the 2004 seminar, Germany expressed the view that Asians and Europeans should discuss together the impact of growing economic interdependence on labor markets in ASEM countries and the conditions required for creating skilled employment (the following relies heavily on Bersick 2004a). The seminar is said to have defined a problematic for ASEM. The central challenge common to Asia and Europe, according to one participant, was how to deal with the phenomenon of jobless growth.

It is doubtful that the challenge is really common to Asia and Europe. One reason that economic growth fails to create jobs in the developed (European) countries is that firms from the latter outsource their production to developing (Asian) countries. Outsourcing then raises profits, which are measured by growth rates. Obviously, in this scenario jobs are not created in the firms' home country; they are created in the developing country, so that growth is not "jobless" in the latter. In another scenario, firms from developed countries expand through mergers with and acquisitions (M&A) of firms in other countries. M&A will raise the profit rates of the firm making the acquisition and of the firm that is the object of the M&A (if it survives) or at the very least, of the individuals selling the firm, in this manner pushing up profit and growth rates in both countries. However, the M&A might involve restructuring of the firm acquired (if not of the firm making the acquisition), and restructuring usually means job losses. Now, M&A are more likely to occur among developed countries, to the extent that their firms possess valuable assets – technology, know-how, name recognition and so on – that many firms in developing countries simply do not possess. This being the case, jobless growth will tend to occur in the developed countries where M&A are more frequent. Only in cases where the object of M&A is a firm from a developing (Asian) country will the possibility of jobless growth occur in developing countries. In a third scenario, highlighted by the Asian financial crisis, individuals, firms and banks from developed countries, instead of investing in production in their home countries, lend their money to their counterparts in developing countries, which then use the loans to fuel manufacturing activity, consumer spending or construction booms. In the short term at least, jobs will be created in the borrowing countries. In the meanwhile, in the home country of the lenders, profit rates will rise, without jobs being created. Again, the phenomenon of jobless growth is observed only in the developed countries. That the problematic of jobless growth is a common challenge is misleading. On the contrary, in some circumstances, it might appear that the Asia–Europe relationship is a zero-sum game (job losses in Europe vs. job creation in Asia).

If the opportunity given to civil society representatives to join in the discussions on the meeting's second day was a sign of openness, the first meeting of ministers of labor and employment, held a few days prior to ASEM 6, raises doubts regarding the scope and inclusiveness of any "social pillar." Predictably, the meeting endorsed a proposal for regular dialogue and cooperation on employment and social policy (Labor and Employment Ministers' Conference 2006: para. 19), a proposal that paralleled that made by Asian and European trade unions meeting at the time of the summit (ICFTU 2006: 1). Yet the ministers failed to identify the topics to be taken up in a future dialogue or the mechanisms for dialogue. The statement did refer to respect and promotion for core labor standards (Labor and Employment Ministers 2006, §6) and implied that regional cooperation could be a "good basis" for interregional dialogue (Labor and Employment Ministers' Conference 2006: 15–16).

This approach bodes ill for a future dialogue. Since core labor standards were raised at the Uruguay Round, there can be no misunderstanding of the positions of ASEAN on these issues. ASEAN has not hesitated to accuse the ILO of rigidly imposing labor standards (ASEAN Labor Ministers 1994: para. 7), which in its view had to be reviewed in order to reflect the economic environment in developing countries [ASEAN Labor Ministers 1992: para. 10; 1994: para. 8; 1996: para. 6(viii)]. This demand was justified by the claim that ILO conventions formulated decades ago had become outdated [ASEAN Labor Ministers 1996: para. 6(vi)]. While awaiting revision of the Conventions, the ILO had to adopt a more flexible approach for the implementation of ILO conventions (ASEAN Labor Ministers 1996: para. 7). Flexibility in turn implied that developing countries would "not be pressured to comply with standards which are mainly based on those of advanced and developed countries" (ASEAN Labor Ministers 1994: para. 8). Needless to say, at the ASEAN level, cooperation on core labor standards is virtually non-existent, making this a poor basis for interregional cooperation.

If the intention to create a social pillar had been genuine, the EU and/or the ASEM Ministers should have proceeded in the same way that dialogue on trade facilitation and investment promotion was organized. A plan similar to the TFAP or the IPAP should have been drafted, identifying concrete targets and organizing a procedure for regular reporting. Approval of the plans would then have been sought from ministerial and summit meetings, paving the way for the holding of regular meetings on specific topics. The process might generate new knowledge, as Todorov's conception of dialogue leads us to expect, regarding the obstacles to implementation of core labor standards in Asian countries and innovative ways of providing assistance to reluctant governments.

With the exception of the ASEM 2 on the Trust Fund, this chapter has dealt with dialogues that failed to take place. In the next two chapters, the focus will shift to issues that have been the object of intensive discussions.

Summary

Consistent with the theoretical framework sketched in Chapter 1, this chapter first surveyed the overall structure of economic relations between Asia and Europe when ASEM was launched in 1996, before the Asia–Europe dialogue was initiated. The relative position of each in relation to the other was described as a combination of strengths and weaknesses. The EU's strengths at the international level were limited in Asia by its considerable trade deficits and European firms' low investment rates. Asia's economic growth is supposed to have encouraged the EU to engage in dialogue with it, but in reality, the Asians are vulnerable to European trade sanctions.

The rest of the chapter discussed failed attempts at ASEM dialogue in the three areas that one or the other party believed to be an area of common interest:

poverty reduction, economic cooperation and social development. ASEM 1 led Asians to believe, in a tacit recognition of the inequality between Asia and Europe, that ASEM would implement poverty alleviation and economic cooperation programs. However, their proposals in these areas could not overcome the obstacle of the EU's unwillingness to engage in dialogue. Meanwhile, the AEBF argued for the establishment of an infrastructure fund to which the Asians were not receptive. The reason was that they wished to control access to the market for infrastructure projects in their countries. These two cases highlight the difficulty, not fully resolved by either Todorov or Habermas, of convincing actors that do not wish to engage in dialogue to do so.

The Asian financial crisis was an exogenous shock that forced the EU not only to dialogue with Asia but also to negotiate the creation of an ATF and to engage in joint action through ATF projects. Thanks to dialogue, European analyses of the causes of the crisis, initially blaming primarily the Asians, and solutions to the crisis that proposed further liberalization changed in significant respects. This result comes closest to meeting the definition of dialogue proposed in Chapter 1. Unfortunately, the decision to make the World Bank responsible for the ATF's implementation introduced into the Asia–Europe dialogue a participant that pursued its own agenda and was not disposed to dialogue. As a result, ATF projects were integrated into larger World Bank projects. With the approaching end of the ATF, the EU has been largely unsympathetic to Asian proposals that ATF be replaced by a more long-term fund.

For their part, civil society groups represented in the AEPF and by trade unions, which are excluded from ASEM dialogue, have long advocated the establishment of a social forum tackling a broad range of issues, including the ILO's core labor standards. As noted in Chapter 1, these groups can be justifiably considered interested parties; yet they are excluded from dialogue. In spite of intense lobbying, particularly prior to ASEM 4 (2002) and ASEM 5 (2004), both Asian and European participants refused to create such a forum for dialogue, let alone take joint action on social issues. One reason for the EU opposition to this may be a fear that it would be compelled to devote financial resources to Asia–Europe joint action.

It was only in 2002 that Asia and Europe started attempts to formulate a social agenda. Efforts so far have been hampered by the fact that they do not really face the same challenges when promoting job creation, which is unconvincingly presented as an area of common interest. The First ASEM Labor and Employment Ministers' Meeting's (held in 2006) main recommendation was that they meet regularly. The meeting simply postponed to a later meeting the task of identifying specific topics for dialogue. If core labor standards are taken up, as their statement implied, the prospects for dialogue are bleak, given the steadfast opposition of ASEAN to what it describes as the rigid implementation of outdated standards.

3   ASEM and multilateralism

Trade and investment undoubtedly are areas of common interest for Asia and Europe. Each group wishes access to the other's markets. Asia wishes to attract European foreign direct investment, and Europe seeks an increase of its firms' investment in Asia. How then can dialogue within Asia–Europe Meeting (ASEM) enable each group to achieve its aims? To put it differently, how does ASEM dialogue generate joint action based on the respective strategies of the European Union (EU) and of the Asian states?

Unlike in the other areas discussed in Chapter 2, it was the EU, the more powerful actor, that had a stake in initiating a dialogue that would facilitate a new World Trade Organization (WTO) round. To this end, the EU attempted to convince Asians that the round was necessary and that the EU positions were worthy of consensus. The EU's objectives were very clearly laid out in its market access strategy, published in February 1996, a month before ASEM 1 [European Commission COM (96) 53 final]. The Commission's argument was that since the Single European Market (SEM) exposed European firms to intensified foreign competition in Europe, European firms should have the opportunity to compete on equal terms in foreign markets. Otherwise, they would not be able to reap the benefits of improved competitiveness deriving from the existence of the SEM. The implication was clear for the European Commission: "Open markets worldwide are one key to securing faster growth and more rapid job creation in Europe ..." [European Commission COM (96) 53 final: 3]. The market opening strategy required that the EU make efforts to ensure that states complied with WTO agreements and action against non-traditional trade and investment barriers. These goals would be pursued at two levels: at the multilateral level, the privileged forum would be the WTO; and at the bilateral level, through high-level visits and missions, bilateral consultations and negotiations of specific agreements.

In Asia, the EU market access strategy was a tacit admission of the weakness of the European position in both trade and investment as compared to that of the United States or Japan. As the European Commission admitted, Japan had since 1985 relocated manufacturing capacity in Southeast Asia on a scale unmatched by the EU or the United States. As I have said elsewhere (Robles 2004: 16–17), the new wave of Japanese investment was a response to a massive revaluation of the yen that the United States and West European countries insisted as the solution to the problem of Japan's massive trade surpluses. To preserve profitability, Japanese firms invested heavily in Thailand, Malaysia, Indonesia and Singapore. Large Japanese firms broke up manufacturing processes into discrete phases, parceling out the labor-intensive, low value-added phases to Japanese production units in different host nations, according to their level of development. The Japanese parent company supplied high-technology inputs to these overseas production sites but kept control over research and development (R&D) and design and precision manufacturing work, which are retained in Japan. Japanese dominance in investment, as the Commission recognized, translated into dominance in trade, since Japanese companies established the same type of sales and distribution systems that European counties found so hard to penetrate in Japan itself.

As the scale of Japanese investment was "unmatched," the European Commission did not even take the trouble to propose that the EU "match" it by competing with Japan using the foreign direct investment (FDI). Instead, the EU could obtain market access if new WTO agreements were concluded that imposed fresh obligations on Asian states and obliged them to modify their domestic laws. For all the emphasis on dialogue among equals as a means of achieving agreement, one cannot help but notice that in the EU's conception, only the Asians are expected to change their views and positions. Of course, reasons would be given to them that would help to convince them of the validity of EU positions. Still, the ever-present risk was that Asians would be seen as objects of persuasion by the EU, which for its part would not change its position. Needless to say, these conditions are inimical to the achievement of genuine dialogue.

On the Asian side, one finds a diversity of interests. At ASEM 1 (1996), the concern of Thailand and Singapore, supported by South Korea, was to neutralize the threats of a fortress Europe, through extension to non-EU members of the benefits that EU members granted to each other (Rüland 1996: 44; Rüland 1998b: 135, Sideri 1996: 16). Interestingly enough, opposition to this proposal came from China, whose initial motive for participation was political rather than economic, and Japan, whose Ministry of Finance was opposed to discussion of WTO issues at ASEM (Bersick 2004c: 114). South Korea's support arose from its concern that its firms had in the 1990s become the targets of antidumping complaints by European firms. At any rate, even had there been a consensus on the Asian side, acceptance of the Thai–Singaporean conception of "open regionalism" would have negated the very idea of regional integration, something that the Europeans could hardly be expected to agree with. The chairman's statement of ASEM 1 offered consolation to Thailand by stressing that regional integration should "benefit the international community as a whole" (ASEM 1 1996: para. 4). In other respects, the European approach prevailed. ASEM's priorities were to ensure full implementation of Uruguay Round agreements; to conclude the unfinished Uruguay Round negotiations on telecommunications and financial services; to pursue the built-in agenda (on agriculture and services) and to consult closely on new issues. Trade and investment between Asia and Europe would be promoted through facilitation and liberalization, involving the simplification and improvement of customs procedures and standards conformance (ASEM 1 1996: paras 11, 12).

If ASEM was not a negotiating forum, within which states would conclude legally binding commitments, how could these goals be achieved? Youth leaders hoped that ASEM could coordinate some positions on certain issues that could contribute to the work of other international organizations (AEYLS 1997c: 1). ASEM 2's final statement contains the clearest statement of the role of ASEM in relation to other multilateral organizations: cooperation within ASEM should lead to "identification of priorities for concerted and supportive action" and should "stimulate and facilitate progress in other fora (ASEM 2 1998a: para. 3)." In this respect, dialogue with ASEM offered the prospect of Asia–Europe collaboration in international organizations, balancing the US tendency toward unilateralism and encouraging Asian countries, with their increased weight in the world economy, to assume greater responsibilities in the international community.

Although the other international organizations could theoretically refer to the entire galaxy of international organizations, in practice, the organization most often named in ASEM documents after the UN is the WTO. To a dialogue on WTO issues, the Asian financial crisis unexpectedly added a possible dialogue on the reform of the international financial architecture. Such a reform emerged as an area of common interest in the wake of Asian demands for European assistance during the Asian financial crisis (Chapter 2). The very meager results of the dialogue and the very modest action that it has given rise to, embodied in the Kobe Research Project, will be discussed before an account of the largely failed EU efforts to use ASEM as a forum to convince the Asians as a group to adopt EU positions on WTO issues is given.

A few words about multilateralism are in order. Multilateralism involves coordinating relations among three or more states in accordance with certain principles (Ruggie 1993: 8, 12). In the post-World War II period, the economic principles of multilateralism comprised the most-favored nation principle in trade, the convertibility of currencies and the freedom of capital flows. These principles institutionalized and regulated a world order dominated by the United States. Political multilateralism's primary goal was the security and maintenance of economic multilateralism (Cox 1992: 495–6). International organizations, as manifestations of multilateralism, embodied the rules that facilitated the expansion of the hegemonic world order and ideologically legitimated the norms of that order. But multilateralism is not merely an element of the existing order; in specific circumstances, it may become a site of struggle between conservative and transformative forces (Cox 1983: 134–8; Cox 1992: 514). Third World countries' challenges in the 1970s and the early 1980s, expressed in the demand for a New International Economic Order, failed, so that by the 1990s, the neoliberal ideology was once more dominant not only within the developed countries but also within international organizations. It is in this structural context of neoliberal hegemony that we must analyze the attempts at dialogue within

ASEM on the reform of the international financial architecture and on WTO issues.

ASEM and the reform of the international financial architecture

One unexpected consequence of the Asian financial crisis was to put the reform of "the international financial architecture" on the ASEM agenda. Regrettably, the little discussion that took place gives the impression that EU member states are reluctant to take into consideration Asian interests in ways that diverge markedly from those of the EU, the United States and the International Monetary Fund (IMF).

ASEM 2's references (ASEM 2 1998b) to cooperation in regulation, supervision and cooperation apparently represented ASEM's input into the international debate (Payoyo 1999: 403). And it is true that the statement represented some progress compared to the unsympathetic European declarations made at the 1997 IMF meeting. Since ASEM 2, other ASEM meetings have unambiguously identified one key (if not the key) problem, the "potential for abrupt and destabilising short-term capital movements" (FinMM 2 1999: para. 7; AEVG 1999: Part II; ASEM 3 2000: para. 12). ASEM participants also agreed that the way forward lay in a deepening of dialogue among themselves (AECF 2000: §16). What then has been the fate of this dialogue?

Rather than making fresh and innovative proposals that can stimulate progress in the IMF, ASEM meetings merely echo those that are made at the IMF. For example, ASEM finance ministers have stressed "the need to examine the question of appropriate transparency and disclosure standards for private sector financial institutions" (FinMM 2 1999: para. 7). The Asia–Europe Vision Group (AEVG) emphasized enhanced transparency in information on foreign exchange reserves and in accumulated external liabilities of the public and private sectors, suggesting that the IMF Special Data Dissemination Standards could be utilized (AEVG 1999: 10). The need to implement codes and standards was highlighted by ASEM 3 (ASEM 3 2000: para. 2; FinMM 3 2001: para. 22). The weaknesses of these types of proposals are well known. Availability of more information as a result of increased transparency and surveillance may not necessarily reduce the volatility of short-term capital flows. The crux of the matter lies not in the supply of more statistical information but in the evaluation of such information, which requires assessments of economic policies and the political situations in the countries concerned. The difficulties involved in making assessments of this kind would explain why private rating agencies failed to predict the Asian crisis (Fitzgerald 2000: 107). Moreover, in the past, speculators have often failed to take account of information that was already available. Nor would availability of more information guarantee that inventors will change their preferences for portfolio investment in favor of FDI (Robles 2001: 34).

In sharp contrast with the very harsh criticism of the IMF heard in the crisis-hit Asian countries, ASEM has adopted a very moderate tone toward the IMF.

After acknowledging the importance of IMF surveillance, ASEM finance ministers ventured in 2001 to call on the IMF to enhance accountability and to ensure that quota allocations reflect developments in the world economy, but without specifying the measures that would enable it to implement these recommendations (FinMM 3 2001: paras 21, 22). The onus was placed on the crisis-affected countries to implement prudent financial supervision, domestic financial reform and corporate governance (AEVG 1999: 11; ASEM 3 2000: para. 12; FinMM 3 2001: para. 22). Only a hint of dissatisfaction with the IMF may be discerned in the AEVG's recommendation that "the major function of the Bretton Woods institutions ... (should) be ... better coordinated" (AEVG 1999: 10). Underlying all these statements are the assumptions that the goal remains the liberalization of capital markets and that the main issue is to implement measures that would enable the developing countries to participate in more open capital markets (Blecker 1999: 92). ASEM finance ministers' statements ignore the growing current of opinion in the crisis-affected countries that financial liberalization had been too hasty.

On two occasions, joint action by Asian and European states was envisaged. As mentioned previously, the 1997 FinMM considered holding regular consultations of financial supervisors on international financial issues and establishing a computerized communication network among the ASEM finance ministers to facilitate information sharing (FinMM 1 1997: paras 4, 9, 16). A few years later, technical assistance and exchange of expertise, e.g. in training of financial supervisors, was identified as one possible task for ASEM (AECF 2000: para. 16). Apart from discussions among finance ministers' deputies, none of these proposals have ever been implemented.

By January 2001, there were signs that some Asian countries were dissatisfied with the lack of progress in international discussions and the absence of an ASEM contribution to them. South Korea was disappointed that the "international community (had) lost its enthusiasm for reform" (Jin Nyum 2001: 2) and challenged the conventional proposals that placed the burden of responsibility for reform on the crisis-hit countries, arguing that the "shortcomings of the international financial system itself" had to be addressed; otherwise strengthening domestic financial sectors would be ineffective. Capital exporting states had to share the burden of reform by developing systems that would hold private investors responsible for their investment decisions. Developing countries had to be allowed to participate in decisions on the reform of the international financial architecture so that their views would not be overlooked (Nyum 2001; Robles 2001: 35–6).

No clearer indication of the absence of dialogue can be found than the failure to reflect these concerns in the chairman's statement. Even worse, the statement went so far as to welcome the progress made in strengthening the international financial architecture (FinMM 3 2001: 21), when there was very little evidence of such progress. As a consolation prize, the meeting adopted a "Kobe research project" proposed by Japan and designed to "facilitate interregional cooperative research and study activities on topics such as the regional monetary cooperation, the exchange rate regimes and the public debt management" (FinMM 3 2001: para. 29). On the final research agenda were exchange rate regimes for emerging East Asian and EU accession countries; requirements for successful currency regimes; lessons for East Asia; regional financial cooperation and surveillance; regional economic integration in East Asia and Europe; and banking sector reform and capital market development.

The Kobe Research Project recommended to ASEM 4 in 2002, that an Asian currency basket system be adopted and an Asian bond market be developed. The first proposal would reduce the vulnerability to external shock of Asian currencies pegged to the dollar, whose value fluctuated against the yen. Pegging a currency against a combination of the dollar, yen and perhaps the euro, would not resolve problems if only some countries switched to basket pegging, while the other currencies continued to be pegged to the dollar. A joint move by Asian states to peg their currencies to a common currency basket could resolve this problem. The Kobe Research Project did not explain how a country that cannot defend its currency against the US dollar can do so for a basket. The second proposal of the Kobe Research Project, an Asian bond market, could reduce dependence on foreign capital investment in stocks and bank loans, which results in the use of short-term borrowing to finance long-term projects. An Asian bond market would channel savings into investment within the region, avoid foreign exchange risk and provide capital projects with a source of long-term financing. Unfortunately, creating an Asian bond market entails the same conditions as those required for the development of domestic capital markets, resulting in a chicken-and-egg problem (Takashi 2003).

Was the Kobe Research project an achievement of dialogue in its epistemic dimension, as described by Todorov? After all, it represents new knowledge, generated through ASEM, distinct from preexisting "Asian" and "European" knowledge. Two circumstances undermine the value of this outcome of dialogue. First, the project was undertaken as a way of avoiding substantive dialogue on fundamental issues that the crisis-affected Asian countries wished to discuss. Indeed, one could even ask if dialogue within ASEM was truly essential to generate the two recommendations, which many others have already made. Second, it is not certain to what extent this new knowledge can be used as a basis for further dialogue between or joint action by Asians and Europeans. What role can or should Europeans play in the adoption of a currency basket and the development of local bond markets? It is noteworthy that the project has as yet not had any catalyzing effect on Asia–Europe dialogue or cooperation in the reform of the international financial architecture.

The Kobe Research Project cannot hide the crisis-affected Asian states' inability to convince the stronger (European and Asian) states to engage in dialogue on international monetary reform that would challenge the status quo. The European countries, as headquarters of some of the world's largest banks, have a vital stake in the status quo, on which part of their structural power in international relations rests. Since the Kobe Research Project's completion, finance ministers' meetings have been confined to welcoming the IMF's initiative to enhance the quality of surveillance (FinMM 4 2002: para. 5; FinMM 5 2003: para. 13). At their 2005 meeting, there was a vague call for "adequate voice and participation, including all ASEM members of the IMF... (to) be assured, and the distribution of the quotas (at the IMF) ... (to) reflect developments in the world economy" (FinMM 6 2005: para. 15). This is not necessarily a concession to the Asian states, since EU members are also IMF members.

Needless to say, the Asia–Europe People's Forum (AEPF) advocated more radical proposals for international financial reform (see Chapter 2). One proposal studiously ignored by ASEM leaders and ministers deserves attention, a foreign exchange transactions tax, first proposed by Nobel Laureate in Economics James Tobin in 1972 and revived after the Mexican crisis (Tobin 1996; Haq *et al.* 1996). A modest tax of 0.5 percent would reduce the volume of short-term (i.e. speculative) transactions without necessarily discouraging long-term ones (FDI). Evasion would be prevented if the tax were linked to transactions for which there were no substitute; if it were imposed by states in which the major capital markets are found and if states imposed higher taxes on transactions with offshore jurisdictions that did not cooperate with other states. States would be given an incentive to cooperate with each other by being allowed to retain a significant portion of the revenues generated by the tax (Porter 1996: 681–2). For others, Chilean-style capital controls of the type in place in Chile are more attractive. Until shortly before the Asian financial crisis, Chile required that portfolio investors keep their funds in the country for at least one year. The government tried to discourage short-term borrowing by requiring that borrowers deposit 30 percent of their loan-proceeds in a non-interest-bearing account for a year (Radelet and Sachs 1998: 40; Grabel 1999: 62). A critic of the Tobin Tax believes that a Chilean-style tax would be more effective (Eichengreen 1999: 80).

Voices representing civil society in Asia and Europe favored the Tobin tax. For Joel Rocamora (1999: 13), a prominent Filipino activist, ASEM should have proposed a mechanism to control fluctuations. In the view of a French proponent, the EU could constitute itself without difficulty into a Tobin zone (Cassen 1998: 14; Cassen 1999: 14). As already mentioned, Asian governments might have welcomed AEPF's rhetorical support for demands for international financial reform but would have been less willing to grant them official participation in the ASEM process because of the nature of their political demands.

One possible explanation for the failure of a dialogue to take place is the absence of all the interested parties in the issue, particularly the United States. As seen in the last chapter, during the first few months of the crisis, the EU was hesitant to take initiatives that could be construed as countering those advocated by the United States. It cannot be denied that proposals for international financial reform that do not enjoy US support are unlikely to make headway. On the other hand, if the US had participated in an Asia–Europe dialogue, it is even more improbable that bold proposals for reform would have been considered. It is difficult to escape the conclusion that European reluctance is responsible for the failure to seize the opportunity offered by the Asian financial crisis to undertake a dialogue on international financial reform.

The EU's reluctance can in turn be attributed to the constraint imposed on EU action by the European integration process, the long-term trend of which has been the liberalization of capital movements. Since the late 1980s, capital movements between members and EU members and the rest of the world have been fully liberalized. Indeed, it is a principle enshrined in the 1992 Maastricht Treaty that external movements must be fully free, like internal movements. The only regulations allowed are those involving FDI; the provision of financial services; the administration of securities to capital markets; and those measures necessary in exceptional circumstances if capital movements threaten to cause serious difficulties to the operation of the Economic and Monetary Union (EMU). Moreover, the EU promotes adoption of liberal policies by third states (Molle 2001: 178–90). Given this structural context, the EU could not envisage proposals that place restraints on international capital movements. One will search in vain in statements made at several years' interval by the president of the European Investment Bank (EIB) and of the new European Central Bank (ECB) for evidence of a specifically European approach to international financial reform, distinct from those of the United States or of the IMF (Maystadt 2001; Trichet 2004). This structural context prevents the EU from taking a broader view of its self-interest, as Habermas would have recommended to great powers, by reconsidering the unquestioned assumption that liberalization of capital movements should be the goal of all countries irrespective of their level of development.

This very rapid survey demonstrates that ASEM has not acted to stimulate dialogue between Asian and European states for the purpose of advancing multilateral discussions on international financial reform, largely owing to unwillingness of the European participants. Much more energy has been expended by the EU on promoting a dialogue between Asians and Europeans on WTO issues, to which we now turn.

ASEM and the WTO

WTO issues were already anticipated as a possible area of Asia–Europe common interest in the report of the ASEAN–EU Eminent Persons Group (EPG), drawn up shortly before ASEM 1. In the Group's opinion, the Association of Southeast Asian Nations (ASEAN) and the EU had to cooperate to promote and maintain openness in the international trading system. To this end, they recommended that ASEAN and the EU implement their Uruguay Round commitments "fully, and on schedule," encourage other WTO members to do so and help "to broker consensus and agreement within the WTO," a function rendered crucial by the emerging "North-South" division of views. ASEAN and the EU could help to bring about a "greater understanding of the conceptual and practical implications of particular policies and ... in negotiations themselves," and to ensure that the 1996 WTO Ministerial Conference reviewed implementation of Uruguay Round agreements; reviewed the unfinished negotiations on financial services and adopt an agenda based on the Built-In Agenda (on agriculture and services). At Singapore, ASEAN and the EU had to "work together to bring about a substantive and successful outcome" (ASEAN–EU EPG 1996: paras 2.8 (i), (iii); 2.9).

The multiplicity and complexity of WTO issues are such that negotiations do seem to require preliminary dialogue for the purpose of agenda setting and identification of possible trade-offs. In its market access strategy, published a month before ASEM 1, the European Commission [European Commission COM (96) 53 final: 17] averred that the EU could reach agreement at the 1996 WTO Ministerial in Singapore if consensus could be worked out beforehand between the EU and the more advanced or significant developing countries. After ASEM 1, all ASEM declarations have portrayed the WTO as the embodiment of the open and rules-based international trading system (e.g. ASEM 1 1996: para. 11; SOMTI 3 1998: 2; SOMTI 4 1999: para. 11; SOMTI 6 2000: para. 17; SOMTI 9 2003: para. 9) and underlined the need to "strengthen further the WTO as the main forum for negotiation" (ASEM 2 1998a: §11; AECF 2000: §16). Like a mantra, they repeat that ASEM should "complement and reinforce efforts to strengthen" the WTO (e.g. ASEM 1 1996: para. 11; CAEC 1996: 4; AECF 2000: para. 16; AEBF 1 1996: 4). The various issues negotiated at the WTO are also specifically mentioned, and the content of ASEM declarations appears to follow very closely the different phases of the WTO's work from one Ministerial Conference to another. These circumstances create the impression that dialogue over WTO issues has indeed taken place between Asia and Europe within ASEM.

Advocates of ASEM as a platform for discussion with Asian countries of issues contested in the WTO (e.g. Rüland 1998b; Dent 1997–98: 515; Geest 2000; Reiterer 2004: 267) have neglected to examine either the contentious issues at the WTO or the specific features of WTO processes that stand in the way of successful negotiations. Without analyses of this kind, they are unable to identify the possible substantive solutions and/or the procedural innovations that dialogue within ASEM could formulate. This circumstance compels us to undertake a somewhat lengthy excursion into WTO issues before assessing the effectiveness of the dialogue that has taken place within ASEM.

North–South inequality and bad governance at the WTO

An advocate of dialogue might plausibly argue that the opposition between developed and developing countries at the WTO renders dialogue within a small group like ASEM all the more necessary. However, the prospects for dialogue, in which only better arguments count and participants are willing to change their positions, are blighted by the inequality among actors – (European and Asian) developed and (Asian) developing countries – created by the Uruguay Round agreements. Before a dialogue can be initiated, this inequality in positions must be recognized by the EU, which is one of its beneficiaries. Over the years, there was little sign of recognition of this situation. Indeed, the EU as the more powerful actor has insisted that WTO issues constituted an area of common interest in

ASEM. The EU exerted pressure on weaker actors to accept WTO negotiations for a new series of agreements, which would only have deepened the inequality. Bad governance at the WTO aggravated this inequality, which inevitably produced resistance on the part of the developing countries to change their views.

North–South disagreement on WTO issues grew as the realization dawned on developing countries that the Uruguay Round, far from being "an important milestone ... in their integration into the global economy" (Martin and Winters 1996: 1), proved to be a millstone around their necks. In practically all areas, the Uruguay Round agreements afforded better treatment to developed countries than to developing countries. In trade in manufactures, the overall reduction in average tariffs on imports from developing countries (37 percent according to Blackhurst *et al.* 1996: 128; 28 percent according to Abreu 1996: 64) was less than the overall reduction on tariffs from all countries (40 percent, according to Blackhurst *et al.* 1996; ibid.). The tariff reductions were below average in products of interest to developing countries (textiles, transport equipment, leather products and fish products). EU tariff reductions on imports from developing countries were lower than reductions made by other developed countries. Overall, products from Asian developing countries faced higher tariffs in developed countries than those imposed on products from other developing regions (Abreu 1996: 64).

In agriculture, tariffs continued to be high: 244 percent for sugar and 174 percent for peanuts in the United States; 213 percent for beef and 168 percent for wheat in the EU; and 353 percent for wheat in Japan (Khor 2000: 16). The EU's minimum import commitments were truly minimal, in part because the EU was allowed to count special arrangements, such as the special protocol on sugar in favor of the African, Caribbean and Pacific (ACP) countries, as part of minimum access commitments. Trigger levels for safeguards against a surge in imports were relatively low, and safeguards did not require proof of injury to domestic producers. Substantial domestic and export subsidies remained in the developed countries as a result of the method of aggregation of commodities and a choice of base periods. Thus, it was estimated that the EU was allowed to subsidize an additional eight million tons of wheat exports and 363,000 tons of beef exports (Hathaway and Ingco 1996). In contrast, developing countries, most of which did not have domestic or export subsidies during the base period, were prohibited from introducing them (Khor 2000: 16).

Regulations in other new areas were characterized by the same structural imbalance in favor of the developed countries. Under the General Agreement on Trade in Services (GATS), only the movement of capital associated with transactions in areas that have been liberalized was allowed. The same treatment was denied to the movement of labor, even if most of the services that the developing countries are able to offer are labor-intensive (Drake and Nicolaidis 1992: 57, 66–7, 73; Das 1998: 1). The Agreement on Trade-Related Investment Measures (TRIMS) prohibited local content requirements, whereby firms must use a specified minimum amount of local inputs, and foreign exchange balancing, which limits the import of inputs by firms to a certain percentage of their exports. It thereby reduced states' ability to regulate FDI. The only concessions that the developing countries obtained were longer transition periods for implementation (five years for developing countries and seven years for the least developed countries) than for the developed countries (two years) (Low and Subramanian 1996: 381–3, 388; Juillard 1996). The Agreement on Trade-Related Aspects of Intellectual Property (TRIPS) imposed a higher degree of protection of intellectual property (patents, trademarks, copyright, geographic indications, industrial designs and layout designs of integrated circuits) than that required by existing intellectual property conventions. For example, the duration of patent protection was extended from sixteen to twenty years; protection had to be offered to pharmaceutical and chemical products, biotechnical, frontier and conventional inventions as well as plant varieties; and strict conditions were imposed on the granting of compulsory licensing (Braga 1996: 349–50, 356). The concessions to developing countries were limited to a moratorium of eleven years for least developed countries and a transition period of four years (instead of two) for other developing countries. Critics have argued that TRIPS would hinder indigenous technological development in the developing countries; restrict competition; increase prices of many crucial commodities, such as food and medicines; increase royalty payments and license fees to transnational companies; accelerate biodiversity loss; and threaten natural ecosystems (Boval 1996: 148; Khor 2000: 18). To cap it all, the provisions of the different Uruguay Round Agreements for special and differential (S and D) treatment of developing countries, whose capacity to implement the agreements was limited, contained little substance and were little more than "best endeavor" clauses.

In spite of developing countries' complaints, the EU insisted in the late 1990s that a further round of liberalization was necessary. The four new apples of discord between (European and Asian) developed and (Asian) developing countries – investment, competition, transparency in government procurement and trade facilitation – were referred to as "Singapore issues," since they were identified at the 1996 WTO Ministerial Conference in Singapore (the following draws heavily on Khor 2000 and Das 2002).

The EU demanded rules on investment and competition that would protect foreign investors' rights and ensure free competition between foreign and domestic investors in developing countries. The EU also sought national treatment (whereby foreign and domestic investors would be treated in the same manner) and most-favored nation treatment (whereby investors from different countries would be treated in the same manner). Developing countries opposed any international agreement prohibiting the imposition of conditions on FDI that would minimize FDI's adverse effects and promote development goals, such as channeling the FDI into priority areas and geographical regions and building links between the domestic economy and FDI. The EU also wanted an international agreement that would enable European firms to participate in government procurement in developing countries, many of which encourage domestic production by restricting or excluding foreign suppliers from government procurement or giving preferences to local firms, suppliers or contractors. The EU's initial goal was to obtain equal access to government procurement contracts. Faced with the developing countries' opposition, it was compelled to agree to limit discussions to "transparency in government procurement." Transparency, in the developing countries' view, would be confined to availability of information on tenders, specifications, rules, practices and final decisions. It would not extend to evaluation of offers, decision-making and appeals against final decisions by unsuccessful bidders. The fourth Singapore issue, trade facilitation, referred to practices very common in developed countries that the latter wish to see adopted in developing countries. One example of such practices is the physical examination of goods by customs authorities in only a small number of cases selected at random. The objection is that practices of this kind could have perverse effects in developing countries, where the chances of leakage (or even smuggling) are higher than in developed countries. Discussions on the Singapore issues were further complicated by the decision to incorporate into the agenda of a new round the negotiations for further liberalization of agriculture.

On the subject of WTO governance, disagreement between the EU and the United States, on the one hand, and the developing countries, on the other, arguably made dialogue more necessary than ever. Unfortunately, the conditions for a dialogue at the WTO were absent. In theory, all WTO member states enjoy the right to participate in deliberation and decision-making in all its bodies and meetings. Over the years, this right was steadily undermined by a series of practices that had not been formally approved by all WTO members. An increasing number of meetings were informal; not all members were invited to them; the organization of meetings was not regulated by any clear rules; no minutes were taken during these informal meetings and no reports of the meetings were provided (Kapoor 2004: 529). The most (in)famous of the informal meetings were the "Green Room" meetings, supposedly named after the color of the wallpaper in the WTO director general's conference room at headquarters. Meetings of this type were held by the working group dealing with Singapore issues at Seattle in 1999 (Friends of the Earth International 1999: 3). Another variation of the informal meeting is the "mini-ministerial," one of which was held in Singapore, on October 13–14, 2001, shortly before the Doha Ministerial in November, to discuss changing the meeting's venue as a response to security concerns raised after 9/11.

One set of actors that can plausibly claim to have a stake in WTO negotiations and yet is totally excluded from official participation comprises representatives of civil society. In comparison to other organizations, the WTO was further behind in efforts to facilitate dialogue with non-governmental organizations (NGOs). Even if 159 NGOs were able to attend the 1996 Singapore Ministerial Meeting (Walter 2001: 68), the WTO General Council ruled that it would not be possible for NGOs to be directly involved in the WTO's work (Lindblom 2000: 7).

In the ideal situation, participants in a dialogue should treat each other as equals. In practice, the interpretation of the consensus procedure of decision-making at the WTO gave more weight to developed countries' views. When the latter reached an agreement among themselves, a consensus was said to be emerging, and pressure was exerted on other states to join the consensus. On the other hand, when a majority of states reached agreement, with a few developed countries holding out, a consensus was said not to exist, and further negotiation was required (Third World Network *et al.* 2003: 3–4).

In the ideal situation, reasons must be given for decisions taken. Yet at WTO meetings, the reasons for selecting members and chairs of working or drafting groups were not publicly given. For instance, at Doha in 2001, the implicit criterion for their selection was their support for the EU and US position on the Singapore issues (Hormeku 2001). Another condition is that participants in the dialogue must take each other's views into account. Unfortunately, at the WTO, developing countries' views tend to be neglected. This was the complaint of many of them regarding the draft declarations transmitted by WTO officials to the Doha (2001) and the Cancun Ministerials (2003) (Hormeku 2001: 3; Khor 2003b) as well as the final declarations of the Doha and Cancún meetings.

With the North–South contradictions at the WTO in mind, it is now possible to inquire into the potential contribution of Asia–Europe dialogue to resolving these contradictions.

ASEM dialogue: superficial consensus, genuine disagreement

Dialogue within ASEM could have fulfilled its function of stimulating progress at the WTO in two ways: by discussing contentious issues in a way that identifies areas of agreement and disagreement, thus clarifying the stakes for states; and by exploring and formulating proposals that can serve as the basis for multilateral agreements. Dialogue could have taken place along the epistemic dimension: its purpose would be to make the Europeans aware of the (Asian) developing countries' reasons for opposition to a new round. If successful, it would have given rise to a new synthesis of the positions of Asians and Europeans, and perhaps of the positions of developing and developed countries.

An ASEM dialogue on WTO issues brings to mind the risk of dialogue for weaker actors, who could be forced to compromise on vital interests by stronger actors who refuse to change their positions (Lynch 2000: 323–39). From Habermas's perspective, the sharp inequalities between participants would ideally be compensated for, at least in part, if the stronger participant (the EU) made an attempt to incorporate some of the weaker participants' views into its own views. Along Todorov's praxeological dimension of dialogue, the requirement would be even more stringent, as noted in the previous chapter: the EU would accept the weaker participants' position, even if the latter were alien or unacceptable to it, as a sign of recognition of the equality of participants.

Based on evidence from three WTO Ministerial conferences (Seattle 1999; Doha 2001; Cancun 2003), it can be safely concluded that ASEM failed to promote a consensus among Asian and European states that could in turn bridge the North–South gap on substantive and governance issues at the WTO. In ASEM, the Asian developing states apparently shared a consensus with the EU on WTO issues. But this did not mean that ASEM prepared WTO discussions as a sort of sounding board; on the contrary, ASEM became an echo chamber of WTO discussions. In addition, Asian developing countries' actions at the WTO contradicted the superficial consensus at ASEM, proving that they had not changed their positions and that bargaining at the WTO was more important for them than ASEM dialogue. The main reasons for ASEM's failure lie in the EU's unwillingness to consider changing its positions, let alone to make concessions; the division within the Asian group between developed and developing countries and the absence of potential allies within ASEM for the Asian developing countries.

Assessing ASEM dialogue on WTO issues presents challenges to any outside observers. Official declarations express the consensus of the participants in terms that are so broad and so general that they can be marshaled to support contradictory positions. There is, however, anecdotal evidence that from the very start it was the EU that put WTO issues on the ASEM agenda and that the Asian states have used ASEM to express their disagreement with the EU on only a few occasions. Let us take the evidence in chronological order.

At ASEM 1 (1996), Germany's chancellor Helmut Kohl reportedly declared that a common position on WTO issues was the highest priority. For Sir Leon Brittan, the European Commission vice president, ASEM was a clearinghouse that could strengthen the bargaining position vis-à-vis third parties, particularly the USA, at the WTO (Bersick 2004c: 222). It was only at the 1999 Economic Ministers' Meeting (EMM), held a few months before the WTO's Seattle Conference, that Asian countries used ASEM as a forum to put on the agenda issues of concern to them. The Korean scholar Lee Chong-Wha, a former government adviser on ASEM matters, reports that the Asian countries, believing that they were being disproportionately targeted by the European Commission for antidumping investigations and penalties and that the use (or even the mere threat of use) of antidumping measures was denying them the benefits of trade liberalization, called for a discussion on antidumping, which was not on the agenda of the new WTO round advocated by the EU (Lee Chong-Wha 2000b).

Some statistics back up the Asian contention. The EU's antidumping investigations against Asian countries rose from twenty-one in 1995 to thirty-eight in 1999; in the same period, investigations directed against South Korea doubled from four to nine (Yoo Choong-Mo 2000: 8). The increase was attributed to the EU's fear that Asian products would flood European markets in the wake of the financial crisis. Yet the virtually unchanged market share of Asian states between 1995 (23.1 percent) and 1999 (24.5 percent) in the EU market provided grounds for skepticism regarding EU allegations of dumping. The European Commission generally denies that antidumping investigations target particular countries and takes pains to establish in its investigations that antidumping duties are justified. As if to counter with an issue that could put the Asian countries on the defensive, at the same meeting the European states proposed to discuss the link between trade and labor standards (Lee Chong-Wha 2000a: 127), which Asian countries consider as a disguised form of protectionism.

The 1999 EMM revealed the differences between Asian and European countries on WTO issues. According to the chairman's statement, only a "substantial number" of ministers supported a comprehensive round encompassing the Singapore issues, as well as linkages between trade and environment and between trade and core labor standards. In contrast, another group of participants argued for negotiations limited to the mandated negotiations on agriculture and services and market access for non-agricultural products (EMM 2 1999: para. 20). Knowing the contradictions at the WTO, it is easy to identify these countries as the Asian developing countries. These divisions reappeared several months later at SOMTI 5 (July 1999). Faced by the EU, Japan and Singapore, which declared themselves once more in favor of a new WTO round, the Asian developing countries insisted again that negotiations should exclude the Singapore issues. They sought concessions from the EU on agriculture and refused to discuss government procurement at all (Bersick 2004c: 225).

Apart from these snippets of evidence, we have to rely on indirect evidence from WTO sources to prove that ASEM played no role in facilitating discussion of WTO issues. The timing of ASEM meetings and WTO ministerial conferences, the one preceding the other, might mislead the observer into thinking that, prior to the latter, the former managed to come up with common positions. The observer who follows WTO negotiations soon realizes that the positions expressed in ASEM declarations are merely reiterations of positions that Asian and European participants already took at the WTO and that ASEM did not bring about any changes in these positions. Second, it will also become clear that the consensus expressed in ASEM declarations was more apparent than real. Third, the EU benefited from unsatisfactory governance at the WTO and was for this reason not inclined to consider improvements in the conditions for dialogue at the WTO. Finally, at the WTO, NGOs are formidable allies for Asian and other developing countries, a circumstance that made the EU even more averse to granting the AEPF a role in the ASEM process.

One early EU (and US) concern was the conclusion of negotiations on telecommunications and services that were extended beyond the Uruguay Round. Japan, Malaysia, South Korea, Singapore and Thailand had been identified by the United States and the EU as part of a group that had to make commitments on market access and national treatment that the United States judged satisfactory if the United States were to make its own commitments. During the Uruguay Round, the EU had cooperated with the United States in exerting pressure on these countries to make such commitments, to no avail (Ahnlid 1996: 83). It was hardly surprising, therefore, that the first ASEM EMM, held a month after the outbreak of the financial crisis, stressed the importance of attaining an agreement on financial services (EMM 1 1997: 4). By the end of 1997, agreements in both financial services and telecommunications had been concluded, to the satisfaction of the EU and the United States.

Following this triumph, the EU focused on convincing Asian states to implement the Uruguay Round obligations. When ASEM was launched in 1996, barely two years had elapsed since the signing of the Uruguay Round's Final Act. At this stage, ASEM participants declared that their priority was to ensure full implementation (ASEM 1 1996: para. 10; ASEM 2 1998a: para. 12; SOMTI

3 1998: para. 2; SOMTI 4 1999: para. 14; FMM 2 1999: para. 19). However, the apparent consensus on the priority of implementation concealed substantial differences in the understanding of implementation. From the developed countries' perspective, this meant that the developing countries had to liberalize without delay: "full and timely implementation of the Uruguay Round" (SOMTI 1 1996: 7). On the other hand, the developing countries sought assistance in implementing the numerous and wide-ranging agreements set out in nearly 22,000 pages of text. As a Singaporean diplomat put it, developing countries were hard put to meet the implementing and notification obligations (Kesavapany 1996: 23). Hence "implementation would need to be judged gradually and over time (SOMTI 1 1996: 7). The fact that these two contradictory positions were incorporated in the same statement demonstrates that a full understanding of each other's position had not been reached. Turning to other issues, Senior Officials' Meeting on Trade and Investment's (SOMTI) regret that little progress had been made in services was not shared by the developing countries. The importance it attached to the linkage between trade and the environment did not accurately reflect the position of developing countries, for whom the linkage would increase production costs and decrease their international competitiveness (Seet-Cheng 1994).

As early as 1996, without considering that states needed time to implement the Uruguay Round agreements, ASEM 1 already called for further liberalization of trade (ASEM 1 1996: para. 11). In July 1996, senior trade and investment officials promised that they would cooperate to ensure the successful outcome of the WTO Singapore Ministerial Conference later that year (SOMTI 1 1996: 7). After the Singapore meeting, the Senior Officials agreed that the aim should be to identify the elements for a future agreement in the area of government procurement, while trade facilitation had to cover rules of origin, observance of agreed deadlines on preshipment inspection and customs valuation (SOMTI 2 1997: 3).

During ASEM's first two years, there was little awareness among developing countries of the Uruguay Round's unfavorable outcomes. At the first ASEM meetings, it was logical that the EU position went unchallenged. The references to government procurement and trade facilitation at the SOMTI meeting provide indirect evidence that little dialogue had taken place. After the 1996 Singapore WTO Ministerial, analysis of government procurement and trade facilitation had barely begun. Thus, the Asian developing countries were hardly in a position to make an informed decision that negotiations on these two issues were necessary, let alone an international agreement. It cannot be excluded that the Asian developing countries acquiesced to ASEM references to these two issues in the belief that they did not commit themselves to anything and that there would be ample opportunities in the future to change their positions.

By ASEM 2, the Asian financial crisis had weakened the position of several Asian states, for whom the priority was European assistance. Agreement in principle to strengthen the WTO as the main negotiating forum for trade and investment rules (ASEM 2 1998a: para. 11) was probably deemed not too high a price to pay for the setting up of the ASEM Trust Fund (ATF). After the London summit, ASEM statements on the WTO emphasized the need for further liberalization through a new round called the "Millennium Round." In the run-up to WTO Ministerial Conferences at Geneva in 1998 and at Seattle in 1999, there were further promises of cooperation between Asia and Europe to prepare the conference (SOMTI 3 1998: 2; SOMTI 4 1999: para. 13).

At the Foreign Ministers' Meeting (FMM 2 1999: para. 19) in Berlin in April 1999, a superficial consensus that negotiations at Seattle "should in all aspects be concluded as expeditiously as possible" masked the divergences referred to earlier. Two months before the ill-fated Seattle meeting, there was for the first time specific reference to "the interests and concerns of the developing countries." Anticipating (wrongly) that a new round would be launched, the economic ministers subsequently asserted that "support for the WTO and consultation among ASEM partners should remain the key element of ASEM economic dialogue and cooperation throughout the Round" (EMM 2 1999: paras 20, 22, 26).

At the WTO Ministerial in Seattle, Malaysia's opposition to both alternatives proposed by the EU and the United States – either the launching of negotiations or undertaking a study with commitments to negotiate at the end (Raghavan 1999: 4) – was proof that at least one Asian ASEM participant did not share in the alleged EMM and FMM consensus. Despite Seattle's failure, the faith of the European Commission and some EU members in ASEM's ability to contribute to advancing the WTO's work was unshaken. The Commission still stressed "the need for deepening our mutual understanding and building alliances in the light of this aim" [European Commission COM (2000) 241: 11]. Nowhere was there recognition that the EU may have to change some of its positions in such a way as to take into account developing countries' views. At ASEM 3, the Danish prime minister reaffirmed his faith in ASEM:

> The breakdown of ... (Seattle) clearly demonstrates how important strong trade policy cooperation between the two regions will be ... in the future. ASEM has the potential to play in important role in bridging the gap on many of the issues which need to be resolved, before agreement on a new round can be initiated.
>
> (Rasmussen 2000: 23)

ASEM Senior Officials declared that to rebuild confidence in the WTO, concrete steps, which they did not specify, would be necessary (SOMTI 6 2000: para. 18). There was no acknowledgment that it was the US and the EU attempt to replicate their Uruguay Round strategy, consisting in striking a bargain between themselves and then presenting a united front to the developing countries, that had provoked the latter's opposition and the meeting's collapse.

That it is the WTO that has an impact on ASEM, rather than the reverse, became obvious after Seattle. References to the concerns and interests of developing countries now started to appear regularly in ASEM declarations. ASEM 3

(2000: para. 11; EMM 3 2001: paras 11–14) recognized that a new round had to strike an overall balance, reflecting the interests and concerns of all WTO members; address implementation issues and address the interests of developing and least developed countries through special and differential treatment, improved market access and technical assistance for capacity building. After ASEM 3, Malaysia reiterated that a new round had to take into account developing countries' concerns, provide for differential treatment for them and exclude environment and labor standards ("Malaysia endorses talks, with conditions," 2000: 2).

Amazingly, the launch of a new round at Doha in 2001 was still declared by ASEM senior officials to be an "absolute priority" (SOMTI 7 2001: para. 14). Undeterred by their lack of foresight as regards the Seattle Ministerial, the economic ministers (EMM 3 2001: paras 11, 13, 14), meeting two months before the Doha Ministerial, reaffirmed their commitment to the launching of a new round. The concerns of the developing countries were expressly cited: improving transparency within the WTO; addressing implementation; improving market access and providing technical assistance for capacity building. Once more, Asian developing countries' actions at the WTO reveal that the consensus on a new round was far from genuine. Indonesia, Malaysia and the Philippines criticized the WTO director general's proposals on implementation as empty and lacking in substantive content (Raghavan 2001a). The Philippines, speaking on behalf of Asian countries, criticized the holding of a "mini-Ministerial" in Singapore, to which many WTO members had not been invited. China, which was not yet a WTO member, joined the developing countries in expressing their "deep disappointment on the lack of any meaningful progress on implementation issues" (Group of 77 and China 2001). At Doha, among the most vocal critics of the EU–US proposal to launch a new round were four Asian ASEM participants – Indonesia, Malaysia, the Philippines and Thailand.

The fate of the Cancun meeting (2003) should lay to rest any lingering illusion that ASEM can facilitate dialogue between Asia and Europe on WTO issues. While ASEM reiterated that "absolute priority" had to be given to the WTO Ministerial at Cancún (SOMTI 9 2003: paras 10, 11), the EMM, held barely two months before Cancún, could not ignore that work at the WTO was making little headway. Asia and Europe were exhorted to "join hands in meeting the challenges and showing strong political will to cooperate constructively in all elements" of the WTO agenda (EMM 5 2003: paras 7, 9, 10). In preparation for Cancún, and following an EU Commission proposal, WTO experts from Asia and Europe held two informal consultations (Hanoi, January 2003 and Paris, June 2003) (Bersick 2004c: 225). The silence over the consultations' outcomes leaves one to conjecture that they were not all that fruitful.

Meanwhile, at WTO headquarters, Indonesia and Malaysia continued to oppose the EU position on negotiation modalities (Khor 2003a). The Draft Ministerial declaration that launched negotiations, as the EU and the United States wished, was criticized by both China and Malaysia (Khor 2003b). At Cancún, the Philippines and Indonesia formed, together with nineteen other developing countries, an alliance aimed at protecting small-scale agriculture employing large numbers of people from foreign competition. China, Malaysia and the Philippines joined sixty-seven developing countries in declaring that in the absence of consensus, negotiations on Singapore issues could not be launched (Khor and Hormeku 2003). Malaysia vigorously condemned the draft declaration's decision to launch negotiations, in a letter to the WTO director general, the United States and the EU (Stuart 2003a).

If ASEM was unable to function as a forum for substantive dialogue on WTO issues, could there at least have been ASEM dialogue on governance at the WTO? After all, there is widespread dissatisfaction with governance at the WTO, especially on the part of developing countries and civil society groups. After Cancún, a consensus apparently had formed that governance at the WTO was in need of reform. For once, complaints were heard from the EU, which characterized the WTO's decision-making as "medieval" and "neolithic" (Raghavan 2003b). The consensus on the need for reform could have created the conditions for a dialogue on WTO governance, to which smaller subsets of WTO members, such as ASEM, could contribute ideas.

In reality, consensus was superficial, thus diminishing ASEM's chances of formulating proposals for reform. The reason was that the EU generally benefited from bad governance in that organization, with informal consultations usually producing the outcomes that favored EU (and US) positions. Bad governance had rarely ever provoked the EU (or the United States) into making protests. Until 2006, when the negotiations were suspended, the EU showed little inclination to enter into a dialogue on the subject in any forum, whether at the WTO or within ASEM.

It is not to be expected that the EU would agree to a reform of WTO governance allowing for NGO participation, precisely because NGOs have proved to be formidable allies for the developing countries. Suffice it to recall that at Seattle, NGOs from developing and developed countries publicly denounced the proceedings and that it was the Third World Network, an international grouping of NGOs, that lobbied successfully for the meeting's suspension (Hormeku 1999: 3). Shortly before the Doha Ministerial, forty NGOs condemned the non-participatory and biased preparatory process; declared the draft to be dangerous and illegitimate; called on the WTO Secretariat and the developed countries not to manipulate the Ministerial and appealed to the Ministerial conference to reject it (Raja 2001). At Cancún, NGOs from developed and developing countries provided technical analysis of the developed countries' proposals to many developing countries. Indeed, one outstanding feature of Cancún was the working partnership between NGOs and developing countries. The EU indirectly confirmed this by blaming NGOs collapse of the Cancún Ministerial (Catholic Agency for Overseas Development 2003: 11).

Having this in mind, we can understand why the EU was wary of any ASEM dialogue authorizing AEPF, which would undoubtedly support the position of the Asian developing countries and contradict EU positions, as a very rapid perusal of their statements will prove. Since AEPF 1 (1996), the AEPF has denounced the Uruguay Round agreements. Instead of further liberalization, the AEPF demanded a focus on the Uruguay Round's impact on small farmers, women and the intellectual property rights of indigenous people. The AEPF demands on intellectual property rights and agriculture would have amounted to a reversal of the Uruguay Round's results (AEPF 1 1996: 4).

If the AEPF could bring potential pressure to bear on the EU, the AEPF's political program would make Asian states, particularly the authoritarian ones, wish to exclude it from ASEM. AEPF 1 had asserted that human rights had to be central to Asia–Europe relations and rejected cultural particularism as a justification for human rights violations. Indonesia's "shameless efforts" to prevent discussion of East Timor at ASEM were condemned. AEPF demanded that the military junta of Burma, which was set to join ASEAN, release political prisoners, recognize the results of the 1980 elections and begin tripartite dialogue with the democratic leader Aung San Suu Kyi (AEPF 1 1996: 5–7). To these demands, AEPF 2 added the respect for the International Labor Organization's (ILO's) core labor standards (AEPF 2 1998a). The contradiction between the AEPF's political agenda and the authoritarian character of several Asian participants makes it painfully clear why the latter would prefer to do without the AEPF's support in any ASEM dialogue on WTO matters.

What accounts for ASEM's failure to act as a forum for dialogue on WTO issues? One major obstacle to dialogue is to be found in its organization as a dialogue between Europe and Asia, forcing each to present group positions. The EU members consistently present a united front, contrary to the hope of Singapore and Thailand that the dialogue would be between individual Asian and individual European states. Facing the EU is a divided Asian group, with the more developed Asian countries, Japan, South Korea, and Singapore sharing the EU views. Japan unequivocally supported a new round covering the Singapore issues. According to its "Basic Strategy" for a comprehensive new round, new rules on trade and investment would create new opportunities for Japanese companies. In agriculture, Japan's goal was to ensure the "coexistence of a wide variety of agriculture," which presumably included the high-cost Japanese and European varieties and to prevent further liberalization of agricultural trade (Japan Ministry of Foreign Affairs 2002). The EU and Japan presented a paper on modalities in transparency on government procurement (Raghavan 2003a) as well as near-identical draft texts on the Singapore issues. Both set January 1, 2005 as the deadline for completing negotiations.

As we have seen, the less-developed Asian countries (Indonesia, Malaysia, the Philippines and Thailand) usually adopted positions contrary to those of the EU and the United States. ASEM's structural weakness for this second group of Asian countries is that it did not include all actors affected by the WTO negotiations in the same way, that is, the African and Latin American countries, with which the Asian developing countries could form tactical coalitions when faced with the united front of the EU and the United States. Since the EU presented itself as a unitary actor in ASEM, there can be no question of forging such an alliance with individual European countries, regardless of their sympathy for some concerns of developing countries. Under these conditions, it would have been rash for the Asian developing countries to suppose that ASEM provided a fresh opportunity of convincing the EU to modify its positions. The alternative would have been to allow like-minded Asian and European states to form ad hoc groupings on WTO issues, a move that would have undermined ASEM, perhaps fatally.

A second advantage that the WTO offered to the Asian developing countries, improbable as it may seem, was the theoretical possibility of bargaining on the basis of an exchange of concessions in different areas. The EU being the party seeking the agreement of the Asian states on all Singapore issues, such bargaining could not take place within ASEM's limited framework. The convergence of interests between the EU and Japan, on the one hand, and the reliance of the Asian developing countries on alliances with developing countries from other regions, on the other, was plain for all to see in the run-up to Cancún.

A further obstacle to dialogue within ASEM lies in the inability or unwillingness of the EU and its Asian allies to incorporate developing countries' views into their positions. In theory, the ASEM process could reduce resistance by holding out the prospect of material concessions that respond to the interests of the Asian developing countries, which could then become allies in the WTO. This theory has not been verified in practice. For instance, Japan's Basic Strategy did not specify what concessions Japan was willing to offer in return for developing countries' agreement on the Singapore issues. On the EU side, it is recognized that further trade liberalization had to be accompanied by special and differential treatment for the developing countries [European Commission COM (1999) 0331: 5]. The EU claimed that the new round was the only way to meet their expectations [European Commission COM (1999) 0331: 4–6]. The brief survey of three WTO Ministerials casts doubt on the veracity of these assertions. On the contrary, it highlights the EU's unwillingness to make substantial concessions to (Asian) developing countries in exchange for further liberalization. At the WTO and in the ASEM process, the EU has relied solely on arguments based on neoliberal ideology to justify a new round [European Commission COM (1999) 0331: 5]. Liberalization was unquestioningly held to be the solution to the 1990s recession, the only alternative being the collapse of the trade system. These arguments were unpersuasive, as European NGOs pointed out: Seattle's failure did not lead to the WTO's disappearance, nor did it invalidate the Uruguay Round agreements (Jenner 2001).

The failure of either the EU or Japan to offer concessions arises from the fact that it was the two that sought the (Asian) developing countries' agreement on the Singapore issues. Consequently, little room was left for bargaining (Hauser 2002: 129; Stuart 2003b; Raghavan 2003c). There was a second reason for the EU, which had to be with the constraints imposed on it by EU policies, specifically the Common Agricultural Policy (CAP). During the Uruguay Round, the European Community (EC) was a staunch opponent of liberalization of agricultural trade. It was largely instrumental in ensuring that the Agreement on Agriculture did not significantly reduce tariffs or increase access to EU markets, through such provisions as exemption of EC compensation payments from reduction in domestic subsidies and the aggregation of commodities to meet minimum access requirements (Hathaway and Ingco 1996: 37, 56). Some observers were aware of the contradiction in the EU's position. One economist pointed out that without liberalization in agriculture, a new round might appear to critics as "a cloak by which to discuss anything and everything, except agriculture" (Lehmann 2000: 111; Sideri 1996: 18). Yet the EU, rather than preparing to make concessions, demanded concessions in its favor for the dismantling of agricultural protectionism that it practiced [European Commission COM (1999) 0331: 5]. Paradoxically the EU, a staunch advocate of the neoliberal ideology, gives the impression of believing that liberalization's negative consequences will not be automatically corrected by market mechanisms in agriculture, for which active state intervention was essential.

Regrettably, even the European Parliament, which sees itself as the champion of the Third World, wishes to safeguard the European agriculture model, on the ground that agriculture also managed the countryside and protected the environment. These functions could not be fulfilled if liberalization triggered migration to cities (European Parliament PE297137, 1999: paras 5, 7, 12, 16). The underlying fear is that liberalization would lose votes for national political leaders and damage the EU's credibility and legitimacy. The (European Parliament) EP's recommendations should force the EU to confront the issue of whether these same arguments are not applicable to other sectors and to developing countries, and if so, whether the whole enterprise of liberalization has not been inherently contradictory. Why it is that only one sector – agriculture – in only one region – Europe – should be spared from the detrimental effects of liberalization? If these detrimental effects are admitted, then perhaps the entire undertaking of liberalization itself needs to be reexamined.

The circumstances of Cancún's collapse give an indication of the amount of pressure necessary to wring concessions from the EU. On the last night of the conference (September 13–14, 2003), Malaysia and India refused a compromise that would have launched negotiations on only two of the four issues. The EU then reportedly offered to "unbundle" the Singapore issues, i.e. leave out investment and competition, negotiate on the other two on condition that the EU position on agriculture was accepted. Faced with Malaysia's objection to government procurement, the EU was reportedly willing to concede this, in order to maintain trade facilitation. The compromise fell through when Japan and South Korea opposed the unbundling of the four issues, perhaps out of a desire to protect their respective agricultural sectors. Still, their resistance might have been overcome had it not been for the refusal of the least-developing and the ACP (African, Caribbean and Pacific) Group to unbundling without concessions on agriculture, particularly on cotton (Raghavan 2003b, 2003c; Stuart 2003b; Catholic Agency for Overseas Development 2003: 8–9). Malaysia's opposition to the EU proposals won steadfast support from other developing countries and further strengthened its hand, something which would not have been possible in a limited forum like ASEM.

That the EU at the WTO was driven to consider modifying its position only at the eleventh hour and under pressure from large coalitions seems to reduce the chances that smaller fora such as ASEM could convince it to enter into a dialogue. The EU's inability to take into account the developing countries' views and interests, which have been repeatedly expressed since 1996, has been remarked upon by European NGOs:

> The tale of Singapore issues is one of startling arrogance and imperviousness both to the arguments and the clearly expressed views of developing countries. For seven years since the Singapore Ministerial, the EC, despite dwindling support from its member states and business, has insisted on their inclusion, only to abandon them altogether a few hours before the scheduled end of the Cancún Ministerial.
> (Catholic Agency for Overseas Development 2003: 9)

The EU's unwillingness to modify its positions also undermines claims that ASEM can serve to counterbalance US unilateralism at the WTO. In reality, the EU and the USA form an alliance at the WTO on agriculture and the Singapore issues. In case of disagreement, they seek first to resolve it between them, before presenting the outcome as a fait accompli to other WTO members. For instance, shortly before Doha, they struck a bargain between themselves (EU support for agricultural negotiations in return for US support for investment and competition), before facing the developing countries. Again, in the run-up to Cancún, they agreed on a common position regarding agriculture, which was then incorporated into the Draft declaration presented to the developing countries.

Whether the possibility of "unbundling" had been floated at the 2003 consultations in Hanoi and Paris is uncertain. Had this been done, the Asian countries would have had time to consider it. Reiterer (2004: 260) suggests that it was no accident that the EU chose to maintain trade facilitation rather than any of the other three issues, at the same time as he denies that Asians and Europeans had succeeded in convincing each other to take each other's interests into account.

There can be little doubt that the divisions between developed and developing Asian countries and the tacit alliance between the EU and Asian developed countries are not passing phenomena; on the contrary, they are rooted in deep-rooted conflicts of interest. In 2005, circumstances were even less propitious for ASEM. As a result of disagreements over participation of Myanmar and the new EU member states in ASEM, ASEM Economics and Finance Ministers' Meetings in 2005 were cancelled, only a few months prior to the December 2005 WTO Ministerial Conference in Hong Kong. Any hope that divergences of interest between Asia and Europe could be addressed through dialogue in ASEM must have vanished at this point. The suspension in July 2006 of the WTO negotiations succeeded in eliciting only an expression of "deep regret" from the sixth ASEM summit in Helsinki, two months later (ASEM 6 2006a: para. 19). One would search in vain for an indication of the hope that ASEM could give impetus to WTO negotiations.

From the actions of Asian states, one may deduce that bargaining at the WTO was more crucial for them than dialogue within ASEM. From the EU perspective, it could still hope to resort to ASEM as an instrument for obtaining consensus on the Singapore issues through the modification of Asian laws in the name of trade facilitation and investment promotion.

Summary

Unlike in the cases of poverty alleviation and economic and social development, it was the more powerful actor, the EU, that insisted on multilateral issues as areas of common interest of Asia and Europe, and that ASEM should be a means of advancing discussions in multilateral organizations, primarily the WTO. This conception was a manifestation of the European market access strategy, which in turn reflected the weak position of European firms in Asia in comparison with their Japanese and US counterparts.

A dialogue on the reform of the international financial architecture only emerged as an area of common interest when Asia demanded European assistance during the Asian financial crisis. In reality, the little discussion that has taken place in ASEM represents a repetition of discussions at the IMF, and proposals for reform have been no more innovative than those floated at the IMF. Other than the ASEM Trust Fund, no evidence has been found that proposals for joint action considered by ASEM finance ministers have been implemented. When Asian states began to express dissatisfaction at the slow pace of international discussions, ASEM decided to launch the Kobe Research Project in 2001. The latter could have been a contribution of dialogue if it had generated new knowledge serving as the basis for joint action, as Todorov's conception of dialogue would have led us to expect. Unfortunately, the Kobe Research Project's recommendations that Asian states peg their currencies to a currency basket and that Asian bond markets be developed have already been put forward by others and do not necessarily require joint Asia–Europe action.

As regards ASEM's contribution to dialogue at the WTO, the prospects for success were diminished by the inequality between participants. To begin with, it was the more powerful actor, the EU, that insisted on WTO issues as areas of common interest that needed to be taken up in Asia–Europe dialogue. As Habermas's analysis of globalization suggests, the impact of inequality could have been mitigated if the stronger actor had taken a broader view of its interests and demonstrated greater willingness to change its positions or even make concessions to the weaker actor. Instead the EU, as the stronger actor, exerted pressure on the developing Asian participants to implement the Uruguay Round Agreements and to accept the EU's agenda for a new WTO round. Dialogue thus entailed for the weaker actor the risk identified by Lynch that vital or essential interests might be compromised by dialogue with a powerful actor. Consequently, Asian developing states gave the impression of agreeing to an Asia–Europe consensus on WTO issues in ASEM. Yet far from advancing WTO discussions, ASEM discussions served little more than to register the state of negotiations at the WTO. Moreover, the actions of Asian developing states prior to and during three successive WTO Ministerial Meetings (Seattle in 1999, Doha in 2001 and Cancún in 2003) prove that they did not feel bound by the consensus expressed in ASEM and that for them, bargaining at the WTO was more important than dialogue at ASEM. ASEM's inability to advance discussions at the WTO can be explained by ASEM's organization as a dialogue between two groups, ignoring the division within the Asian group between developing and developed countries. As an examination of WTO negotiations reveals, the latter generally take the same positions as the Europeans. Unlike in the WTO, Asian developing countries were unable to form coalitions within ASEM with like-minded (developing) countries. A second explanation can be found in the developed (Asian and European) participants' unwillingness to modify their positions, much less to make concessions to the developing countries, which were the only participants in the dialogue expected to change their positions. The European attitude cannot be reconciled with the requirements that each side treats the other as an equal partner, that each should be willing to consider the other's position and that each should be willing to change its position. NGOs could have been valuable allies for the latter in ASEM, as they have been at the WTO, had it not been for their political agenda stressing democratization and human rights.

4 ASEM as a lobby for the modification of Asian laws

The European Union's (EU's) attempt to use Asia–Europe Meeting (ASEM) as a lobby for the modification of the legislation of Asian participants is a function of ASEM that has escaped most observers' attention. Not surprisingly, Asian states have never openly admitted that the modification of their laws is an area of common interest in ASEM. The significance of this function for the EU becomes obvious once we understand the specific nature of the market access problem facing European firms in Asia. From the perspective of the EU, whose firms lag behind their Japanese and US counterparts in investing in East Asia, the market access of European goods is linked to foreign direct investment (FDI) presence, and both allegedly face non-tariff barriers in Asia.

In conventional economic theory, FDI is a substitute for international trade. When a firm invests in a foreign country and starts production there, it ceases to export to it. In Asia, at least, this linkage is different, and it poses special problems to EU firms. As the EU's New Asia Strategy admitted, Japanese firms that were investing in Asia from the mid-1980s onwards were also creating the sales and distribution networks that European firms had been unable to penetrate in Japan. In the 1980s, the linkage in Southeast Asia was the basis of the argument that in order to increase trade with Southeast Asia, European firms had to invest there. In this view, European FDI in Southeast Asia would not substitute trade but would instead intensify trade between the two regions. The Japanese experience was said to prove that production in the host country would inevitably create demand for capital goods, raw materials and intermediate goods supplied by parent companies. FDI would also make it possible to circumvent tariff and non-tariff barriers. By reducing production costs, FDI would stimulate demand in the host country. FDI was even anticipated to have a potential imitation effect in the home country, encouraging other companies to engage in production overseas. Ultimately, FDI would increase the parent company's international competitiveness (Hiemenz 1987; Hiemenz *et al.* 1987: 38–9; Langhammer 1989: 120–1; Gross 1988: 81–2; Eschborn *et al.* 1992: 172). The European Commission endorsed this conception of the role of FDI in its 1996 Communication on ASEAN–EU relations. As the Commission succinctly put it, "access to the Southeast Asian market requires large-scale investment in ASEAN member states" [European Commission COM (96) 314 final: 15].

A policy of encouraging European FDI in East Asia must recognize that European integration itself creates structural incentives for European firms to invest within the EU, notably by creating a larger internal market and implementing a European regional development policy. In the late 1990s, a series of programs, such as European Community Investment Programs, European Investment Bank (EIB) lending to Asia and Latin America and Asia-Invest, was instituted by the Commission as a way of altering these incentives (Robles 2004: 112–18). The Asia-Invest Programme was extended from 2003 to 2007, with a total appropriation of thirty-five million euros. These programs, no matter how useful they were in providing technical assistance and promoting networking and partnership, were small scale and had a limited duration. By their nature, their impact could only be felt in a limited number of sectors and by a limited number of firms. A strategy that modifies the domestic laws of Asian countries would have more far-reaching consequences from the European perspective. At a very low cost, if not minimal, favorable conditions, as defined by Europeans, would be created for European firms that wish to export to Asia or to invest there in all economic sectors.

The EU's New Asia Strategy explicitly declared:

> It is necessary to undertake all the appropriate steps to obtain from Asian partners modifications of their legislation and administrative regulations which hamper the development of European trade and direct investments. Basic concerns include Standards and Quality Control; Intellectual Property Rights and the negotiation of Mutual Recognition Agreements on standards, testing and certification.
>
> [European Commission COM (94) 314 final: Part IV, 2.2.1]

The strategy would explain the EU's remarkably unenthusiastic response to the proposal put forward by the Asia–Europe Vision Group (AEVG) that ASEM participants "set the goal of free trade in goods and services by the year 2025" (AEVG 1999: 9). ASEM 3 did not so much as allude to the AEVG's recommendation. Sir Leon Brittan, the Commission's vice president at the time, simply declared that ASEM should not promote regional trade liberalization (Ton Sinh Thanh 1998: 94). The reason is obvious: free trade would simply have bloated the European trade deficit with East Asia, with no guarantee of increased market access of European goods and investment in Asia.

If Japan is the competitor of and the model for the EU in Asia, it behooves us to examine the Japan–EU Regulatory Reform Dialogue (RRD) as a paradigm for dialogue within ASEM. It is argued here that the RRD is both a positive and a negative model for ASEM. It helps us to understand the kind of changes in Asian domestic laws desired by the EU; at the same time, its inherent limitations clarify the EU's rationale for dialogue through ASEM. The second section of this chapter will analyze the conflicting explanations provided by Asians and Europeans for the relatively low level of European FDI in Asia and their preferred solutions. These differences were clearly articulated during the preparation of the ASEM Investment Promotion Action Plan (IPAP). The last section will examine the implementation of the IPAP and the Trade Facilitation Action Plan (TFAP).

The Japan–EU dialogue as a paradigm for ASEM

A study of Japan–EU relations is instructive for an analysis of broader Asia–Europe relations, in that the cycle observed since the 1970s of Japanese trade surplus–European protests–Japanese response seems to set a pattern that is being replicated as other Asian countries have industrialized and increased their capacity to export.

In this pattern, the appearance of Japanese (Asian) surplus arouses concern in Europe. Europeans are unaware that as late as 1968, Japan had trade deficits with Europe. Similarly, the rapid increase in European imports from Southeast Asia and China in the last two decades tends to obscure in European minds the fact that, for very long periods, Europe enjoyed trade surpluses with them. Faced with accumulating surpluses, Europeans are tempted to attribute Japanese (Asian) success to dumping, that is, the sale of goods at abnormally low prices in Europe. In the case of Japan, the European "explanation" ignored the role of industrial planning and substantial investments in plant and equipment that created Japan's competitive advantages. In the 1990s, Europeans were unable to resist the temptation to transpose to the cases of Southeast Asia and China, the same explanation for Japanese success.

The evolution of EU policy responses to Japanese and Asian surpluses also follows a remarkably similar pattern. Not realizing that Japanese surpluses resulted from Japanese long-term planning and investment, the European Community (EC) sought from the late 1960s to the mid-1970s to limit Japanese exports to the EC (Wilkinson 1990: 174). This approach has also been adopted toward Southeast Asia and China. In the Japanese case, the most widely used instruments were Voluntary Export Restraints (VERs). As regards Southeast Asia (Robles 2004) and China, successive reforms of the EC's Generalized System of Preferences (GSP) restricted the range of products for which they could claim tariff reductions. In all three cases, increases in exports also provoked a rise in the number of antidumping complaints filed by European firms, most of which were decided by the European Commission in favor of the firms and entailed the imposition of tariffs on the allegedly dumped imports.

The effectiveness of trade restrictions vis-à-vis Japanese (East Asian) products in enhancing European goods' competitiveness is a matter of debate. An independent study commissioned by the European Parliament pointed out as far back as 1993 that ball bearings produced in Europe needed the protection of antidumping measures against imports from Japan for fifteen years. The length of protection inevitably prompted the conclusion that European products did not become any more competitive following the imposition of antidumping duties on Japanese ball bearings (European Parliament 1993: 172). In the case of personal fax machines, the difficulties encountered by the Dutch company Philips in competing with Japanese products were attributable to the fact that it entered the market five years after Japanese firms did so (Yano 1999: 32). The lag was so substantial that Philips needed the protection of antidumping measures in order to catch up.

To relieve the pressure from EU members and European trade unions for protection against imports from Japan, the European Commission switched in the late 1970s and the 1980s to a strategy of demanding reduction of Japanese tariffs and abolition of non-tariff barriers. Ironically, the reduction of Japanese tariffs, which at the end of the General Agreement on Tariffs and Trade's (GATT's) Tokyo Round (1979), were among the lowest in the developed world, coincided with continued increases in Japanese trade surpluses. The logical conclusion, according to Endymion Wilkinson, a European Commission official who served many years in Japan, was that the surpluses were "not the result of a closed Japanese market but of a successful Japanese export drive" (Wilkinson 1990: 176). This was confirmed by the observation that European companies were also losing market shares in the United States (Wilkinson 1990: 215). In the 1980s, the need to face the Japanese challenge became one of the driving forces for accelerating European integration, embodied in the Single European Market. By the mid-1980s, when "pretty much everything had been tried" (Wilkinson 1990: 197), European attention shifted to Japanese non-tariff barriers. Japanese institutions that allegedly constituted structural impediments to imports came under heavy criticism from Europe. Following this pattern, the EU has been exerting pressure, since the mid-1990s, on the Association of Southeast Asian Nations (ASEAN) and China to remove what the EU perceives to be non-tariff barriers in these countries.

There seems to be a consensus between Japan and the EU that since the mid-1990s, trade frictions have become less acute in their relations. The growth of Japanese FDI in Western Europe is one reason often cited for the improvement. Another is the inauguration in 1994 of the RRD, which focuses on modification of Japanese regulations as a means of increasing access of European goods to and investment in Japan. Faced with an EU request to initiate dialogue, Japan had little choice but to accept. Initially, the RRD tended to be one-sided, because only the EU made demands. More recently, Japan has been putting forward its own demands, giving the RRD the character of a disguised negotiation. The RRD is said to have the merit of being non-confrontational, but it is a little-known fact that it can be backed up by the threat of sanctions embodied in the European Trade Barriers Regulation.

The Japan–EU regulatory reform dialogue: disguised bargaining between equals

In their 1991 Joint Declaration, Japan and EC members affirmed that they would pursue equitable access to their respective markets, removing obstacles, whether structural or other, impeding the expansion of trade and investment, on the basis of comparable opportunities (EU–Japan 1991). Under the 2001 Action Plan for

EU–Japan Cooperation, both sides agreed that the aim of the dialogue was "to develop an appropriate regulatory framework" (EU–Japan Summit 2001: 9). The expression of mutual interest should not mask the fact that initially only one actor – the EU – had an interest in the RRD. It is not too far-fetched to assume that Japan consented to it in order to demonstrate its willingness to reduce Japanese trade surpluses with Europe and to increase European FDI in Japan. Thus, the RRD, at least initially, did not meet two crucial requirements for an ideal dialogue: that the participants should consider each other as equals and that they should be willing to change their positions. However, since the late 1990s, Japan has given the impression that its interest in the RRD had increased, as indicated by a growing number of Japanese requests for regulatory reform in the EU. Certainly, Japan and the EU are in a position either to offer substantial concessions or to cause considerable harm to each other. In recent years, the RRD has become more balanced, with each side presenting reform requests to the other. Its name should not mislead us: change in the legislation of the other party is the goal. In this sense, the RRD is more akin to an institutionalized negotiation.

For Europe, the RRD's premise is that Japanese informal barriers need to be removed. One group of barriers is administrative. Regulation is said to be excessive in Japan, with the number of Japanese laws and regulations on the economy estimated at 10,000. Second, the Japanese bureaucracy has the discretionary, if not arbitrary, power to interpret and implement these laws. Among the practices incriminated by Europeans are inspection of each unit of consumption goods; the incompatibility of Japanese standards with international standards; insufficient intellectual property protection; administrative guidance; and systematic preferential treatment of local suppliers in government procurement. Trade barriers arising from private firms' practices include the *keiretsu* system, the distribution system, difficulties in recruitment of qualified staff, high start-up costs and other practices such as the importance of personal contacts (Kohl *et al.* 1999: 61–3).

Ten years after the RRD's initiation, the EU believed that it had "proved its worth as a systematic but non-confrontational way to address problem issues" for European firms (European Commission 2004: 3). One example of progress cited by the EU was the increased autonomy and resources of the Japan Fair Trade Commission (JFTC), which the EU wished to be empowered to enforce competition rules and to review administrative guidance by ministries (European Commission 1999a: 2; 1999b; 2001a: 11). The JFTC's importance was illustrated when it broke up a cartel at Narita airport between the two providers of fumigation and warehousing services for plant, fruit and vegetable imports (European Commission 2001a: 12; 2002a: 15). Presumably, European exporters to Japan would have more choice of service providers after the JFTC's ruling. Another RRD achievement was the sharp reduction in the approval time for drugs to a maximum of twelve months (European Commission 1999a: 14; 2001a: 25; 2002a: 3; 2003a: 34). A third positive result was the passing of Japanese legislation in July 2003 allowing for free association between

European and Japanese lawyers. Previously, Japanese lawyers were prohibited from entering into partnership with or being employed by foreign lawyers licensed in Japan, thus limiting opportunities for foreign lawyers to practice in Japan and allegedly deterring foreign investment in Japan (European Commission 1999a: 9, 26; 2000a: 15; 2001a: 8–9; 2002a: 12–13; 3; 2003a: 3–4). On the other hand, little progress had been made in the areas of transport and sanitary and phytosanitary rules (European Commission 2004: 3).

It is essential to examine the types of arguments that the EU puts forward in order to convince Japan to modify Japanese legislation, as the EU arguments may be mobilized again in a dialogue with other Asian countries. The following analysis cannot claim to be exhaustive, since the documents of the RRD for 1994–98 are not available online. For the following period, three EU approaches to regulatory reform in Japan can be identified. First, the EU urges Japan to implement the relevant World Trade Organization (WTO) agreement and/or ruling; second, the EU suggests that Japan look to the EU model for a solution and third, the EU simply asks Japan to change a Japanese law or regulation that is inconvenient for European companies.

The first approach was exemplified in the EU request that Japan change the procedure for acceptance of varieties of fresh fruits and vegetables. In February 1999, a WTO Appellate Body, acting on a US complaint, had ruled that Japan's policy of "varieties testing," testing for every single variety of fruit and vegetable before granting import authorization, was inconsistent with the WTO's Sanitary and Phytosanitary (SPS) Agreement. The EU, pointing out that SPS approval in Japan could take up to twenty years for some citrus fruits, requested application of this ruling to European exports (particularly, Spanish Clementina and Salustiana oranges, French golden apples and Italian fruits and vegetables) to Japan. By 2004, the EU was able to report that Japan had lifted the restrictions for Spanish oranges and Belgian tomatoes. However, the hearing planned for Italian fruits and vegetables had not yet taken place, and processing of approvals remained very slow (European Commission 2001a: 35; 2002a: 44–5; 2003a: 44; 2004: 39–40).

Second, if no relevant WTO agreement or ruling exists, the EU recommends that Japan consider adopting EU practices. In the area of government procurement, the EU complained that in 1999, no EU construction company was able to obtain a single contract (out of 580 contracts awarded). One alleged reason for this was the requirement that foreign experience be certified by the Japanese government prior to bidding, which the EU considered as potentially discriminatory against European firms. The European Commission pointed out that in the EU, procuring bodies evaluated foreign and domestic experience on an equal footing. On this basis, the EU requested that no distinction should be made in Japan between foreign and domestic experience. Another Japanese practice criticized by the EU was that of fixing a price ceiling for bids. Because the ceiling was kept secret, the practice allegedly favored leaks and bid rigging and also failed to take into account new technology. EU procuring bodies were said not to use price ceilings, although they publicly announced the budget available for a given project (European Commission 2004: 11–13; 2003a: 16–17; 2002a: 18).

When no existing WTO or EU rules support the EU request for change, the EU requests that the practice be abolished, for the simple reason that it causes inconvenience to EU exporters to Japan. One finds a good example of this strategy in the European challenge to Art. 10 of the Japanese Road Vehicles Act, which laid down that control devices for operating motor vehicles should be located 500 mm to the left or to the right of the steering wheel. The regulation obliged some European companies that placed their defroster switch on one model outside the 500 mm range to reconfigure the control panels of vehicles exported to Japan, at additional cost. In the EU view, the increase in the Japanese population's average height since the Act was passed in 1951 meant that non-application of Art. 10 would not affect safety. The EU wished the regulation to be relaxed "without delay" (European Commission 2001a: 9–10).

Whenever the EU argues for regulatory reform in Japan, on the basis of a WTO agreement or ruling, there appears to be very little room for dialogue. The other two strategies of the EU may leave Japan with several options, but one wonders whether in the EU view there is room for dialogue. For example, since 1999, the EU has objected to working practices on the Japanese waterfront that are said to pose problems for European shipping and for which it holds the Japan Harbour Transportation Association (JHTA) responsible. Under JHTA agreements with various parties, consultations must be held between the JHTA and shipping lines prior to any changes that might decrease employment or adversely affect working conditions. Shipping lines are required to consult the JHTA for approval of changes in their operations, including what the EU considers as minor issues, such as substitution of vessels. For the EU, the JHTA's large discretionary power and de facto restraint on free competition in the provision of harbor service inhibit price competition. The EU asserts that the JHTA fulfills an obsolete regulatory function (European Commission 1999a: 10–11; 2000a: 18; 2001a: 24–5; 2002a: 31–2; 2003a: 31–2; 2004: 25–6). From the harbor employees' point of view, substitution of vessels might not necessarily be a minor matter as it might increase or decrease demand for their services. One might ask if the position of the EU, which prides itself on a social model able to reconcile capitalism and welfare in Europe, appreciates sufficiently the importance of preserving employment in Japan.

Japan's assessment of the RRD is positive, at least on the surface. Thanks to the RRD, the initial confrontational character of Japan–EU economic relations is acknowledged to have receded. Dialogue had become a means for a constructive exchange of opinions regarding technical regulations and the business environment (Government of Japan 2003: 2). The EU claims that it has responded to Japan's requests regarding driving licenses, data protection and the implementation of a Community patent system (European Commission 2004: 3).

On the matter of driving licenses, Japan's request stemmed from a European Directive on Driving Licenses (1991/439/EEC), which required non-EU nationals to surrender licenses issued by their countries when obtaining EC model licenses. As a result of the directive, Japanese citizens who surrendered their licenses in Europe could not drive cars when they returned to Japan. In 2001, the

EU proposed that Japan allow its nationals to drive in Japan by attaching a photo-copy of their Japanese driving license to the license issued in Europe. Japan responded that this procedure would violate the Japanese Road Traffic Law. In 2004, the EU then proposed that the Japanese license should be surrendered to the Embassy of Japan in the EU member concerned, and Japan accepted this proposal (Government of Japan 1998; 2001a: 21; 2001b: 12–3; 2004: 8, 50–1).

No information is available online on data protection. As regards the Commun-ity Patent System, the EU Council of Ministers decided to establish it in March 2003, but it had not yet been implemented by EC regulations as of November 2004 (Government of Japan 2004: 1, 22). Japan acknowledges that its requests for EU accession to the Protocol regarding the Madrid Arrangement concerning the International Registration of Marks and cancellation of antidumping duties on pro-fessional cameras that could not be used as broadcasting cameras have been met by the EU (Government of Japan 2003: 6–7; 2004: 8).

Japan's approach to the RRD is reflected in the nature of the solutions it seeks, which may consist in application of WTO agreements and/or rulings, application or adoption of EU rules and regulations and modification of national legislations of EU members. In the last two cases, Japanese requests are addressed either to the EU (twenty-seven requests between October 2000 and November 2004) and to EU members (twenty-four in the same period) or to EU members only (nineteen in the same period).

It is interesting to note that some Japanese requests concerning implementa-tion of WTO agreements and EU rules still concern tariff barriers against Japan-ese products. For example, Japan pointed out in 2004 that under the WTO's Information Technology Agreement (ITA), tariffs on IT-related products had been eliminated in the EU. Japan requested that digital audiovisual and house-hold electrical appliances, which were subject to a tariff rate of 14 percent, be reclassified as IT items to make them eligible for zero-tariff in the EU (Govern-ment of Japan 2004: 21). Japan observed also in 2004 that the European Com-mission had changed the tariff classification of certain plasma display panels (PDP), with computer terminals subject to zero tariff, as video monitors, which were subject to a 14 percent tariff. Japan reminded the EU that there were no manufacturers in the EU of flat display panels [including PDP and liquid crystal display (LCD)] and that the WTO ITA covered PDP and LCD monitors for IT products (Government of Japan 2004: 19).

On several occasions, Japan requested that the EU adopt new regulations as solutions to problems encountered by Japanese firms in Europe. For instance, Japan requested that the EU consider integrating standards concerning the shape of plugs and sockets for electrical outlets and telephone, as well as a unified system for approval of automatic scales. With common European standards, Japanese firms would be able to manufacture products with common speci-fications for Europe (Government of Japan 2004: 17). Another long-standing Japanese request involves the establishment of a European Private Company law making cross-border mergers possible. The Statute for a European Company adopted by the EU applies only to public companies, whereas most Japanese companies operating in Europe, particularly in the United Kingdom, Germany and the Netherlands, are private companies. Another Japanese request seeks introduction by the EU of a system whereby financial activities, products and licenses approved by one member would be automatically approved in other EU members, with no additional procedures required (Government of Japan 2001a: 2, 12; 2001b: 4, 8; 2003: 5, 13; 2004: 10, 31–2).

A second group of problems raised by Japan requires action by the EU and one or more members. Japan reported in 2004 that France had ordered that shipment of microwave ovens from Japan be stopped, due to non-compliance with the EU's Low Voltage Directive. After re-inspection at the EU level, the order to stop shipment of microwave ovens to Europe was withdrawn; yet, neither the EU nor France notified the company importing the microwave ovens of the withdrawal. Japan's request was twofold: first, inspections had to be carried out carefully and promptly; and second, the results of inspection had to be published and communicated in writing to the firms concerned (Government of Japan 2004: 16–17).

A very large number of Japanese complaints have to be addressed to members if the latter have sole competence in the matter. The nature of Japanese complaints gives us an insight into a unique source of Japan's bargaining power vis-à-vis the EU, one which few Asian countries can match – the ability of its firms to invest in Europe. This source of strength might compensate to some extent for the RRD's one-sided nature. The complaints deal primarily with employment regulations, which in the Japanese firms' view represent obstacles to Japanese FDI in Europe. A sampling of the complaints is provided below.

1   *Working hours*: In January 2000, the weekly working hours in Belgium were reduced by one hour, while annual paid holidays were increased by six days: "work hours are getting shorter in Belgium" (Government of Japan 2004: 26–7).

2   *Dismissals*: The "last-in, first-out" rule in Sweden, which made it difficult to dismiss employees who were not familiar with new technology, should be relaxed. In France, the category of protected employees (*salariés protégés*), which included workforce delegates (*délégués du personnel*) and trade union delegates (*délégués syndicaux*), could not be dismissed even if they made mistakes that caused losses to the companies or they had "rebellious attitudes on other problems" (Government of Japan 2004: 28). In Japan's view, the relevant laws on employee protection had to be improved.

3   *Overtime*: In Spain, overtime was limited to eighty hours per year; if the limit was exceeded, companies had to provide vacations to their employees. This regulation made it difficult for Japanese firms "to promptly cope with a sharp increase of their production and sales" (Government of Japan 2004: 25).

4   *Temporary work*: In Spain, temporary work contracts were limited to six months and could be extended for only six months. Japan requested an amendment of the law enabling companies to conclude contracts for the

time period of their choice without restriction (Government of Japan 2004: 24).

5   *Wages*: In Belgium, it was forbidden to cut salaries of individual workers. In Japan's view, the determination of individual workers' wages had to be made on the basis of each company's capacity (Government of Japan 2004: 26).

6   *Disability*: In the Netherlands, employers were obliged to pay 100 percent of wages in the first year and seventy percent in the second year to employees who became unable to work due to illness. In the absence of a requirement to produce a medical certificate, it was impossible in some cases to confirm the impact of illness on the employees' ability to work. Japan believed the certification method had to be revised (Government of Japan 2004: 26–7).

The largest number of Japanese requests concerned work and residence permits for Japanese nationals in Europe. In France, a renewed business identity card (*carte d'identité de commerçant étranger*) was required to apply for residence permits, but a renewed residence permit was required to apply for renewal of the business identity card. In Italy, the number of work permits issued was quite small both for independent business operators (including board members) and for dependent workers (including managers). Moreover, the announcement of the number of work permits was delayed every year. In Portugal, applications for renewing work permits were accepted only one week before the expiration of the work permit. In Spain, applications for renewal of work permits could only be sent by e-mail one month before the expiration of the current permits, but sometimes responses to the e-mail were received after two months (Government of Japan 2001a: 25; 2001b: 15; 2003: 20–1; 2004: 47–8).

In the last few years, some expressions of dissatisfaction with the RRD can be discerned in Japanese government documents. In 2001, Japan stressed that the purpose of dialogue was "not to criticize each other, but to share findings and experience concerning regulations, and to build up better frameworks by learning from each other" (Government of Japan 2001b: 2). Many European observers have admitted that while in theory the dialogue is a two-way exercise, in practice, Japan had few complaints to raise, at least until recently, and the dialogue came to revolve around EU concerns over Japanese practices (Dent 1999: 101; Gilson 2000: 100; Cardwell 2004). The one-sided focus on Japanese practices might explain why Japan felt it necessary to emphasize that the RRD's object was not to enable one party to criticize the other and why Japan has increased the number of its requests to the EU, in an attempt to make the dialogue more balanced.

In at least two instances, Japan has complained about the absence of reciprocity, that is, the EU's failure to make a concession identical to that made by Japan. For example, in spite of the Japanese amendment that allowed foreign lawyers to work with Japanese lawyers, several EU members failed to lift their restrictions on Japanese lawyers' activities in their countries. France still required Japanese lawyers to pass a special examination before they could provide services pertaining to Japanese laws. Germany continued to prohibit Japanese lawyers from providing services on Japanese laws in Germany. In another case of non-reciprocity, Japan reported in 2004 that it had introduced a "No Action Letter" system, partly due to an EU request, which allowed a firm to make prior inquiries regarding the relationship of its planned activities to prevailing laws and other firms' activities. No such system existed in the EU, and so Japanese firms had no means of determining whether their products will be subject to EU regulations (Government of Japan 2004: 12, 29–30).

Another source of Japanese dissatisfaction arose from the lack of or delays in EU response. In 2004, replies had not been given to many Japanese requests put forward in 2002 (Government of Japan 2004: 9). Of course, the EU is not the only party that can be faulted for such delays. Japanese inaction probably accounts for the repetition of EU requests from one year to the next. As we have seen above, several years pass before Japan modifies its legislation in response to EU demands. One reason for delays on the European side can be found in the nature of Japanese requests, which concern matters within individual members' competence. As the EU has reminded Japan, EU legislation on employment only laid down minimum requirements, a fact that Japan acknowledged (Government of Japan 2001b: 2). Japan realized that working conditions, which were often unique to each member state, were outcomes of different historical evolutions and were thus very sensitive issues. That said, Japan believed that the EU might benefit from listening to viewpoints of non-EU members, which if implemented could create jobs and enhance European competitiveness (Government of Japan 2004: 24).

Individual members do respond to Japan. Belgium replied in 2000 to the Japanese complaint over the inability to cut salaries of individual workers, although Japan deemed the Belgian reply insufficient. Spain explained in June 2003, in response to Japanese inquiries made in November 2002 and March 2003, that there were four different types of temporary labor contracts, and that Spanish laws were flexible enough to allow companies to face changes in demand by hiring temporary workers. Japan was not convinced. Portugal referred the Japanese request for extension of the period for submission of renewal applications for work permits to the Portuguese Immigration Service (Government of Japan 2004: 24, 26, 48). Italy created special counters for accepting applications for work permits in Milan and Turin (Government of Japan 2001b: 15). Individual members also have dialogues with Japan that allow Japan to raise its concerns with them. The Japanese request regarding the "last-in, first-out" rule in Sweden was also discussed in a Japan–Swedish Trade and Economic Consultation. As regards residence and work permits for Japanese nationals in the EU, after what Japan qualifies as a "frank exchange of views," it concluded that the Japanese position had been understood by each member (Government of Japan 2001b: 8, 28). Finally at the EU–Japan Summit of 2004, the EU declared that it would further facilitate procedures for obtaining visas and work and residence permits for Japanese residents in EU members. One can still sense some Japanese frustration due to the occasional lack of responsive-ness of individual EU member states. In recent years, Japan has urged member states to participate more actively in the RRD, especially when matters within their competence are discussed, and urged the EU to encourage members to do so (Government of Japan 2001b: 2; 2004: 7).

The account so far should have convinced us that Japan and the EU seek to change each other's views and practices without always being willing to change their own views and practices. While they profess to gain a better understanding of each other's practices (e.g. on employment in individual EU member states) through the RRD, this does not prevent either from demanding that the other side's practices be changed or that the other accept that its own practices cannot be changed. Sometimes, there is no effort at understanding at all, as demonstra-ted by the EU criticism of Japanese government procurement or of the Japan Harbor Transport Association.

In the effort to change the other's views, each adopts strategies – such as appeals to WTO Agreements or to their respective legislation – that leave very little room for taking into account the other's position and practices, and even less room for reaching a compromise. Initially it was presumed that Japan was the participant whose views and practices were to be changed. The imbalance in the RRD's first five years or so became a source of concern even for some Euro-pean observers. As a German task force remarked, "the one-sided focus on results of negotiation while simultaneously neglecting Japanese points of view will be successful only in the short term and motivate both sides to behave in an *ad hoc* manner in the future" (Kohl *et al.* 1999: 73) Since then, the imbalance has been corrected somewhat, as Japan has presented an increasing number of requests to the EU and its members. Perhaps the changing Japanese attitude is one of the lessons learned from the experience of the RRD.

Whatever may be the reason for the increase in Japan's demands, it has accentuated the RRD's character as a bargaining exercise, in which there is a more or less explicit trading of concessions, accompanied occasionally by a demand to achieve reciprocity (foreign lawyers in Japan and Japanese lawyers in Europe). Thus, the RRD gradually took on the form of an institutionalized yet disguised negotiation. Each side brought to the bargaining table strengths and weaknesses that to some extent compensated each other. Japan, which is aware (and made aware) of its huge trade surpluses with the EU, demonstrates its will-ingness to reduce them by listening to EU complaints. For its part, the EU is increasingly compelled to pay attention to Japanese complaints if it wishes to attract Japanese FDI in the EU. Japanese firms continue to be vulnerable to tariff barriers imposed by the EU, as well as to differences in regulations among member states. Conversely, EU firms are apparently hampered primarily by non-tariff barriers in Japan.

The primary reason why the RRD is called a dialogue is that it appears to exclude recourse to sanctions if a satisfactory response to a request is not forth-coming. The request is simply repeated or elaborated upon, from one year to the next, until the other side's inertia (or resistance) is worn down. The EU approach is presumably to be contrasted with the US unilateral, sanctions-based approach. The fact that it takes years for one side to obtain responses to its requests without any untoward action being taken against the other seems to provide confirmation of this. It is not widely known that, after the Uruguay Round's conclusion, the EU adopted a Trade Barriers Regulation that is backed up by the threat of recourse to WTO settlement and eventually by trade sanctions.

The EU Trade Barriers Regulation: an instrument of dialogue?

EU Council Regulation 3286/94 of December 31, 1994, more widely known as the "Trade Barriers Regulation," grants an explicit role to European private actors in securing market access for European firms throughout the world. This role is to be contrasted with the indirect role that firms and other private actors, e.g. the EU–Japan Business Roundtable, play in the RRD, which consists primarily of providing Japan and the EU with information that constitutes the substance of complaints and/or reform suggestions.

Under the Trade Barriers Regulation (TBR), European companies have the right to submit complaints to the European Commission if a foreign trade barrier in a non-EU member is covered by a WTO agreement. European industries can file complaints based on alleged violations of a broader range of international rules. Industries are defined as all EC producers of goods or providers of services identical or similar to or competing with the foreign products or services; or consumers or processors of the products or consumers or users of the service that are the objects of the trade barrier; or all producers or providers whose combined output constitutes a major proportion of the total EC product of products and services. EU action on these complaints will seek to remove injury on the EC market resulting from obstacles to trade or adverse trade effects in non-EC markets resulting from obstacles to trade. Adverse trade effects occur when trade is prevented, impeded or diverted, or the supply of inputs to EC companies is affected.

The TBR is unique in that it does not seek to protect EU markets from imports but rather to remove barriers to trade – barriers to EU exports – in the markets of non-EU countries. The types of practices that may be incriminated are very numerous. These include import restrictions and licensing procedures; export restrictions; quotas; measures causing internal discrimination between domestic and foreign products; excessive and discriminatory sanitary and phytosanitary regulations; draconian antidumping laws; export subsidies and failure to protect intellectual property rights (MacLean 1999: 73).

Once a complaint is submitted, the Commission consults an Advisory Committee to determine if there is sufficient evidence to justify an examination. If an examination is initiated, the Commission informs the state concerned and may request information from importers, traders, agents, producers and trade associations. The Commission must submit its report to the Advisory Committee within five months, or exceptionally, within seven months. The procedure may be suspended or terminated if the country concerned removes the obstacle to trade or if it is willing to negotiate a settlement. If no satisfactory solution is reached and the investigation supports the complaint, the EU may request the WTO Dispute Settlement Body to initiate consultations, and if necessary, to initiate formal dispute resolution procedures. Should the WTO decision be in favor of the EU and the other country does not implement the decision, the EU may take retaliatory measures such as suspension or withdrawal of a trade concession; an increase of customs duties; import charges; or quantitative restrictions (Sánchez Rydelski and Zonnekeyn 1997: 157–9). European commentators have stressed that retaliation will be exceptional compared to voluntary compliance or an agreement with the state concerned. The Commission is said to be more interested in compliance, since retaliation is not likely to remove the foreign trade barrier (Bronckers and McNelis 2001: 440, 443). The TBR'S alleged advantage is that it encourages negotiation, undertakings or agreements (MacLean 1999: 70).

In the first few years following the TBR's adoption, only one case was brought against Japan. In the case involving imports of finished leather in Japan (April 1997 to February 1998), it was alleged that Japan had granted subsidies to the leather industry in violation of the WTO Agreement on Subsidies and Countervailing Measures and the WTO Agreement on Import Licensing Procedures. No agreement was reached with Japan; hence the Commission decided to pursue WTO action. The fact that only this case was brought to the WTO is cited as proof that the TBR encourages negotiation and has not become an instrument of unbridled unilateral action (MacLean 1999: 95), similar to the notorious Section 301 and Super 301 of the US Trade Act. The argument is not necessarily conclusive. One reason for the paucity of cases under the TBR might be that there are other routes for referring cases to the WTO. Another might be that there already exist EU legal instruments applicable to other complaints (e.g. dumping, subsidies).

RRD records since 2000 do not provide evidence of any EU or EU firms' attempts to take action under the TBR in case Japan refused to comply with an EU request. Such action would not be allowed under the TBR in the first place if the European complaint concerned Japanese regulations not covered by any WTO Agreement or other international trade rules. If a WTO agreement can be invoked, perhaps the RRD's existence obviates the need to resort to the TBR. EU firms might prefer the RRD if they feared that retaliation under the TBR would not necessarily lead to modification of Japan's regulations and could even increase prices for European consumers (Kohl *et al.* 1999: 67–8).

On the other hand, it cannot be entirely excluded that the implicit threat of resort to the TBR may be in the minds of RRD participants, all the more so because of the TBR's link to the considerably strengthened WTO dispute settlement system. Thanks to the TBR, the EU is in a position to exert pressure on other countries, especially the developing countries (Sundberg and Vermulst 2001: 1005), for several reasons. First, the types of measures that can be addressed under the TBR are numerous. Second, all WTO agreements can be invoked. Finally, the European Commission actively seeks complaints under the TBR; for this purpose, it has constructed a database and conducted seminars on the TBR. Paradoxically, TBR investigations appear to have no legal basis in WTO law. Moreover, neither the process nor the solutions appear to be transparent: "One may wonder whether there are sufficient guarantees that the due process rights of interested parties, especially respondents, are sufficiently safeguarded in the course of such fishing expeditions" (Sundberg and Vermulst 2001: 1005).

Sundberg and Vermulst conclude that the TBR's settlement component may end up being an obstacle to trade. Japan is, of course, not a developing country. The size of its market gives it bargaining power vis-a-vis the EU that few developing countries possess. European firms would have to compare the costs and benefits of pursuing a complaint through the RRD or under the TBR. For its part, Japan, when faced with a request in the RRD, would have to determine whether to accede to the request or to risk a complaint under the TBR (or under any other EU procedure, for that matter).

Regardless of the actual use of the TBR against Japan, it is part of the RRD's overall context. The possibility of resort to sanctions accentuates the character of the RRD as a disguised negotiation; it is magnified by the size of the EU market, an advantage in any dialogue with Asian countries.

This rather long excursion into the Japan–EU RRD should clarify the EU's interest in an ASEM dialogue on trade facilitation and investment promotion. The EU wishes Asian countries to modify Asian laws and regulations that the EU sees as similar to Japanese laws and regulations. This being the case, one might ask to what extent the EU will marshal in the ASEM dialogue on trade facilitation and investment promotion the same arguments that it uses in the Japan–EU RRD.

The RRD's inherent limitations reveal the potential advantages of ASEM for the EU. As noted earlier, modification of Japanese laws and regulations is slow and piecemeal. First of all, the European Commission cannot make any requests for change if it does not receive information from European firms regarding the obstacles that they face. Second, it may take years before Japan acts on complaints. Even when such modifications are made, they may concern only very narrow areas of legislation. The same limitations are inherent in the TBR's application: European firms have to be encouraged to file complaints, their complaints must be examined and the outcomes must be negotiated with the other country, at the risk of aggravating tension with the latter. Through ASEM, the EU can address its demands on a broad range of issues to a large number of participants. Even if the Asian states do not modify their laws and regulations simultaneously, the EU can still hope that the time lags will not be too great, and/or that the modifications introduced in different countries will tend to converge along the lines desired by the EU.

With these considerations in mind, we can now turn to the ASEM dialogue on trade facilitation and investment promotion.

The rationale for ASEM dialogue on trade facilitation and investment promotion

Differences in understanding of and approaches to trade facilitation and investment promotion seem to create the need for dialogue between Asian and European countries in these two areas. It is the EU, a powerful international actor whose firms are weaker in Asia than Japanese and US firms, that urged the Asians to engage in a dialogue, through which it hoped to bring the latter round to its views in the two areas. However, in ASEM's first two years, the EU preferred not to redefine its interests to take into account Asian views. While discussing the IPAP with the Asian countries, the EU pursued parallel negotiations for a Multilateral Agreement on Investments at the Organisation for Economic Cooperation and Development (OECD), in which only Japan and South Korea are represented.

In trade facilitation, the TFAP was initially presented by the EU as complementary to the WTO's work. In doing so, the EU sought to counter the impression that ASEM was duplicating the WTO's work and to prevent the Asians' opposition to EU views on the Singapore issues from being carried over into ASEM. That said, the TFAP's contents make it obvious that it constitutes another means for convincing Asians to implement Uruguay Round agreements and to accept the EU's agenda for a new WTO round.

The TFAP originated from a proposal by the European Commission in July 1996 (Pou Saradell 1996). It was the Commission that prepared the final draft adopted by the Economic Ministers' Meeting in 1997, during which the Commission added standards harmonization, public procurement and regulatory transparency (Ton Sinh Thanh 1998: 5). The TFAP gave the impression of being simply a framework for dialogue: "TFAP has its value in its potential for building understanding, and should be a catalyst of progress on the discussion of trade facilitation issues. It shall promote understanding among ASEM partners in these areas." (TFAP 1998a: 2) The plan's priority areas were customs procedures; standards, testing, certification and accreditation; public procurement; quarantine and SPS procedures; intellectual property rights; mobility of business people; and other trade activities. The rationale for the choice of priority areas was that they "were not sufficiently covered in other fora" (TFAP 1998a: Part 2), e.g. the WTO.

The explanation is only partial and somewhat misleading. Intellectual property rights and SPS procedures are covered by WTO agreements. They were therefore included to remind the Asians to implement them. Customs procedures and government procurement were not yet regulated by WTO agreements, but they were two of the four Singapore issues that the EU wished to see on the WTO agenda. As we have seen in Chapter 3, developing Asian countries' resistance to internationally binding agreements on the Singapore issues gradually built up as their implications became clear and was openly manifested at successive WTO Ministerials. In this light, the TFAP was a new opportunity for the EU to circumvent resistance at the WTO. Discussion within the TFAP framework would complement EU action at the WTO to obtain their consent to a new round. Dialogue would be but a preliminary to the actual reduction of non-tariff barriers, which could be achieved if concrete goals and guidelines for successful achievement were set (TFAP 1998a). Little wonder that, according to a Filipino official interviewed by Bersick (quoted in Bersick 2004c: 222) in 1999, Asian participants were increasingly under the impression that the EU was using the ASEM as a forum to achieve its WTO goals more quickly.

The IPAP's preparation revealed fundamental differences between Asians and Europeans regarding the very meaning of investment, the reasons for low levels of European investment in East Asia, and the means of investment promotion. The IPAP surveys reported that European investors were seeking greater investment activities in Asia, but investment was understood in a very broad sense, so that it included even trade (IPAP 1997: 6). In this view, representative offices to support local distribution are also considered "investment" (IPAP 1997: Annex 1, 6). The surveys demonstrated the persistence of the well-known attitude of European companies, whose main interest is exporting to Asia rather than investing there (Robles 2001: 9).

In Asia, and notably in Southeast Asia, states seek to attract FDI, so that they can accelerate and diversify their industrial and export capacities. Over two decades ago, a Singaporean economist declared that ASEAN wished to attract skill-intensive and knowledge-based industries to move from Europe to Southeast Asia (Lim 1980: 252). Having just abandoned import substitution in favor of export-oriented strategies based on labor-intensive manufacturing, ASEAN countries were particularly anxious to encourage EC investment in industries that were labor intensive, relied on ASEAN raw materials and raised their technological capabilities (AEMM 1 1978: 28). For this reason, the sectoral distribution of European FDI, which was concentrated in "traditional" industries, gave cause for concern. Well into the 1990s, the largest European investor in Southeast Asia, the UK, was heavily represented in chemicals, mechanical engineering, food and drink and energy. The investments of Germany, the second largest investor, were directed towards the chemical and electrical engineering sector, and those of the Netherlands in mining, oil and chemicals, metal processing and mechanical engineering and food and drink (Hilpert 1998: 63–5; Robles 2001: 8–9).

Europeans with experience in Asia give some reasons why European firms should increase FDI there. Relying on local distributors and licenses is said to have a long term disadvantage: the task of building up reputation and image is left to distributors, making it very difficult for the company to assess market potential and very costly to take over local activities when the decision is made to invest (Lasserre and Schütte 1999: 147–8). The reasons for low EU FDI in Asia could lie either in structural conditions in the host countries or in the countries of origin of investors. Not surprisingly, Europeans tend to stress the first set of factors and Asians, the second. European analyses emphasize that the legal, administrative and business environment in Asia is unfavorable. Three major obstacles were identified in IPAP. First and foremost was the alleged lack of transparency and instability of interpretation of laws. Europeans stressed that all laws and regulations had to be stable and available to all, and implementation, predictable and consistent. A widely cited example is China, where the legal system resulting from the combination of economic reform and decentralization was complicated at all levels and lacked transparency, thus creating the breeding ground for corruption (Li Jinxiang 1998: 166). A second complaint was the lack of protection and/or enforcement, particularly of intellectual property rights (e.g. patents and trademarks) and trade secrets. Finally, Europeans complained of lack of control over the business enterprise resulting from local content require-ments and ownership restrictions (e.g. the prohibition of 100 percent ownership and the requirement to form joint ventures with local companies) (IPAP 1997: Annex I, 3–4; Jinxiang 1998; Robles 2001: 9–10).

The difficulties involved in setting up and running joint ventures, as described by Lasserre and Schütte (1999: 186–7, 208–9, 223–34), provide partial explanations for the European preference for wholly owned companies. In the first place, partner selection is usually very difficult. Not only is it under-taken at a time when the firm's experience in the host country is limited, but also the information available in and on Asia is often unsystematic and sketchy. Once the joint venture is set up, failure to understand the local partner's strategic logic as well as the political and cultural complexity of the local environment can lead to failure. And a successful joint venture might simply mean making a competitor out of the local partner, who saves on research and development (R&D) by obtaining technology from the European partner. Lasserre and Schütte (1999: 192) cite the example of Sukree Botiratanangkul, the head of a Thai textile conglomerate, who entered into a joint venture with the French company Rhône-Poulenc in order to acquire continuous polyester fiber techno-logy. After intense conflict between the two, the Thai partner bought back the shares from Rhône-Poulenc and became a major producer and exporter of fibers. If the European firm responds to the local partner's increased competitiveness with a further shift in production from Europe to Asia, the long-term risk may be "hollowing out" of the European company in its home country – the breaking of the link between production, development and marketing (Robles 2001: 10).

It is only too easy for Asians to respond that these so-called obstacles have not deterred Japanese and US companies from investing: "If the Americans and the Japanese have been able to ensure themselves a place in Asia, what stops the Europeans from doing the same?" (Seet-Cheng 1994: 2). Similarly, an Asian youth leader asked why, despite the lack of transparency, Japanese, US and even East Asian firms continued to invest in Asia. The Europeans were hard put to find replies, citing the difficulty of persuading head offices in Europe that Asia was a worthwhile market and the ability of Japanese and American investors to circumvent barriers that European investors found daunting (AEYLS 1997c: 2, 3; Robles 2001: 10–11).

More importantly, the success stories of some European firms in Asia suggest that the alleged obstacles are far from insuperable. For example, by the mid-1990s, Volkswagen had the largest local supply network of foreign manufacturers in

China and controlled 59 percent of the home-produced car market, with total market share of 40 percent. In 1995, Volkswagen sales in China surpassed for the first time sales in the whole of North America (Lehmann 1998: 76). For the Asians, if the Japanese and America succeed, then the obstacles to European investment may "have been self-imposed ... (and are) the result of outdated attitudes and perceptions" (Seet-Cheng 1994: 2). The negative attitude towards investment in Asia is captured in a term widely used in Europe, "delocalization," implying export of highly paid European jobs to countries or regions where labor costs are low. Fears of competition for jobs and "social dumping" would explain why European companies prefer to consider Asia as an export market, rather than as a region for foreign investment.

Consistent with its focus on the environment for investment in Asia, Europe defined its interest before ASEM 1 in terms of the drafting of a multilateral investment code (this paragraph is based on Rüland 1996: 38, 40–1). Part and parcel of efforts to stimulate European investment would have been better protection of patents and other intellectual property rights and less discriminatory bidding procedures for public works projects. Predictably, the EU failed to convince Asian countries (other than Japan and Singapore), that support for a global investment code was also in the Asians' interest. Indonesia objected that if foreign capital "could enter all sectors unimpeded, it would threaten the existence of SMEs" (*Jakarta Post*, March 1, 1996: 1, cited in Rüland 1996: 40–1; Bobrow 1999: 116). Underlying the idea of a global investment code was an "unbalanced approach with all freedoms given to the investing country but no corresponding freedoms for the receiving country" (*Financial Times*, March 3, 1996: 1, cited in Rüland 1996: 41). The Southeast Asian countries were supported by the ASEAN Chambers of Commerce and Industry. As expected, the Asia–Europe People's Forum (AEPF) also objected to a multilateral investment code which "would abolish the power and legitimate right of states and peoples to regulate the entry, conditions, behavior, and operation of foreign companies and foreigners in their countries" (*Jakarta Post*, March 1, 1996: 1, cited in Rüland 1996: 41).

The same divergence of views was reflected within the ASEM Government and Private Sector Working Group that prepared the IPAP. Three options were identified: the status quo (i.e. no need for ASEM investment principles), need to consider binding ASEM investment principles and adoption of non-binding ASEM investment principles. Predictably, the Europeans emphasized the importance of legally binding principles (IPAP 1997: Annex 5, 5). The survey of European investors did not reveal any moves toward convergence of European and Asian interests. Europeans favored a binding investment code, which would cover national treatment, transparency and market access. Asian respondents were divided, with Asian firms that were competing in international product markets expressing themselves in favor of a binding code (IPAP 1997: Annex 1, 5; IPAP 1997: Annex 7, 4). In general, Asians were less likely than Europeans to focus on an investment code and more likely to consider investment promotion, even though most also confessed to not being aware of the importance of

European perspectives on the issues (IPAP 1997: Annex 7, 4). At the Asia–Europe Business Forum [AEBF 1 (1996)], the need for stable, transparent and non-discriminatory market-driven investment frameworks was stressed by the Chairman's statement. The Forum's first two sessions again mentioned protection of intellectual property rights; non-discriminatory licensing arrangements; improved regulatory regimes; and dispute settlement procedures (AEBF 1 1996: 9; AEBF 2 1997; Robles 2001: 12).

The persistence of differences of opinion among Asians and Europeans leads the observer to question the consensus on IPAP apparently achieved at the second Economic Ministers' Meeting [EMM (1999)]. The IPAP would aim at improving frameworks of investment policies and regulations within ASEM. For an ASEM initiative to be approved, it had to be distinct from country-specific or subregional issues; of concern to investors and have a direct beneficial impact on the investment environment; it did not duplicate other bilateral, regional or ASEM projects; and it had to be achievable, without being too ambitious or too complex (IPAP 1997: 8–9). Under the first, third, fourth and fifth criteria, the IPAP would definitely exclude consideration of any programs similar to Asia-Invest, the European Community Investment Partners (ECIP) or the lending program of the EIB, which provided financial resources to firms in both Asia and Europe. Thus investment promotion in ASEM would not entail assisting firms to obtain market information, search for partners, carry out feasibility studies and enter into partnership agreements for purposes of production or marketing. The only activity left, by implication, is the modification of Asian legislation. This aim was not explicitly stated, perhaps because to put it so bluntly would have provoked Asian defensive reactions. The second criterion sent a clear message that the IPAP's purpose went beyond mere dialogue, and that it had to be translated into concrete action, which in the IPAP context could only be obtained through modification of Asian countries' respective laws.

In accordance with these restrictive criteria, only two pillars of IPAP were identified. Under Pillar I, IPAP listed the establishment of an ASEM Virtual Information Exchange; an ASEM Decision-Makers Roundtable to promote partnership and networking; and an ASEM Business-to-Business Exchange Programme enhancing cultural understanding. The second component arguably duplicated the AEBF, while the third overlapped with existing projects sponsored by the EU, such as Asia-Invest. Understandably, these components were never implemented. The divergences of interest between Asia and Europe rendered more arduous the task of identifying activities under Pillar 2, which identified only one activity, a high-level dialogue on key investment issues. The only guideline that was set was nevertheless significant: the Investment Experts' Group (IEG) should be open to input from business (IPAP 1997: 17–18). Nowhere was it explicitly stated that in practice only Asian countries' regulations were to be modified. To do so would have been tantamount to an admission that the EU did not consider the Asians as equal partners whose views deserved to be taken into account by the Europeans, or that the EU did not have to modify its own regulations.

The failed negotiations for a Multilateral Agreement on Investments (MAI), carried out in secret among developed countries at the OECD give us an idea of the kind of modifications of domestic legislation that the Europeans would have wanted the Asians to implement. That the EU participated in MAI negotiations, initiated one year before ASEM 1, and continued in parallel with the IPAP's preparation makes it obvious that the Europeans were unwilling to take into account Asian countries' views. Asian countries had been among the developing countries identified by the US and the EU as objects of pressure to ratify the MAI once they had agreed on the MAI between them. Ironically, it was opposition in both the EU and the USA to the MAI, after the leaking of the MAI provisions by an non-governmental organization (NGO) and the prestigious French newspaper *Le Monde*, that forced postponement, and finally, the collapse of negotiations in October 1998 (OECD 1998; Lefort and Page 1998; Société Française pour le Droit International 1999).

An MAI would in any case have been unacceptable to the Asian developing states. As already pointed out by the Indonesian Foreign Minister at ASEM 1, the provisions of such a MAI were unbalanced, in that only states assumed obligations, while all the rights were granted exclusively to investors (and primarily to foreign investors). The MAI would have restricted states' power to regulate the activities of foreign, and in some cases, domestic investors (the following is based on Wallach 1998; Albala 1998; Lefort and Page 1998; "MAI Provisions and Proposals," 1998). Foreign investors would have had a general right of entry in all economic sectors, enabling them to purchase, without restriction, land, natural resources, telecommunication services, foreign exchange, and so on. States would have been prevented from identifying sectors or industries that they considered central to economic development or essential for national security and from reserving these sectors to domestic companies. Numerous strategies to limit inflows of foreign investment, such as imposing a ceiling on foreign borrowing by domestic banks, and imposing a reserve requirement for portfolio investment, would have been prohibited. At the same time, states would have been prevented from taking measures against capital flight (MAI, Chapter III, National Treatment 1; Chapter IV, 4.2 and 4.1) (OECD 1997; MAI Provisions and Proposals 1998: 12; Robles 2001: 16–17).

Another series of provisions would have obliged the state to guarantee "full and constant protection and security" to investments. States would have been prohibited from imposing performance requirements, such as domestic content requirements, domestic purchasing requirements balancing of imports and exports, local sales restrictions and mandatory exporting requirements [MAI, Chapter III Performance Requirements 1(b)] (OECD 1997); or from requiring that an investor hire local managers, specialists or executives, and that executives, managers and members of boards of directors be of a specific nationality [MAI, Chapter III, Temporary Entry 1(a)(ii) and 2; Nationality Requirements] (OECD 1997). At present, performance requirements constitute, in developing countries, the counterpart to the incentives to FDI; their aim is to ensure that FDI stimulates local industry, increases export capacity, generates jobs and facilitates transfer of technology. A final set of MAI provisions would have obliged states not to impair the operation of, and to provide protection for, foreign investment during periods of strife, defined to include wars, revolutions, civil insurrection and "disturbances and other states of emergency" (MAI, Chapter IV.3, Protection from Strife, OECD 1997). The latter two concepts were broad enough to make states responsible for protection of foreign investments even against riots caused by food or fuel shortages, strikes and social chaos resulting from natural disasters (MAI Provisions and Proposals: 15, OECD 1997). States would have been under a duty to provide compensation when they directly or indirectly expropriated investments or profits of foreign investors or took action that has the "equivalent effect" of expropriation (MAI, Chapter IV.2, Mandatory Compensation for Expropriation, OECD 1997). According to critics, the reference to "equivalent effect" and "indirect" expropriation opened the door for investors to challenge state regulations, intended, for instance, to protect public health or preserve the environment, if their effect was to reduce the value of an investment (Robles 2001: 16–17).

It is true that in response to the Asian financial crisis, many ASEAN member states had considerably liberalized their restrictions on FDI (Robles 2004: 42–5). The difference is that these liberal provisions were short-term measures, intended to be in force for a specified period of time: the ASEAN states did not renounce on a permanent basis their right to regulate FDI. The MAI was objectionable in that it would have bound states for at least five years; even if they withdrew, they would still have been bound for fifteen years (MAI, Chapter XII, 3, OECD 1997; Robles 2001: 17).

The European failure to convince the Asians to agree to a binding investment code would explain the EU desire to pursue negotiations in a separate forum that excluded developing countries. It is at once an obvious indicator of the strength of the EU vis-à-vis Asia, and proof of the inability to comprehend the structural differences between capitalism in the West, particularly of the Anglo-American brand, and "East Asian" capitalism (e.g. Stubbs 1998: 68–80; Lasserre and Schütte 1999: 117–39). Most Asian states do wish to attract FDI. Nevertheless, they also wish to ensure, through appropriate regulation, that FDI contributes to achievement of development objectives, such as job creation, transfer of technology and enhancement of export capacities (Khor 2000). In East Asia, it is widely accepted that the state can intervene in the economy to secure these goals. State intervention is not limited to providing the appropriate environment but can also assist industrial sectors and even specific firms in acquiring a comparative advantage that will make them competitive in the domestic and international markets. The state maintains close links with firms through economic, political and social networks, far closer than comparable links between state and business in most Western countries. Firms themselves are organized into networks in which banks may participate and which are characterized by mutually interlocking ownership. The very different capitalist structures of East Asia create the impression among outsiders that the state confers undue advantages on domestic capitalists, which place obstacles to the entry to the market of European firms. Sometimes, the operation of these structures is perceived as reflecting a culture based on corruption rather than on the arms-length transactions of the market in the West. These structural features would have made it unlikely, in the absence of some strong compelling circumstance, that European and US views on liberalization of investment rules would have been adopted by Asian countries (Robles 2001: 17–18).

If it is doubtful that dialogue alone could change Asian views, Europeans could at least have achieved a better understanding of the operation of capitalism in Asia, and Asians would have gained an insight into European perceptions. Instead, relying on their membership in a forum from which most Asian states are excluded, the European states preferred to accelerate negotiations for an agreement that reflected primarily their views. The MAI's failure only spurred the EU and the USA to redouble their efforts to negotiate an agreement on FDI at the WTO (Robles 2001: 18). With respect to the Asian states, implementation of the IPAP would, in the EU strategy, replace the MAI and that of the TFAP would complement the EU strategy at the WTO. If the ASEM dialogue succeeded, then the EU would achieve its objectives even in the absence of a multilateral agreement. Indeed, one European Commission official implied that ASEM would inevitably create pressures for the conclusion of such an agreement: "In order to increase the effectiveness and predictability of this voluntary approach (through ASEM), some form of legal framework could be envisaged in the long term: ..." (Reiterer 2002: 205).

The "voluntary" implementation through ASEM will be the object of the last section.

The implementation of TFAP and IPAP

The implementation of TFAP and IPAP makes it obvious that the purpose of the "dialogue" is to convince Asian participants (who are not identified as such) to change domestic laws and regulations that are alleged to constitute non-tariff barriers for European goods and barriers to investment for European firms. For all the reminders that the two plans are voluntary and non-binding, ministers and officials have repeatedly stressed the need for concrete steps (EMM 2 1999: para. 9). As the EU Commission put it succinctly, economic dialogue should have a genuine impact on trade and investment conditions facing economic operators [European Commission COM 2000 (241): 5]. The advantage of ASEM for the EU, according to a European Commission official, is that it brings together the officials who implement non-tariff barriers, obstacles to investment and the Most Effective Measures to attract FDI. These officials would be subject to pressure from their European counterparts to implement TFAP and IPAP. Networking would make it easier to achieve the consensus that is elusive at the WTO (Yoo Choong-Mo 2000; Reiterer 2002: 194). A survey of the TFAP and IPAP reporting process reveals that when Asians present justifications of existing policies that are considered detrimental by the EU to European interests, these tend to be dismissed.

That TFAP must be implemented is clear from the fact that "deliverables" by 2000 were set (SOMTI 3 1998: 1–2). In the area of customs procedures, the deliverable was "accelerated implementation" of the WTO Customs Valuation Agreement. In the area of standards, testing, certification and accreditation, work should aim at "accelerated alignment of national standards to international standards." For quarantine and SPS procedures, timely implementation of the WTO SPS Agreement and close consultation in the WTO's SPS work were two deliverables. In the area of intellectual property, full and timely implementation of the WTO Trade-related Intellectual Property Rights (TRIPS) was a major deliverable. As part of the effort to persuade the Asians to agree to negotiate government procurement at the WTO, workshops and seminars on the topic were to be organized. Another area that was not yet regulated by a WTO agreement, distribution in the retail sector, was to be the object of an exchange of views (TFAP 2000). In 1999, the need to remove non-tariff barriers in a more concrete manner was stressed, through ASEM's "non-confrontational, non-binding, voluntary and informal nature" (SOMTI 5 1999: 4; EMM 2 1999: para. 9).

Since the TFAP's seven priority areas were obviously EU concerns, Asians recommended that antidumping be included in the list, as a way of redressing the balance. In order to neutralize this demand, core labor standards were put forward by the EU (Lee Chong-Wha 2000a: 123). In 2000, antidumping was added, though not as a priority area; e-commerce became a priority area (May 2000). Consolidated deliverables and concrete goals for the period 2000–02, as well as a "Consolidated and Prioritised List of the Major Generic Barriers to Trade," were approved by ASEM 3 (2000), which also decided that members would report individually and voluntarily to SOMTI every year (TFAP 1998b; 1998c; SOMTI 6 2000: paras 4, 5; ASEM 3 2000: para. 10). To the first set of goals were added formulation of common positions in the WTO on customs procedures; close consultation at the WTO regarding technical barriers to trade; recognition of the WTO SPS agreement as a benchmark for trade policies; and implementation of TRIPS in intellectual property. Asian countries, though not singled out as such, were to be encouraged to accept the WTO's Government Procurement Agreement. Although there was as yet no WTO agreement on trade facilitation, the WTO work in this area was to be supported.

The first progress reports were discussed at SOMTI 7 (July 2001) (TFAP 2002). Another set of deliverables was adopted for 2002–04 (SOMTI 8 2002: para. 14). In 2003, it was suggested that members should report more comprehensively on a biannual basis starting SOMTI 11 (SOMTI 9 2003: para. 34). From the very outset, activities were organized so as to pave the way for implementation of WTO agreements or expeditious conclusion of new agreements and their implementation ahead of such conclusion. Between 1998 and 2002, working groups on standards, testing, certification, accreditation and technical regulation and SPS and quarantine met several times (SOMTI 8 2002: paras 2–13; SOMTI 9 2003: paras 24–34).

The attempted linkage between IPAP and the WTO is no less obvious. The IEG (IEG 1 1998: 2–3) declared openly at its very first meeting, that its work would facilitate that of the WTO. In 1999, the EU went further and claimed that the IEG might be a "good basis to complement the work of the WTO Working Group on Trade and Investment." Faced with this obvious attempt to put WTO issues on the ASEM agenda, unnamed ASEM participants objected that WTO work might be duplicated. Although the EU insisted that in ASEM discussion on WTO investment issues was useful and would not prejudge WTO work, the suggestion was not taken up (IEG 2 1999: 1, 2). Undeterred, the European Commission took another tack, in the form of a "bottom-up approach." The Commission explained that this did not require initial agreement by Asian states on abstract investment principles. In any case, such an approach would never have been successful, given the Asians' skepticism on the need for a legally binding code. Instead, the Commission presented in 1999 an allegedly non-binding list of "Most Effective Measures" in attracting FDI, compiled on the basis of questionnaires. EMM 2 (1999: 11) approved the list in October 1999 and decided that ASEM participants would voluntarily report every year on progress in implementing the list. Subsequently, obstacles to investment were identified with input from the AEBF. Steps taken to abolish these obstacles would also be reported to SOMTI, the first reports being submitted to IEG5 (July 2001).

The TFAP and IPAP reporting process focused on implementation of the TFAP's "Consolidated and Prioritised List of Major Generic Trade Barriers among ASEM Partners" (TFAP 1998b) and the IPAP's "Most Effective Measures to Attract Foreign Investment and the Obstacles to Investment" (IPAP 1999). The reporting process provides unambiguous evidence that ASEM "dialogue" is far from a dialogue between "equals" in which each participant is prepared to change its views and practices. As in the Japan–EU dialogue, only the Asian participants are expected to change their views and practices.

Several practices in TFAP's list of major trade barriers reflect primarily the views and interests of European firms and the EU. Under public procurement, the barriers to be removed included requirements that companies must have a minimum level of domestically held shares and domestic content in products and requirements of technology transfer and counter trade. These restrictions can be justified in developing countries as means of stimulating local production and promoting local Research and Development. The same argument may be made in respect of distribution: requirements of domestic partnerships and joint ventures, limitations on foreign ownership for specific activities, the promotion of local products and the obligations imposed on large foreign retailers to buy local products for their supermarkets, even limitations on the ownership and lease of real estate should not be considered solely as trade barriers, but as instruments for achieving other goals, e.g. an increase in local companies' market share. The TFAP complained of widespread infringement of intellectual property rights, yet it was silent on impact of IPR abuses on the cost of pharmaceuticals and on competition between local and transnational corporations in developing countries. The TFAP, by identifying limits on duration of business visas as barriers, seems to take for granted that business people have some kind of right to very long, if not unlimited, stays in foreign countries. The TFAP sections on standards and conformity assessment and on SPS procedures assume as a matter of course that international standards are better than national standards and that differences between national and international standards are by definition undesirable. All in all, the TFAP's list gives the impression that European firms wish to have untrammeled freedom of action in their operations in Asia.

Careful perusal of the first reports on implementation of the list, submitted in 2001, confirms ASEM's character as a lobby through which the EU attempted to modify laws and regulations of the Asian states (European Commission ASEM Counsellor 2001). As in the Japan–EU RRD, EU practices are held up as models to the Asians. Unlike in the Japan–EU RRD, the EU has in general refrained from arguing that Asians should modify specific regulations solely because these are inconvenient for European firms. There are also practically no references to WTO rulings that favor EU positions, perhaps because the Asian countries had not yet been parties to WTO dispute settlement procedures.

As in the Japan–EU RRD, the EU has not been very receptive to Asian views. The very few Asian complaints in an eighty-nine-page report were, except for one, not reported by the European Commission in its fifteen-page synthesis (TFAP 2002). The only complaint it noted was the Malaysian report that EU requirements for the transportation and storage of palm oil for human consumption using containers made of stainless steel and coated with epoxy resins increased transportation costs, as such containers were not readily available (European Commission ASEM Counsellor 2001: 52; TFAP 2002: 15). Apart from this exception, observations by Malaysia, China and Japan that defended existing Asian practices or objected to EU practices were ignored by the European Commission. Such behavior is hardly a reassuring indicator of EU willingness to consider modifying its own practices in response to these objections, even if for the moment, the EU has no choice but to accept that these countries wished to maintain their practices.

The Malaysian, Chinese and Japanese observations deserve some attention. Malaysia pointed out that the EU was the most active user of antidumping measures and countervailing measures on imports from Asian countries, resulting in trade harassment. It revived the proposal for an early warning system, already raised at the ASEAN–EU Joint Cooperation Committee (JCC) in previous years (European Commission ASEM Counsellor 2001: 53). Malaysia justified the use of export subsidies by referring to "socio-economic development objectives" and asserted its sovereign right so set licensing procedures. A "buy local products" campaign was explained as a means for creating awareness among consumers to buy local goods and to encourage local manufacturers to produce quality products; it was not a campaign against imported products. Malaysia argued that a country can deviate from international standards that are ineffective or inappropriate to fulfill legitimate objectives, such as protection of human health or safety, animal or plant life or health, or the environment, or for reasons owing to fundamental climatic, geographical, technological or infrastructural problems (European Commission, ASEM Counsellor 2001: 37, 43, 48, 51). In at least one instance – when the Commission reported that there were no restrictions in Malaysia on any form of commercial activity including the import, export and distribution trade – there seemed to be a major discrepancy with the Malaysian report (TFAP 2002: 15).

On international standards, China reported that it would not adopt them if they were unacceptable because of fundamental climatic or geographical factors or fundamental technological problems (European Commission, ASEM Counsellor 2001: 13). Under standards and conformity assessment, Japan gave at least four reasons for its proposal to revise the list of "Major Generic Trade Barriers." In Japan's view, differences between national and international standards, resulting in stricter standards and certification requirements for foreign products than for domestic products, should not be regarded as trade barriers, given that the WTO's Technical Barriers to Trade Agreement does not seek regional or interregional harmonization. Conformity assessment procedures and results differ in countries because they seek to achieve objectives specific to countries. Japan pointed out that it could not automatically accept the results of conformity assessment in exporting countries without knowledge of the technical competence of the relevant bodies in the latter. Finally, Japan reminded ASEM participants that nothing in the WTO's Technical Barriers to Trade Agreement required the publication of texts other than in the language of the country concerned (European Commission, ASEM Counsellor, 2001: 21–2).

In the area of investment promotion, IPAP cannot mask the inequality in the relationship between Asian and European actors, whether states or firms. Only firms from the more developed Asian states, primarily Japan and South Korea, are in a position to invest in Europe, so that at least in the short term, investment promotion will benefit primarily European firms that invest in Asia. IPAP advocates might respond that host countries benefit from FDI as much as the countries of origin. Indeed for this reason, developing countries do adopt measures to attract FDI. Among the IPAP's "Most Effective Measures to Attract Foreign Direct Investment" (MEM), several are already implemented in Asia. In many countries, investment promotion agencies have been set up; capital flows and other transactions related to FDI have been liberalized; incentives (e.g. tax breaks, subsidies, grants and special infrastructure) are provided; transparency and predictability of the investment climate and government efficiency have been enhanced; and bilateral and regional investment agreements have been concluded (MEM Nos. 1, 2, 5, 6, 7, 8). Asian countries' policies should convince the observer that they are willing to provide incentives to FDI.

Yet the IPAP's list seeks to diminish the ability of states to regulate FDI to the benefit primarily of firms and the EU. Performance requirements (such as local content, export and transfer of technology) are identified as obstacles to investment (Obstacle No. 5); and their removal is said to be an effective measure to attract FDI (MEM No. 4). The list ignores that states impose performance requirements as a means of increasing demand for local production of parts and/or increasing revenues. Restrictions on investment that involve foreign ownership (e.g. the obligation to form joint ventures) and the prohibition of investment in some sectors, also mentioned in the two lists (Obstacle No. 3;

MEM No. 3), do involve discrimination, but they may be necessary in order to redress the balance between powerful foreign and local firms, to promote transfer of technology and/or to maintain national control over strategic industries or sectors. Limitations on the number of intracorporate transferees and on the employment of foreigners in management (Obstacle No. 7) undoubtedly affect the ability of a firm to conduct its operations. Without such restrictions, few citizens of the host country might ever reach higher management positions in foreign-owned firms or in joint ventures.

These sections of the "Most Effective Measures" require that the state refrain from interfering in firms' operations. Other sections compel the state to remove a very large number of alleged obstacles encountered by firms. Complaints are registered over capital tax and excessive compliance expenses (Obstacle No. 4); local financing difficulties and high interest expenses on real estate rents (Obstacle No. 6); high employment costs and lack of skilled labor in certain countries (Obstacle No. 7); and political risk, restriction on practice of foreign lawyers and restrictions on retail stores (Obstacle No. 8). Even different trade practices, cultural differences and language barriers are classified as obstacles (Obstacle No. 8). The bias of the list in favor of firms is manifested when the absence of strikes is included in the category of measures that would improve the domestic economic environment and infrastructure (MEM No. 9). One can legitimately ask if this last is a tacit European encouragement to Asian states to suppress the right of workers to organize and bargain collectively, in flagrant contradiction to the European position on respect for core labor standards (Lim 2003: 138). For all practical intents and purposes, the state is required by the "Most Effective Measures" list to provide perfect conditions for FDI and to refrain from imposing specific obligations on investors.

It should be pointed out that the coverage of the TFAP and IPAP lists is much broader than that of the WTO Agreement on Trade-Related Investment Measures (TRIMS), whose Annex prohibits only five such measures: the requirement that a firm purchase domestic products; the requirement that a firm's purchase of imported products be limited to an amount related to the volume or value of local products that the firm exports; restriction of importation by a firm of products generally or to an amount related to the volume or value of local products that the firm exports; restriction of access to foreign exchange for the purpose of importation to an amount related to the foreign exchange inflows attributable to the enterprise; and restriction of the exportation by a firm of products. On the other hand, the scope of the MEM and the Obstacles to Investment overlaps to a great extent with that of the failed MAI.

It must be obvious by now that Asians and Europeans have encountered extreme difficulties in reconciling the contradictions between those who see certain practices as justified on development grounds and those who denounce them as "trade barriers" or "obstacles to investment." If the EU had been interested in dialogue, the inequality of wealth and power between the Asians and the Europeans should have been reason enough for the EU to adopt a broader view of its self-interest and accommodate itself to the existence of practices that the

Asians consider justifiable. As it is, the only option open to the Asians under the TFAP and the IPAP seems to be the abolition of their trade and investment practices considered objectionable by the EU.

It could be objected that Asians demonstrated their willingness to cooperate with the EU under TFAP and IPAP. After all, reporting was voluntary and informal, with no formal or legal sanctions attached to non-compliance. Conceivably, an Asian state that realizes that the EU is unwilling to make concessions could cease to participate in ASEM. Yet none have done so. Furthermore, they have gradually implemented deliverables under both plans.

That said, the Asian states' actions are susceptible of a wholly different interpretation if we bear in mind that some of them are weaker actors that find themselves compelled to engage in a dialogue whose outcome may threaten their interests. In this alternative view, Asians participate in the dialogue precisely because it is voluntary and therefore cannot oblige them to take divergent positions at the WTO or in other contexts. Even this attitude may be changing in a more negative direction. In 2002, signs of Asian dissatisfaction with TFAP were expressed at the ninth SOMTI:

> Some ASEM partners were of the view that ASEM's deliverables should be linked with the WTO in the light of the forthcoming round of negotiations. While recognizing the importance of linking ASEM's work with the developments in the WTO, some ASEM partners emphasized that the basis of SOMTI's work is on trade facilitation between Asia and Europe and therefore specific activities of TFAP should continue to focus along this line.
>
> (SOMTI 8 2002: para. 14)

The first view implied that unnamed (probably Asian developing) countries preferred to wait for the outcome of WTO negotiations before they could consider reducing their trade barriers and reporting on them to ASEM. As mentioned in Chapter 3, at the WTO the developing Asian countries, cooperating with Asian, African and Latin American countries, had better chances of obtaining concessions from the EU than within ASEM. The second view, which was probably expressed by the developed Asian countries and the EU, was aware of the implications of linkage, and precisely for this reason, wished to continue with the TFAP regardless of the increasing reluctance of the first group of states.

Although the first group's opinion was in effect ignored, there is no denying that after SOMTI 9 (2003), TFAP and IPAP activities slowed down. States stopped submitting reports on the MEM to attract foreign investment from 2000 onwards and reports on generic trade barriers from 2002 onwards. In 2003, the IEG ended its work, and its mandate was not renewed. To be sure, TFAP working groups on Standards and Conformity Assessment, on Intellectual Property Rights, on e-commerce and on Distribution met several times between 2002 and 2005. Yet they made little headway in taking "immediate action for the reduction of trade barriers," as required by the Senior Officials (SOMTI 10 2005: para. 8). Under the IPAP only one seminar was held between 2003 and

2005, prompting calls for more action not only from the Senior officials but also from ASEM 6 itself (SOMTI 10 2005: para. 12; ASEM 6 2006a: para. 21).

An explanation for the loss of momentum may be found in developing Asian states' reluctance to continue participating in a dialogue in which their views were not fully taken into account and in which they were expected to change their views without any concessions being made to them by the EU. The signing of the Philippine–Japan Economic Partnership Agreement (JPEPA) on September 9, 2006, at Helsinki, on the eve of ASEM 6, provided graphic evidence that for ASEAN, dialogue with the EU was accorded a lower priority than bargaining with other states on the very same issues taken up at ASEM. In other words, as suggested earlier, ASEAN states acted as though dialogue with the EU did not oblige them to engage in joint action with the EU. Significantly, in the context of bargaining with the USA or Japan, ASEAN states proved more willing to grant the unilateral concessions that the EU attempted to obtain through dialogue within ASEM. Singapore had already concluded an Economic Partnership Agreement that included free trade with Japan in 2002, followed by a free trade agreement with the USA in May 2003. Of course, Singapore would have been willing to enter into a similar agreement with the EU, given the convergence of its views on WTO issues with those of the EU. Nevertheless, it is remarkable that the Singapore–US FTA incorporated provisions on labor cooperation and the environment, which Singapore had always refused to countenance in the WTO. Similarly, the Economic Partnership Agreements of Japan with Malaysia, the Philippines and Thailand lay down rules on several WTO, TFAP and IPAP issues that the EU could not persuade them to accept through dialogue. For instance, the Philippines granted Japan national treatment in practically all matters relating to investment in the Philippines (JPEPA, Article 89) and agreed to provisions on customs procedures (JPEPA, Articles 52–4). In exchange, Japan committed to grant Filipino careworkers' entry and temporary stay in Japan without any quantitative restriction (JPEPA, Article 110, §3).

It was perhaps fitting that the EU response was also announced at ASEM 6, but the response may bode ill for ASEM. It represents a tacit admission that the dialogue in which the EU had resisted changing its points of view had not succeeded in convincing other participants to change their views and to engage in joint action with the EU solely on the basis of EU views. As Malaysia put it, ASEM had not produced favorable results on economic cooperation (Damodaran 2006). Consequently, the EU may have realized that the time had come to renounce dialogue in favor of bargaining.

The European Commission President acknowledged to European journalists that the EU was considering negotiations for free trade agreements with ASEAN starting in 2007, as proposed by an ASEAN–EU Vision Group report submitted in May 2006 (ASEAN–EU Vision Group 2006; Ricard 2006). A month later, the EU plan was confirmed, and Korea was added to the list of negotiating partners [European Commission SEC (2006), 1230: 14, 16]. The EU had until then resisted such a possibility when raised by ASEAN in September 2004 (Agcaoili 2004). In place of FTAs, the EU proposed at ASEM 5 in Hanoi, the negotiation of Partnership and Cooperation Agreements (PCAs) with individual ASEAN states (European Commission 2004), which only held out the possibility of an FTA in the long term. The official reason given was that the EU gave priority to the WTO negotiations, through which it hoped to obtain developing countries' agreement to the Singapore issues. In the Asian case, the EU still placed its hopes on ASEM, through the TFAP and the IPAP as a means of achieving the same goal. These plans were stymied when WTO negotiations reached an impasse and were suspended, at practically the same time as the TFAP and IPAP working groups' activities were slowing down, and the ASEAN states were negotiating FTAs with Japan and the USA. Conscious of the risk that its firms would be put at a disadvantage in relation to Japanese and US firms, the EU felt that it had little option but to enter into negotiations for FTAs [European Commission SEC (2006), 1230]. Of course, it is by no means guaranteed that negotiations will be successful. One potential obstacle to success might be ASEAN's insistence that negotiations be carried out between the EU and ASEAN as a group, i.e. with the participation of Myanmar, but to overcome this, the EU could simply negotiate with individual ASEAN members. Whether ASEAN would accept this procedure is an open question ("Myanmar an Obstacle as EU Pushes for FTA with Southeast Asia," 2006; "FTA with EU May Cut Myanmar Out," 2007).

Since a two-year deadline has been set for completion of FTA negotiations, one might therefore ask whether the EU's new strategy calls into question ASEM's utility as a forum for Asia–Europe dialogue. First, instead of treating the Asian ASEM participants as a group, the EU now openly distinguishes between subgroups of Asian participants – on the one hand, ASEAN and South Korea, and on the other hand, Japan and China. FTAs with the latter are excluded, since these merely raise the specter of increasing the EU's already large trade deficit. Second, ASEM would hardly be appropriate for negotiations with ASEAN and with South Korea. It is therefore highly likely that separate fora will be organized for the purpose. Finally, the scope of future negotiations covers the same issues as those in the TFAP and the IPAP. In view of the need to devote human resources to negotiations rather than to dialogue, interest in the TFAP and the IPAP might decrease even further.

Whether trade facilitation and investment promotion are pursued through dialogue in ASEM or bilateral bargaining, they would entail modification of Asian states' legislation in the interest of European firms and to a lesser extent, Asian firms. Civil society groups have long proposed an alternative vision for ASEM work in trade and investment, aiming at economically and socially sustainable development, democratization, gender equality and food security (AEPF 2000: 8). Plans for trade and investment had to incorporate the International Labour Organization (ILO) core labor standards and respect for international standards of environmental protection, health and safety (AEPF 2000 para. 8; ASEF *et al.* 2004: 9; ICFTU 2004: para. 6). Such an agenda is not calculated to encourage either the Asians or the Europeans to accept civil society's demands for participation in the official ASEM process.

Summary

ASEM's function as a lobby for the modification of Asian laws is one of ASEM's most important functions from the EU perspective, although Asian states have never openly expressed their agreement to this goal. The modification of Asian laws was explicitly declared in the EU's 1994 New Asia Strategy and accounts for its refusal to consider the AEVG's proposal of an Asia–Europe FTA by 2025, which would simply have bloated European deficits with Asia.

Given the EU's goal, it is essential to examine the Japan–EU RRD as a paradigm for the kind of dialogue with Asia that the EU wishes to see in ASEM. The fact is the pattern of Japan's economic relations with Europe, marked by cycles of rising trade surpluses – European protests – Japanese responses, seems to be replicated in European relations with ASEAN and China. In the bilateral context, it was the EU that sought the RRD, which was far from meeting the conditions for dialogue when it was initiated. In the dialogue, only Japan was expected to change its positions, and the EU expected it to do so if a WTO ruling existed that supported the EU's position; if an EU rule existed that the EU wished Japan to adopt; or if the Japanese regulation was inconvenient to EU firms. With the passing of time, Japan has also put forward its own requests for regulatory reform, concerning primarily the working conditions of Europeans and Japanese employed in Japanese firms in Europe. Japan is aware that it has to demonstrate its willingness to reduce its huge trade surplus; on the other hand, the EU is eager to attract Japanese FDI to Europe. In these circumstances, the RRD has taken on the character of an institutionalized negotiation, where bargaining takes place. It is only called dialogue presumably because no sanctions are brandished. It should not be forgotten, though, that the threat of application of the EU's Trade Barriers Regulation is part of the context of the so-called dialogue.

As in the Japan–EU dialogue, it was the EU, which combined strengths as an international actor and weakness in Asia, that urged the Asians to engage in a dialogue on trade facilitation and investment promotion, but once more, only the Asians were expected to change their views. This attitude obviously contradicts one of the fundamental requirements of dialogue laid down by Todorov and Habermas. In the area of investment, the EU preferred a binding code that would have granted the widest possible degree of freedom to firms. In fact, the EU was already negotiating such a code at the OCDE, in which most Asian ASEM countries were unrepresented. The exclusion of interested Asian parties from the dialogue was undoubtedly another violation of the requirements for dialogue. In ASEM, it was the EU that lobbied for the adoption of the TFAP and the IPAP, which led to the adoption of supposedly non-binding lists of measures that ASEM participants were encouraged to adopt. The measures themselves were compatible with the EU's agenda at the WTO or went beyond them. If implemented, they would benefit mostly the EU and European firms, since they obliged governments to provide near-perfect conditions for firms and to refrain from imposing specific obligations on them. The reporting process instituted for the TFAP and the IPAP revealed that the EU was for the most part unwilling to listen to Asian participants' views, in another obvious contradiction with the requirements of dialogue. It is likely that Asian developing countries continued participating in the reporting process because they felt compelled to do so as weaker actors and because they realized that they could not be obliged to take different actions at the WTO. In the last few years, TFAP and IPAP activities have lost momentum. At the same time, developing Asian states negotiated free trade agreements with Japan and/or the USA, through which they granted to the two countries concessions that they were unwilling to grant to the EU through dialogue. Their actions confirm that for them, bargaining in a bilateral context was more important than dialogue within ASEM, and that they only participated in ASEM dialogue because they did not feel constrained by the apparent consensus that emerged from the dialogue.

5 ASEM as a forum for political and cultural dialogue

Singapore's proposed agenda for Asia–Europe Meeting 1 (ASEM 1) included political issues, but its understanding of the areas of common interest was restricted to deepening of mutual understanding of the Asian and European security situations and United Nations (UN) restructuring and democratization (Bersick 1998: 50–61). In the latter case, some form of Asian–European joint action would presumably have followed a dialogue. Cultural issues were not mentioned at all. The European Union (EU), in keeping with a June 1991 declaration that "respecting, promoting and safeguarding human rights" was to be a cornerstone of its relations with non-European states, insisted on a formulation of areas of common interest that encompassed human rights, democracy and the rule of law. Failure to put these issues on the agenda would have provoked protests in Europe (Nuttall 2000: 155). As a compromise, the phrase "for greater growth" was added to the "comprehensive partnership," upon the Asians' insistence, thus emphasizing the priority of economic issues over political issues (Bersick 2004c: 100).

ASEM's possible agenda for political dialogue can be subdivided into security issues (regional and international), on the one hand, and human rights, democratization and the rule of law, on the other. Asian resistance to discussion of the latter issues has failed to have them removed from the agenda but has successfully relegated them to cultural dialogue (Bersick 2004c: 105). This subtle shift in emphasis justifies a separate discussion of human rights that will be taken up in a separate section. The 9/11 and its aftermath enhanced the willingness of Asians and Europeans to engage in a security dialogue, presumably as a prelude to joint action to combat international terrorism. In this new context, a dialogue between cultures and civilizations is presented as a specific, and indeed, unique ASEM approach to the problem. There is a risk, though, that the increased willingness to engage in a security dialogue and undertake joint action will come at the expense of a human rights dialogue, which at the outset was the least likely area of common interest for Asia and Europe. To assess the prospects of the human rights and cultural dialogue within ASEM, we shall examine the experience of bilateral dialogues between the EU and two Asian actors in each field, China and Japan, respectively, as possible paradigms for ASEM dialogue.

ASEM security dialogue: regional and global issues

Within the broad field of security, the European Commission's New Asia Strategy started from the premise that "(t)he maintenance of peace and stability in Asia is an important factor ... for the promotion of the Union's interests in this region." At the same time, it assumed that with the increasing strength of individual Asian countries, Asia would wish to play a more prominent role in international relations [European Commission COM (94) 314: Part III.1]. Consequently, a political dialogue had to encompass regional as well as international security issues. This dialogue did not make much headway until 2001. Since 9/11, the fight against international terrorism, requiring joint Asian–European action at regional and global levels, has given a new impetus to the ASEM security dialogue and might possibly serve to bridge the gap between the dialogues on regional and global security issues.

ASEM and regional security in Asia

In theory, nothing prevents an ASEM security dialogue from taking up regional security issues in Asia and in Europe. In practice, the focus of the dialogue has been somewhat one-sided, in that regional security issues in Asia receive more attention than European security issues. One factor explaining this imbalance is the difference in degree of integration attained in the respective regions. Since the 1970s, the EU has been pursuing the aim of speaking with one voice and acting jointly in international affairs. Despite considerable difficulties, the EU has been gradually acquiring instruments that enable it to enter into a dialogue with Asia as a more or less unitary actor. In Asia, on the other hand, the Association of Southeast Asian Nations (ASEAN), the only regional organization capable of sustaining an institutional relationship with the EU, lacks the material resources that would allow it to bring to bear its influence on European security issues. Japan and China, which do possess such resources, are not in a position to speak on behalf of Asia as a region in the absence of an Asian regional organization.

The second reason for the imbalance in the security dialogue lies in the structure of the Asian regional security relations, which continues to be characterized by a balance of power (Hänggi 2004: 96–7). Hence, Asian regional stability poses specific – perhaps unique – challenges to the EU. In Asia, the possibility of limited conflicts involving one or more major powers remains latent. Indeed, some of the most dangerous centers of conflict are to be found in Asia [quoted in (Hansen 2000: 1)] (Robles 2003a: 19). The balance of power structure, in which the United States plays a pivotal role through its bilateral alliances, has hampered the conceptualization by Europeans and Asians of a European interest in the region's security. However, this failure did not stand in the way of the EU playing a security role in Asia on at least two occasions, though ASEM was bypassed in the process. In ASEM itself, serendipity – the holding of ASEM 3 in Seoul shortly after the awarding of the Nobel Peace Prize to South Korean President Kim Dae-Jung – and South Korea's determined pursuit of its "sunshine policy" account for the prominence in the ASEM security dialogue, for a few years, of the situation in the Korean Peninsula.

In the early 1990s, the notion that Europe had security interests in Asia was not widely shared. For some German scholars, the Europeans no longer had any such interests (Eschborn *et al.* 1992: 160). In the mid-1990s, following the end of the Cold War and with the growing European awareness of rapid economic growth in Asia, Europeans and even Asians started to assert that Europe had a "strong and increasing stake in Asian security" (Godemont *et al.* 1995: 1). The goal of EU action envisaged by the European Commission was quite ambitious: "to demonstrate to the Asian countries ... (Europe's) ability and commitment ... to make a positive contribution to the peaceful development and stability of the region" [European Commission COM (94) 314 final: Part 2, para. 2.1].

There have been numerous and sometimes contradictory European attempts to define a European security role in Asia. The European Commission identified maritime security, denuclearization, fight against drugs, preventive diplomacy and conflict resolution as areas of dialogue with ASEAN [European Commission COM (1996) 314 final: 11]. Some European scholars, writing on the eve of ASEM 1, presented what Segal (1997: 134) has called a "laundry-list" – a mass of ideas without any clear priorities – of European security roles: support for the Korean Peninsula Energy Development Organization (KEDO); sharing of experience on the formulation and operation of nuclear free zones, handling of ethnic conflict and ensuring maritime security; and cooperation with Asia in the effort to integrate China into the international order (Godemont *et al.* 1995). Whether or not the EU indeed has the capacity to pursue these interests depends largely on the structural contexts of action in Europe as well as in Asia. These render it difficult for the EU to use ASEM as a forum for security dialogue with Asia (Robles 2003a: 20).

The structural constraints on possible action in Asia by the EU, whether the latter is conceptualized as a security system or as an actor, are well known. As a security system, the EU will, by its very nature, be likely to contribute little to Asian security. In Europe, the EU was able to exercise a "silent disciplining power" on non-EU members by holding out to them the prospect of accession. This incentive obviously cannot function vis-à-vis states that have no prospect of membership in the EU. Sometimes, the question has been asked whether the European security system can be a model for Asia (Krause and Umbach 1998). The near-unanimous response of Asians and Europeans is negative (Dosch 1998). If this were the case, much of the rationale for European dialogue with Asia, that is, sharing of European experience with Asia would vanish (Robles 2003a: 22).

Segal (1997: 131) argues that from a US perspective, the existence of a European security system, though geographically confined, could still have a beneficial effect on Asian security. If the Europeans assumed a greater share of the burden of ensuring security in Europe, US resources would be freed, enabling the United States to bear more burdens in Asia. Assuming that a causal linkage exists between the European security system and Asian security, Segal's approach would force one to consider any setback in the evolution of a European security system and/or US opposition to any such security system as threats to Asian security. In Europe itself, the continued development of the European security system could hardly be motivated by the desire to enable the United States to divert resources from Europe to Asia. Segal's conception seems to entail a contradiction: Europe can take action in the area of Asian security by concentrating on European security. It is almost as if European action in the Asian security sphere would be achieved through inaction.

The EU's capacity as a security actor is conditioned by the Common Foreign and Security Policy's (CFSP's) goals, which are broad enough to extend to action in Asia, and its regional priorities and resources, which compel the EU to lay stress in practice on other regions in the developing world. Among the CFSP's specific objectives are those of safeguarding the EU's common values, fundamental interests and independence; strengthening the security of the EU and its member states; preserving peace and strengthening international security; and developing and consolidating democracy and the rule of law and respect for human rights and fundamental freedoms. To avoid stretching EU resources in the effort to achieve these extremely broad objectives, the Lisbon European Council (1992) identified factors that would enable the EU to determine its common interest: geographic proximity, important political interests in political and economic stability and threats to EU security interests. The areas where joint action would be particularly beneficial were Central and Eastern Europe, especially the ex-USSR and the former Yugoslavia, the Maghreb (North Africa) and the Middle East. A 1991 Maastricht "Declaration on Areas which could be the subject of Joint Action" specified four security areas in which EU members had important common interests: the Organization for Security and Cooperation (OSCE) in Europe, disarmament and arms control in Europe, nuclear non-proliferation and the economic aspects of security. From this cursory survey, we may conclude that although certain issues, e.g. nuclear non-proliferation, undoubtedly have Asian dimensions, Asia as such is not a priority region for the CFSP. Apart from Central and Eastern Europe (including Russia), the regions of greatest concern to the EU are those that are geographically closest to it: the Maghreb (North Africa) and the Middle East (Robles 2003a: 23).

In Asia, several structural features of the security architecture will determine the EU's ability to use ASEM as a forum for dialogue that could pave the way for joint action with Asian states. The first is the overwhelming preponderance of the United States in the regional balance of power, which is such that Europeans readily admit that they are in no position to challenge the US "hard security" role in the region. For the moment, any action under this heading remains within the competence of individual EU member states (Lim 2004: 11). A second obstacle is the inability or unwillingness of the Asians themselves to agree on a security role for Europe in the region. Möller (2002: 30) goes so far as to assert that China neither wants nor expects Europe to play a role in Asia. Third, there exists an alternative security forum, the ASEAN Regional Forum (ARF), to which the Southeast Asians attach immense symbolic importance and in which the EU already participates (Lim 2004). Finally, the very weakness of the ARF means that in certain circumstances the EU could conceivably make a contribution to Asian security with the collaboration of only a few Asian states and bypassing the ARF and ASEM.

The process leading to the establishment of the KEDO illustrates the potential of EU action in Asia and the limits of dialogue within ASEM as a forum for promoting a European contribution to Asian security. The immediate threat to Asian security came from North Korea's possession of nuclear reactors capable of producing weapons-grade plutonium suitable for nuclear weapons, which could threaten not just South Korea but also Japan. The United States and North Korea signed a Framework Agreement on 21 October 1994 and pursued negotiations that culminated in the establishment of KEDO on March 9, 1995 by the United States, South Korea and Japan. Under the agreement, the North Korean reactors would be replaced by two Light Water Reactors for electricity, which would be safer from nuclear accidents and more difficult to use in the production of weapons-grade plutonium. They would be under monitoring, supervision and control by the International Atomic Energy Agency (IAEA). In return, the United States undertook to supply 500,000 tons of heavy oil; provide formal assurances against the threat or use of nuclear weapons by the United States and reduce barriers to trade, investment and communication (Lim 1999: 22–3; Robles 2003a: 24).

The EU's decision to accede to the KEDO Agreement was largely a response to Japan's demand that the EU participate in KEDO in return for Japanese support for reconstruction in the former Yugoslavia. By a Joint Action of March 5, 1996, the EU agreed to cofinance the KEDO. Under the Accession Agreement signed on July 30, 1997, the EU would contribute European Currency Unit (ECU) fifteen million a year for five years. As Paul Lim puts it, "EU participation in KEDO has been hailed as (an expression of) EU concern for the peace and stability of Asia, nuclear safety, and nuclear non-proliferation" (Lim 1999: 22).As was to be expected, South Korea, the United States and Japan were KEDO's primary contributors. The 5.96 percent contribution of the EU and its members appears to be very small until it is compared with the one-fourth of one percent contribution of six ASEAN members; China made none at all. EU participation in KEDO is all the more significant because of the structural differences between the security situation in Northeast Asia and that in Southeast Asia. Now, war is not very likely to occur among the member states of ASEAN, whereas this danger looms large in Northeast Asia (Robles 2003a: 25–6) (see Table 5.1).

In the case of East Timor, the EU circumvented the ARF and ASEM. Following the fall of the Suharto regime and an agreement between Portugal and Indonesia to organize a referendum in East Timor on autonomy or independence, the European Commission offered to provide one million euros for monitoring the referendum and €15–20 million for long-term development assistance. The European Parliament as well as the EU observer mission to East Timor requested that a UN police force be deployed in the territory that would

Table 5.1 Total financial support by countries to KEDO March 1995 to December 2001 (US$)

Country/organization	Total	Percentage
Total	1,376,905,507	
Republic of Korea	604,542,477	43.91
United States	310,886,000	22.58
Japan	292,603,930	21.25
Europe		
EAEA (EURATOM)	82,118,897	5.96
Italy	1,821,429	0.13
Germany	1,011,485	0.07
United Kingdom	1,000,000	0.07
The Netherlands	790,192	0.06
Finland	645,593	0.05
France	503,778	0.04
Greece	25,000	0.001
Subtotal Europe	87,916,374	6.39
ASEAN		
Singapore	1,600,000	0.12
Indonesia	974,907	0.07
Brunei	423,690	0.03
Malaysia	300,000	0.02
Thailand	300,000	0.02
The Philippines	150,000	0.01
Subtotal ASEAN	3,748,597	0.27

Source: KEDO Annual Report, Appendix I.

take over responsibility for maintaining peace and order during the referendum. Probably out of deference to Indonesia, a major purchaser of weapons from several European states, this call was not heeded.

The massacres and forced resettlement that had compelled 250,000 East Timorese to flee to the mountains and 200,000 others to seek refuge in West Timor prompted several members of the European Parliament to denounce ethnic cleansing by Indonesia and demanded that the EU freeze all forms of cooperation with Indonesia. Finland, which at the time held the EU Presidency, urged Indonesia to end the violence and to request that the UN Security Council, authorize an armed presence. NGOs and trade unions joined in the appeal to the EU to support the sending of a peacekeeping force. The major powers, negotiating at the UN, refused to do so, again in deference to Indonesia (Cahin 2000: 144–8). Nevertheless, the violence reached such levels that in September 1999, the EU imposed sanctions on Indonesia, banning the export of arms, munitions and military equipment to Indonesia. Bilateral military cooperation between Indonesia and EU member states was also suspended (Robles 2003a: 26–7).

In brief, KEDO and East Timor lead us to believe that the EU can play a role in Asian security by engaging in a dialogue with only one or two Asian countries (Japan and South Korea), and if necessary take joint action against an Asian country (Indonesia). This being the case, the rationale for a dialogue forum like ASEM might come into question. Paradoxically, on at least one occasion, when the Southeast Asian states sought European cooperation through ASEM, it was the Europeans who shrank from the opportunity. Paul Lim reports that at ASEM 1 (1996), ASEAN requested that the European states accede to the Treaty on the Southeast Asia Nuclear Weapons-Free Zone (SEANWFZ), signed at Bangkok in December 1995, barely three months before ASEM 1. The most relevant provisions of the Treaty for non-Southeast Asian states would have required them not to test, use, station or transport nuclear weapons inside Southeast Asia and not to dispose on land in the territory of the Southeast Asian states or dump at sea or discharge into the atmosphere within Southeast Asia radioactive material or wastes [Article 3, §§1(a),(b), (c) and 3(a), (b)]. The European states refused (Lim 2004: 2). Another issue on which the Europeans could have been placed on the defensive was that of the European weapons to Asian states. Only the Asia–Europe People's Forum (AEPF 2000: paras 6.1, 6.2) has been bold enough to demand that ASEM members develop binding mechanisms for controlling arms imports and exports and adopt Asian and European codes of conduct on the arms trade. Needless to say, there has been no echo of these demands in ASEM's official declarations.

It was the determination of South Korea, the host of ASEM 3, to use ASEM as a platform for its policy toward North Korea that was responsible for the unexpected prominence at ASEM 3 and ASEM 4 of the situation in the Korean Peninsula in the ASEM security dialogue. As late as a month before the summit in October 2000, it was feared that there would be no theme for ASEM 3 and thus no reason for heads of state or government to attend it (Bersick 2004c: 230–1). The awarding of the Nobel Peace Prize to South Korean President Kim Dae-Jung shortly before the summit ensured that the situation in the Korean Peninsula would be the center of attention at ASEM 3. As Lim (2004) put it aptly, ASEM 3 was a very good public relations coup for the host country. A few years earlier, South Korea had campaigned for a European contribution to KEDO (Camroux and Park 2004: 178). Now the South Korean president was determined to obtain European support for his "Sunshine policy" that took the form of an ASEM Declaration for Peace on the Korean Peninsula.

The Declaration's formulation reflected European attention to South Korea's concerns. For instance, the Europeans originally wished for a reference to "weapons of mass destruction." When South Korea warned that this might provoke North Korea, the Europeans agreed to omit the phrase. A number of European states (Finland, Germany, Italy, Portugal, Sweden and the UK), took advantage of the opportunity to establish diplomatic relations with North Korea. Such moves were interpreted by observers as a message to the United States that the European states wished to pursue an independent course. At ASEM 4 (2002), another "Political Declaration for Peace on the Korean Peninsula" was adopted in which references were made to the naval clash in the Yellow Sea, the implementation of inter-Korean cooperation projects; the holding of the second inter-Korean summit and the resumption of the US–North Korea dialogue (Lim

2004: 14–16). Seen against the background of the US president's declaration earlier that year that North Korea belonged to the Axis of evil, ASEM's support for inter-Korean reconciliation was again deemed as the expression of a desire to pursue an alternative approach (Bersick 2004c: 158). North Korea's launching of seven ballistic missiles on July 7, 2006 prompted an expression of serious concern from ASEM 6, which also emphasized the need for denuclearization in the Korean Peninsula and urged North Korea to return to six-party talks (ASEM 6 2006a: para. 4). Barely a month after ASEM 6, North Korea detonated a nuclear device on October 9, 2006; yet, neither ASEM leaders nor foreign ministers appear to have issued any collective statement, perhaps a telling indication of the limits of the very modest one-issue political dialogue on regional stability in Asia. Attempts to initiate a dialogue on the international security situation have also encountered serious difficulties.

ASEM and international security

The list of international security issues that are claimed to be areas of common interest for Asia and Europe resembles the UN General Assembly's agenda. Neither traditional nor non-traditional security issues have been neglected in declarations of ASEM summits or foreign ministers' meetings (FMM). Among the traditional issues that have been touched on at one time or the other are UN reform; arms control, disarmament and non-proliferation of weapons of mass destruction and the new international order/global strategic balance. Among the non-traditional issues that have on different occasions been the object of discussion are international terrorism, transnational crime, drug trafficking, trafficking in persons, anti-personnel landmines, small arms and light weapons, legal and illegal migration, welfare of women and children, health-related issues (e.g. HIV/AIDS and SARS) and environmental issues (see the tables in Hänggi 2004: 103–6, 108–9). At one meeting, the foreign ministers (FMM 6 2004) dealt with multilateralism; non-proliferation of weapons of mass destruction; international terrorism; Korea; Iraq; and the Middle East; international public health; migration and Myanmar [not to mention the World Trade Organization (WTO), sustainable development and the dialogue of cultures and civilizations]. European scholars have been no less ambitious when proposing dialogue topics. Europe was said to have a role in creating an environment that would make China more likely to accept the Comprehensive Test Ban Treaty; Europe could share its experience with Asian states that wished to participate in peacekeeping; Europe and Asia could discuss ways to advance conventional arms control; they could share their experience in dealing with Russia; they could consult with each other about the United States and its global role and lastly – just to make sure that nothing was left out – they could discuss general concepts of security (Godemont *et al.* 1995; Mahncke 1997).

The contentious nature of practically all of these issues simultaneously makes dialogue essential and arduous. In these circumstances, it is legitimate to ask what the purpose of dialogue is: understanding or joint action. Certainly, the EU's New Asia Strategy envisaged joint action: the UN Conventional Arms Register was to be improved in coverage and efficiency; the IAEA's safeguards system was to be reinforced and made more credible; and the Biological and Chemical Weapons Conventions were to be implemented (European Commission COM (94) 314 final: Part III, para. 2.2). After nearly a decade, it is painfully obvious that the activities listed by Hänggi under traditional and non-traditional security issues are confined to declarations and statements. It is not clear if there has been any actual impact on the policies of each Asian and European state subscribing to the declaration or even if dialogue has actually taken place. Skeptics have pointed out that ASEM participants choose topics for dialogue that are non-controversial (Hänggi 2004), that is, topics on which there is no disagreement among them. It is plausible to assume, though, that on some issues, such as UN reform, substantial differences of opinion exist among ASEM participants. Given the very limited amount of time available, the very large number of issues on the table and the fact that the dialogue is not necessarily an input to a negotiation process, ASEM discussions may produce only very general expressions of opinion that leave differences unresolved and prevent joint action from being envisaged. Discussions remain at a very high level of generality, with final declarations containing the least common denominator or worse, empty formulas (Möllers 2000: 1). If ever ASEM was vulnerable to the charge of being a mere talk shop, the blame must be attributed to the discussions of global issues, particularly at Summits and at FMMs. A Filipino official interviewed by Bersick complained that "Ministers speak at length, and that is called dialogue" (Bersick 2004c: 101).

Perhaps, this pitfall could have been avoided if the proposal made at ASEM 1 and at FMM 5 for meetings at UN headquarters of Asian and European representatives, who are presumably familiar with the details of these issues and could engage in coalition-building with non-ASEM participants, on the sidelines of UN meetings, had been pursued systematically (ASEM 1 1996: para. 7; FMM 5 2003: para. 5). Only one such meeting was held, in June 1996, between the EU troika (at that time comprising Spain, Italy and Ireland), on the one hand, and Singapore and Japan, on the other (Bersick 2004c: 227).

The major obstacles to the pursuit of fruitful dialogue between Asia and Europe were identified by Germany when objecting to the discussion of reform of UN finances within ASEM: the matter was already being studied in a UN working group, so that establishment of another dialogue forum would not contribute to progress in the discussions, particularly since the Asian group did not constitute a homogeneous group (Bersick 2004c: 227). In other words, not all parties interested in these issues were represented in an Asia–Europe forum. Conversely, it would be rash to suppose that all Asian (and even European) states were equally interested in all the topics listed under the heading "international peace and security." For instance, corruption may be widespread in Asia, but precisely for this reason the willingness to discuss it might be absent. Even worse, dialogue participants might feign interest in dialogue even if they are unwilling or unable to take concrete action following the dialogue.

Since 2002, the foreign ministers (FMM 4 2002; FMM 5 2003: para. 8) have grappled with the challenge of making ASEM dialogue on international peace and security more efficient and effective. Tacitly admitting the limitations of the "laundry-list" approach to agenda setting, they agreed that agendas would henceforth be "focused on a few key international and global issues of mutual interest" (FMM 6 2004: 6). An exchange of views would no longer take place for the sake of exchanging views. Rather specific goals would be set, and result-oriented programs or projects would be designed. Political dialogue would concentrate on strengthening multilateralism and addressing security threats (FMM 7 2005: Annex, para. 1).

The foreign ministers' choice of key issue does not augur well for political dialogue, for the new themes are no less broad than the earlier themes and can hardly provide adequate guidelines for the choice of prioritized areas. Scholars have not been very helpful in identifying areas where ASEM could have a comparative advantage. It will certainly be a challenge to identify issues on which all Asian and all European participants can achieve consensus. Perhaps the possibility of only subsets of Asian and European actors forming a coalition, with or without the collaboration of non-ASEM participants, will have to be considered. In addition, if concrete goals and specific programs or projects are to be implemented, ASEM participants will have to confront once more the issue of funding for these activities. As we have seen, the EU has used the pretext that ASEM is a dialogue among equals in order to preempt discussions of development issues and economic/industrial cooperation (see Chapter 2).

In any effort to make political dialogue as a basis for action, ASEM may well have to confront once more the issue of civil society participation. If dialogue requires that all interested parties must be allowed to participate and treat each other as equals, the negotiating history of two recent international conventions provides proof that civil society organizations can claim to be interested parties that are capable of entering into a dialogue and contributing to joint action. During the preparatory process of the Rome Statute of the International Criminal Court (ICC), the World Federalist Movement convened and designed an NGO coalition in favor of the ICC. Larger organizations circulated and promoted new research. Working alongside them, smaller groups carried out networking, information dissemination and coalition building. NGOs became partners in the negotiations, especially in a consultative role with an increasing number of states. In particular, they forged an alliance with the Like-Minded Group, comprising states that had a clear general vision of a strong, independent ICC. EU member states, except France and the UK, were part of the Like-Minded Group. In recognition of the NGOs' contribution to the process, the Preparatory Commission's plenary and informal working group meetings were opened to them. Civil society experts also participated in intersessional meetings. At the Diplomatic Conference in Rome in July 1998, NGOs adopted more aggressive tactics. They set up thirteen teams covering each part of the ICC and assumed greater responsibility to provide daily information and analysis to all participants (Benedetti and Washburn, 1999: 1–39; Kirsch and Holmes 1999).

In the International Campaign to Ban Landmines (ICBL), an umbrella network of 160 NGOs from forty states, the ICBL and the International Committee on the Red Cross (ICRC) played a key role in delegitimizing and delegalizing landmines. The NGOs worked effectively with a core group of small and medium states, notably Austria, Belgium, Canada, Denmark, the Netherlands and Norway, whom they pushed to take positions consistent with their domestic, social and political policies. Subsequently, France, Germany and the UK were brought into the campaign. In short, NGOs forged closer relations with states than they had ever done before by sitting in official delegations, participating in their government's deliberations, helping to organize conferences and focusing activity at sub-national levels (Warkentin and Mingst 2000: 245–8).

These examples are relevant, notwithstanding possible objections that ASEM is a dialogue process and not a negotiating forum. Civil society participation and support might well be the additional element that could facilitate dialogue and joint action in view of the ambitious nature of the objectives, the small number of ASEM participants and the limited resources that they are willing to put in joint action.

ASEM and the fight against terrorism

Prior to ASEM 4 (2002), international terrorism was usually mentioned in the context of the fight against transnational crime. In the wake of 9/11, it rose to the top of the agenda of ASEM 4 and became an ASEM priority area. This political dialogue is claimed to be likely to produce an approach to the fight against international terrorism that compares favorably to the US approach. A slightly different picture emerges upon detailed analysis of ASEM declarations on terrorism, highlighting a much greater degree of convergence between the US position, on the one hand, and the ASEM position, on the other.

For the elements of a supposedly distinct ASEM approach, one can turn to the Copenhagen Declaration on Cooperation against International Terrorism. Upon closer examination, some of these elements may ultimately turn out to be compatible with a US approach. The condemnation of "all acts of terrorism as criminal and unjustifiable, irrespective of their motivation" (ASEM 4 2002c: para. 1) is a standard formula contained in UN resolutions for which the United States has voted. The statement that "acts of international terrorism constitute one of the most serious threats to international peace and security" is not very far removed from UN Charter language of "threat to the peace," which can justify UN Security Council measures to maintain or restore international peace and security. Acknowledgment that "the proliferation of weapons of mass destruction to terrorist groups is a serious threat to global peace and security" (ASEM 4 2002c, para. 4) echoes a US position. The insistence that the fight against terrorism "must be based on the principles of the UN Charter and basic norms of international law" (ASEM 4 2002c: para. 1) is widely perceived to be at the heart of the difference vis-à-vis the US unilateral approach. This argument ignores the fact that states disagree on the content of the basic norms of international law. In the US view, preemptive self-defense is allowed under international law; moreover, the Iraqi breaches of UN Security Council Resolution 687 (1991), adopted after the conclusion of Operation Desert Storm, revived the authority to use "all necessary measures" granted to the coalition under UN Security Council Resolution 678 (1990). Other states might disagree with the US legal views, and to this extent, there is indeed a difference between the UnitedStates and those other states. In the absence of an impartial (judicial) authority to adjudicate these claims, the superiority of one against the other cannot be definitively established. Finally, advocacy of a comprehensive approach, which comprises political, economic, diplomatic, military and legal means and takes into account root causes of terrorism "without acknowledging these as justifications for terrorist and/or criminal activities" (ASEM 4 2002c: para. 2), can be reconciled with the US approach. After all, since 9/11, the United States has increased its economic assistance to the Philippines, where armed groups reputedly linked with Al-Qaeda are active.

An effort was made at ASEM 4 to generate a consensus that would represent a unique Asia–European perspective distinct from US views. If the effort had been successful, it would have been evidence that dialogue had taken place. According to a news report, France, Japan and Germany tabled a resolution on September 22, 2002 that declared the principle of a preemptive attack illegal and illegitimate. The Japanese prime minister cited the attack on Pearl Harbor as an example of the dangers of a preemptive approach. The resolution was not approved due to the refusal of the UK, Italy and Spain, all close US allies, to change their views. The Summit had to content itself with a statement that Iraq had to fully cooperate with the UN, which seemed to an observer to be a green light for US plans to overthrow Sadam Hussein (De Beer 2002). Similar attempts to generate a distinct Asian–European perspective through dialogue may well share the same fate as there are divisions within each of the two groups – between those supportive of the United States (e.g. the Philippines, the UK and Italy) and those critical of the United States (e.g. Malaysia and France).

At least ASEM dialogue on terrorism has the potential to constitute a new area of common interest, going beyond dialogue to encompass joint action. Some of the measures enumerated in the Cooperation Programme on Fighting International Terrorism are simple reminders to Asian and European states to support the work of the UN through implementation of UN Security Council Resolution 1373 (Bantekas 2003; Rosand 2003); accession to and implementation of international conventions and protocols on terrorism; and implementation of the Organization for Economic Cooperation and Development's (OECD's) recommendations regarding anti-money laundering. Other measures are to be implemented within the ASEM framework. In the short term, an ad hoc informal consultative mechanism enabling ASEM participants to "confer expeditiously" on international events was to be established. An ASEM Seminar on Anti-terrorism was held in China in 2003, with other seminars likely to follow on underground banking. Singapore also proposed that links be established among the European Police Office (EUROPOL), ASEAN Chiefs of Police Conference

(ASEANPOL) and the law enforcement agencies of China, Japan and South Korea at the 2002 FMM. In the medium term, ASEM participants undertook to cooperate to enhance customs communication networks; combat financial crime and money laundering; improve air and maritime security; assist each other in capacity building for implementation of UN Security Council resolutions and the OECD recommendations; and enhance cross-cultural understanding and build mutual confidence through a dialogue on cultures and civilizations. In the long term, activities would promote human resource and economic development, notably through the Trade Facilitation Action Plan (TFAP) and Investment Promotion Action Plan (IPAP) (ASEM 4 2002b).

Those Asian countries that have attempted to use ASEM as a means to obtain development assistance will perhaps express satisfaction at this new impetus. There is, however, a risk that these countries and their citizens are increasingly identified with new security threats. This tendency may result from the blurring of internal and external security threats in Europe, which leads external security agencies to look for new adversaries within national borders (e.g. immigrants) and internal security agencies to look for adversaries beyond their national borders (Bigo 2000). While the new habits might facilitate cooperation with Asian countries, it may well be more difficult to treat the latter as equal partners, as required by Todorov and Habermas. The reason is that the categories of individuals associated with the threats (e.g. Islamic groups, illegal migrants, suspected terrorists) come mostly from Asia. Preventing identification of Asian countries with the security threats should be one of the objectives of a security dialogue with the EU. Another goal should be to ensure that the human rights of the individuals concerned are respected. Asylum and extradition procedures should be fair; victims of trafficking should be adequately protected; and terrorist suspects should be guaranteed a fair trial and protection against torture, cruel, inhumane or degrading treatment and the death penalty (Human Rights Watch 2002).

From the preceding discussion, it should be obvious that ASEM security dialogue cannot be divorced from a dialogue on human rights.

ASEM and the dialogue on human rights

It is impossible to recapitulate here all of the dilemmas associated with the international protection of human rights. We can only identify here those that are the most relevant for Asia–Europe dialogue and those that make it difficult for states to agree that human rights are an area of common interest. A state that seeks to advance respect of human rights beyond its borders must very often address itself to a state that violates these rights. This is only one aspect of a broader paradox. Human rights, defined as rights that human beings possess by virtue of their being human (or alternatively, so that they can become human), are intended to protect individuals against the state's arbitrary power. Yet, enforcement of these rights requires that the state limit or restrain itself (Dhommeaux 1989: 400). This being the case, the state will not necessarily be "the best watch-

dog" of the implementation of human rights law. If the state itself institutional-
izes violations of basic human rights, as was the case in Nazi Germany, appeal
to the state will be futile (Robles 2004: 131–2). For this reason, the protection of
human rights, whether at the national or international levels, will require the
action not just of states but also of a very large number of individuals and NGOs
(Cassese 1991: 70–2).

The difficulties inherent in inter-state dialogue are further aggravated in the
case of Asia–Europe relations by divergent regional trends. Since the 1990s,
promoting and safeguarding human rights have been a cornerstone of European
relations with developing countries. In the post-war period, regionalism has been
considered in Europe as a solution to contradictions inherent in protecting
human rights at national and global levels. Within the EU, a system combining
incentives and sanctions has been developed that is intended to enhance the
EU's ability to influence human rights protection in other countries and regions.
In contrast, among developing regions, Asia is unique in that it is the only one
that lacks a regional system for the protection of human rights. If anything, it
seems that a de facto consensus exists among Asian states against the international protection of human rights (Robles 2004: 132–41).

A consistent EU approach to dialogue with Asia is hampered by the existence
of contradictions in the liberal ideology in which the conception of human rights
is embedded. The earlier, classical liberalism, which treated the defense of property rights and the limiting of state power as unconditional principles, is challenged by a version of liberalism in which equality of rights and opportunities is
accorded a positive role and state intervention in the economy is accepted
(Richardson 1997). Classical liberalism's economic and political doctrines may
also come into conflict. A free-market economy may operate under undemocratic conditions; conversely, a democracy may pursue protectionist policies or
allow state intervention in the economy (Strange 1994: 216). When the EU,
which simultaneously advocates a free-market economy and democratic principles inspired by classical liberalism, is faced with a partner that could be convinced to modify its economic organization along liberal lines but resists respect
for human rights and democratization, the question of trade-offs arises. The
EU's market access strategy is in danger of trumping the EU's policy of promotion of human rights and democracy.

The EU faces this dilemma in its dialogue with Asia (for Southeast Asia, see
Robles 2004: 131–41). In EU relations with Asia, it is obvious from the very
outset that only one group is interested in a human rights dialogue in ASEM. In
1994, the European Community's (EC's) New Asia strategy declared that the
EU had to contribute to the development and consolidation of democracy and
the rule of law as well as the respect for fundamental rights and freedoms in
Asia [European Commission COM (94) 314 final: Part III, para. 2.2], a priority
that was reaffirmed in the 2001 Strategic Framework for Enhanced Partnerships
[European Commission COM (2001) 469 final: 15]. In contrast, the conception
of dialogue advocated by Singapore, which originally proposed ASEM, was
hedged about by so many restrictions – it should be based on reciprocal respect;

it should be held in a positive spirit with the aim of understanding and learning from each other; ASEM participants should not accuse each other; they should avoid efforts to accommodate pressures from lobbies and the international media – that one European diplomat exclaimed: "all that's left to talk about is the color of the wallpaper" (Lim 2004: 8). The most vigorous defenders of an ASEM human rights agenda are the Asian and European NGOs meeting in parallel summits at the AEPF, which since ASEM 1 has stressed that human rights should be central to Asia–Europe Relations and fully discussed at ASEM (AEPF 1 1996: 5; see also AEPF 2 1998b: 2).

Over a decade, the EU has not been successful in convincing the Asian ASEM participants to engage in a dialogue on human rights, democracy and the rule of law. In the first four ASEM summits, the reference to human rights, if it appeared at all (cf. ASEM 2 1998a) was disguised under the term "fundamental rights," which was said to be one of the bases of the partnership, together with mutual respect, equality and non-intervention in domestic affairs (ASEM 1 1996: para. 5). Under a restrictive reading congenial to authoritarian states, the last three would neutralize any attempt to bring civil and political rights into the discussion. It was only at ASEM 3 that the EU finally succeeded in persuading China and other Asian states to accept a commitment "to promote and protect all human rights" (ASEM 3 2000: para. 8) and to uphold "respect for democracy, the rule of law, equality, justice and human rights" (AECF 2000: para. 5). It is said that China, Malaysia and Singapore agreed to these phrases in order not to embarrass the host, South Korean President Kim Dae Jung, a former dissident. China also wished to avoid deadlock when its turn came to preside over ASEM meetings in 2001 (Hänggi 2004: 100). Nevertheless, authoritarian states wishing to subordinate the observance of civil and political rights to alleged imperatives of economic development could be satisfied with the reference to the right to development as a human right. Conversely, the EU and human rights NGOs, which refuse to see economic and social rights prevail over civil and political rights, would find support for their position in the reference to the universality, indivisibility and interdependent character of human rights, as expressed in the declaration of the 1993 Vienna World Conference on Human Rights (ASEM 3 2000: para. 8). Clearly, ASEM 3 did not generate a new consensus, since these statements merely repeat well-known and contradictory views.

A hasty reading of the AECF might create the impression that very narrow limits are set on political dialogue in general. According to the Framework, the focus of dialogue should be on "issues of common interest"; its purpose should be to enhance mutual awareness and understanding; ASEM participants should proceed "step-by-step in a process of consensus building" and no issue should be excluded beforehand, but "wisdom and judiciousness" should be exercised in selecting the topics for discussion (AECF 2000: para. 12). For good measure, Paribatra (2000: 150–3) adds that the dialogue should be non-country specific and non-confrontational. In reality, these restrictive conditions apply primarily to the human rights dialogue, which Asians consider to be divisive and thus wish to avoid. From the European perspective, a dialogue on issues with respect to which agreement already exists does not appear to be particularly useful (Van Haute 2000: 4). Indeed, such a discussion cannot even be properly called a dialogue if we recall that it is precisely the existence of either uncertainty or a difference of views among participants as regards joint action that necessitates dialogue.

Will dialogue between Asia and Europe be possible once the Asians feel more at ease in the ASEM setting? To answer this question, it might be instructive to examine the record of one significant bilateral dialogue on human rights – that between China and the EU. The record so far gives very little cause for optimism. On the contrary, the China–EU dialogue might even be considered as a paradigm for the failure of Asian and EU dialogue on human rights to take place at ASEM.

The China–EU dialogue as a paradigm for ASEM

The parties that may be supposed to have an interest in a human rights dialogue must be identified and their interests described, if we are to understand the evolution of the dialogue.

The interests of participants in a dialogue

There is a widely shared feeling in Europe that China's human rights record, while it has made progress in the last two decades, still requires substantial improvement. For this purpose, the EU believes that the most appropriate instrument at its disposal is dialogue with China. Whether the ongoing official dialogue meets the key conditions required for genuine dialogue identified above is an open question. The EU proclaims its commitment to a dialogue, but this commitment is subject to (economic) pressures that may affect its willingness and capability to defend its position on human rights. Moreover, it is far from obvious that the interest in dialogue is shared by China, whose willingness to envisage changes in its human rights policies and practices is subject to debate. The dialogue's chances of success are further vitiated by the refusal of China to allow a set of interested actors – Asian and European human rights NGOs – to participate in the dialogue.

The European Commission has observed that the human rights situation in China has improved, in that there is greater freedom of choice in education, employment, housing and travel. China has passed civil and criminal laws, signed key international human rights instruments and taken steps to develop the electoral process at the local level [European Commission COM (1998) 181 final: 2]. Chinese and Western scholars point out that the setting up of non-state-owned enterprises created a private sphere, free from state intervention, and thereby provided some room for free choice. Such choice, even if restricted to economic activities, still constituted a degree of political liberty (Zhao Chenggen and McGough 2001: 160). Despite the progress accomplished, few would disagree with the European Commission [COM (1998) 181 final: 1] that China is still far from meeting international human rights standards.

There is a broad consensus in Europe that dialogue with China is the only means available to Europe in this field. The existence of a consensus is in sharp contrast to the situation in the United States, where there is often fierce debate as to the appropriate way to deal with China. Europe believes that its interest lies in working together with China and sharing responsibilities in global governance. These would include reconciling the interests of developing and developed countries; promoting peace and stability in Asia and addressing climate arms control, non-proliferation, climate change and other global issues [European Commission COM (2003) 533: 8; COM (2000) 552 final: 4]. Achieving a partnership of this type would clearly be difficult, if not impossible, to reconcile with a strategy of confrontation and a resort to sanctions.

European interests in a dialogue also result from some weaknesses in the EU position vis-à-vis China. In the unlikely event that the EU adopted sanctions, EU institutions would be too weak to make the threat credible. The EU would not be able to compel member states to cease investing in China, given the EU institutions' lack of competence over foreign direct investment (FDI). Furthermore, no provision in the EU allows for mobilization of military instruments as a means of safeguarding democracy (Youngs 2001: 39–40). A third obstacle to the adoption of a sanctions-based approach is the tension between the EU's economic and political goals. In many economic areas, the EU finds itself in the position of seeking concessions from China, such as transparent economic governance; removal of restrictive regulations and non-tariff barriers; protection of intellectual property rights and compliance with international technical standards. At the WTO, the EU seeks Chinese support for the Singapore issues [European Commission COM (2003) 533: 16]. Of course, the argument can plausibly be made that it is also in China's interest to solve these problems, if it wishes to continue attracting FDI. Still, the need for Chinese cooperation in all these areas would seem to make a strategy of confrontation over human rights counterproductive.

All EU member states subscribe to the above-mentioned goals in trade and investment. At the same time, individual member states continue to formulate and implement national policies toward China. The primary goal is to improve their trade balances, uniformly in deficit, with China. As a result, a tacit division of labor emerges between EU institutions (primarily the European Commission) and member states. The latter defend their national interests, concentrating on promoting trade with or investment in China, and leave sensitive topics such as human rights to be handled by the European Commission (Sandschneider 2002: 34, 39, 42). In short, European human rights policies toward China are subject to two sorts of tensions: the tension between economic and political goals and the tension between EU policy and member states' policies.

The fate of EU sanctions imposed against China in the wake of the June 1989 Tiananmen massacre underscores the challenges that the EU faces in reconciling these interests, which may at times resemble efforts to square the circle. The EU had decided to raise the issue of human rights in China at the UN; request permission for independent observers to attend trials and visit prisons; interrupt military cooperation; impose an arms embargo; suspend high-level contacts; postpone new projects and reduce cultural, scientific and technical cooperation programs. One would have thought that the dramatic context would be conducive to unanimity among the EU members. In reality, the discussion was marked by profound disagreement between Germany and Italy, on the one hand, said to favor a milder approach, and France, on the other hand, which advocated a stronger approach. By October 1990, Italy, which held the EU presidency, was demanding the resumption of dialogue with China. The EU gradually lifted sanctions, then removed China from the list of non-market economy countries and increased EU official development assistance from twenty million ecus in 1991–94 to seventy million ecus in 1995–99 (Baker 2002: 50; Algieri 2002: 70). Unlike other developing countries, China has not been compelled to sign an agreement with EU that includes a clause on conditionality, whereby EU sanctions can be imposed on the recipient in case of gross human rights violations or interruptions of the democratic process (Youngs 2001: 167).

In an effort to explain the move away from sanctions, the European Commission cited in 1995 [COM (1995) 279 final: 5] the danger that "frequent and strident declarations" would dilute the message and provoke "knee-jerk" reactions from China. In the Commission's view, the EU had to combine carefully timed public statements, formal private discussions and practical cooperation. The EU would support continued reform in China while raising the Chinese human rights situation at the UN as well as in bilateral dialogue. Contrary to this policy, the EU gradually stopped raising the Chinese human rights record at the UN after 1995. In 1990, and from 1992 to 1996, all EU member states sponsored a draft resolution on China's human rights situation record at the UN Commission on Human Rights. In 1997, EU unity broke down, when a draft resolution was sponsored by only ten member states. France, Germany, Italy, Spain and Greece refused to cosponsor the draft. The French attitude may have been dictated by a desire not to upset China a few weeks before a scheduled visit of French President Chirac to that country. Be that as it may, in successive years, it was not even possible for the EU to agree to cosponsor a resolution (Baker 2002: 55–7). France did not hesitate to call the annual exercise at the UN Commission on Human Rights a farce (Youngs 2001: 170).

The EU–China bilateral dialogue on human rights, which was initiated in January 1995, was suspended by China in 1996 after the EU sponsored a draft resolution at the UN Human Rights Commission on the situation in China. The EU has made the bilateral dialogue appear to be an alternative to the public shaming of China, in the hope that quiet diplomacy would yield tangible results (and incidentally avoid Chinese non-cooperation in trade and investment). The dialogue would be backed up with concrete, EU-funded cooperation programs that would promote the rule of law (e.g. through the training of lawyers and judges) and strengthen civil society (through training centers for officials implementing the village governance law; the promotion of consumers' rights; and assistance to the most vulnerable groups) [European Commission COM (1998) 181 final: 2].

In the annual dialogue (resumed in November 1997), China gave the impression that it was willing to engage in "serious and results-oriented dialogue," in the course of which all subjects of concern, even the most sensitive, would be addressed [European Commission COM (1998) 181 final: 2]. Some Europeans think it is a good sign that the Chinese do not accuse the Europeans of ulterior motives whenever the latter raise human rights issues with China (Yahuda 1998: 198). However, a willingness to change one's position is a precondition for dialogue. Whether China fulfills this condition is an open question.

Evidence for China's willingness to engage in a human rights dialogue not just with the EU but with other countries goes back to the early 1990s, when China received fact-finding missions from Australia, France, Britain and Switzerland. Chinese scholars declare that China does not deny in principle the "righteousness" of freedom and other human rights but insist that Europe must understand and respect differences in ideas, values and cultures (Zhang Yunling 1998: 197). It is openly admitted that China is suspicious of Western pressure on it, which could slow down growth and increase political instability. Sometimes, a thinly veiled warning is given that China and Europe cannot afford a breakdown over "minor interruptions," like human rights (Zhao Gancheng 1999: 111, 117).

Doubts about China's willingness to consider changing its human rights policy through dialogue with the West arise from an analysis of the reform process initiated in the late 1970s. It cannot be denied that the aims of economic reform, alongside improvement of the population's living standards, were to strengthen state capacity and to preserve the Chinese Communist party's control of the country. Reform was in no way identified with political liberalization and democracy, as the events at Tiananmen amply demonstrated. Since then, there is little sign of a change in goals. As one Chinese author put it succinctly, China would continue to build socialism (Zhao Gancheng 1999: 121).

Human rights NGOs constitute one set of actors whose interest in a human rights dialogue is not tempered by the need to protect economic interests (like the EU) or to preserve the political status quo (like China). Recognition of their potential contribution to the dialogue came when France, as EU president, invited human rights NGOs to participate in the September 2000 dialogue. This was far from the institutionalized participation that the NGOs themselves demanded, yet China refused the inclusion of the NGO Human Rights in China, which had been invited by the EU. Chinese human rights NGOs do not have representation at all. In other words, "dialogue excludes those in China who are most actively engaged in promoting human rights inside China" [Fédération Internationale des Ligues de Droits de l'Homme (FIDH) 2000: 1]. The Chinese attitude was consistent with China's policy of limiting the growth of NGOs in almost all areas. Möller (2004: 15) points out that in 1998, 163,000 NGOs were registered in China, which only seems to be a large number if we do not know that 300,000 were prohibited. Not that the NGO presence would necessarily guarantee a voice in the dialogue. In the United Kingdom and Australian dialogues with China, little time is provided for NGO meetings with Chinese officials.

One obvious reason for the Chinese attitude toward NGOs in general is that the latter's assessment of the Chinese human rights record is far grimmer than that of the EU. The human rights situation in China is said to be terrible for a country that has not suffered foreign invasion for over fifty years or major civil unrest for over twenty-five years; that has not been subject to country-wide natural disasters; and that has enjoyed unprecedented economic growth for over thirty years (Baker 2002: 46). Another reason for the Chinese attitude is that human rights NGOs, unlike the EU, do not hesitate to advocate the use of sanctions.

In these circumstances, it is only proper to ask whether dialogue can yield a consensus conducive to the improvement of the human rights situation in China.

The evolution of the dialogue

The China–EU dialogue is an ongoing process; neither partner has indicated any desire to discontinue it. For this reason, any evaluation may appear to be premature. On the other hand, a decade seems to be sufficient for a preliminary assessment of the difficulties encountered by dialogue when one party is not interested (China), another must keep in mind its economic interests (the EU), and a third is marginalized (human rights NGOs).

Initial assessments of the dialogue were cautiously optimistic. The European Commission [COM (1998) 181final: III, para. 1] was heartened that China appeared willing to discuss even the most sensitive subjects. In 1997, China agreed to meet European NGOs, released prisoners and approved EU human rights projects worth one million euros (Youngs 2001: 179). In 2003, the Commission asserted that through dialogue, it had obtained information on human rights in China; enhanced China's awareness of international standards and EU best practice; and helped to build trust and confidence. China had signed the International Covenant on Economic, Social and Cultural Rights (ICESCR) and announced in October 1998 that it was preparing to sign the International Covenant on Civil and Political Rights (ICCPR). It had invited the UN High Commissioner for Human Rights to visit China (September 1998 and March 2000) (Baker 2002: 61) and promised to enhance cooperation with the UN, particularly the UN Commission on Human Rights, the Special Rapporteurs on Torture and on Education and the Working Group on Arbitrary Detention. The EU and China had also discussed individual cases of human rights violations, with China offering to provide information on individual cases between the rounds of the dialogue [European Commission COM (2003) 533: 12–3].

Human rights NGOs' assessments were more critical. To begin with, two of the achievements attributed to the dialogue – China's signature of the two human rights covenants – were in reality the results of US, not European, pressure. More significantly, the apparent consensus in the dialogue was not translated into concrete improvements in the Chinese human rights situation. When

China ratified the ICESCR, it declared that Chinese law would prevail over the Covenant's article on the right to form trade unions. China has so far failed to ratify the ICCPR. Restrictive conditions forced indefinite postponement of the visit of the UN Special Rapporteur on Torture and reduced the usefulness of the visit of the UN Working Group on Arbitrary Detention (FIDH 2000: 4; 2004: 10).

To cap it all, the human rights situation actually began to deteriorate in 1997. In 2000, the Commission itself was forced to recognize the worsening situation, characterized by repression of political dissidents and minorities, arbitrary detention, extensive use of the death penalty, restrictions on religious freedom, the right of association and free speech and the failure to observe the International Labor Organization's (ILO) core labor standards [European Commission COM (2000) 552 final: 6]. In response, the European Council announced in 2001 benchmarks for judging China's human rights situation, benchmarks that human rights NGOs had long advocated: ratification and implementation of the ICCPR and ICESCR; cooperation with UN human rights mechanisms; compliance with UN guarantees for the protection of those sentenced to death; provision of statistics on the use of the death penalty; reform of administrative detention; introduction of the judicial supervision of procedures and respect for the right to a fair trial and the right of defense; respect for the fundamental rights of all prisoners, progress on access to prisoners and a constructive response to individual cases raised by the EU; freedom of religion and belief; respect for the right to organize; and respect for cultural rights and religious freedoms in Tibet and Xinjiang (FIDH 2004: 4–5; Human Rights Watch 2000: 1). Unfortunately, the situation continued to deteriorate. In 2001, revealing of state secrets became punishable by death, while a democratic experiment in city districts was suspended. In 2002, a prohibition was imposed on reporting workers' demonstrations or the Tiananmen massacre (Möller 2004: 13). To mark the UN International Anti-Drugs' Day on June 26, 2002, 150 people were executed (FIDH 2004: 10). As a result, in March 2002 and March 2003, the EU foreign ministers felt compelled to express their concern once more over the grave setbacks [Tang Shaocheng 2003: 514; European Commission COM (2003) 533: 12].

In the last few years, expert seminars, in which academics are the main participants, have become the main forum for China–EU dialogue on human rights. Seminars have been held on the death penalty, torture, the right to education, transparency and regulation of the mass media [European Commission COM (2003) 533: 12]. From Todorov's epistemic perspective, it might be contended that the value of dialogue in expert seminars lies in the possibility of exchanging information that would enable Europeans to understand China's difficulties in implementing human rights treaties and Chinese to understand European benchmarks. It is somewhat disheartening to note that the conditions in which the seminars are held are hardly more favorable to reaching a consensus conducive to the improvement of the Chinese human rights situation. Chinese participants confine themselves to presenting Chinese law, with practically no mention of actual practice or explanation of reasons for violations. From one session to the next, the content of presentations changes very little. Not all interested parties, for example, journalists or human rights NGOs, are allowed to participate in the seminars. Restrictions on participation are aggravated by the failure to disseminate seminar presentations and conclusions or to report them in the media in China and in the EU (Woodman 2002: 1). Not surprisingly, the FIDH concluded in 2004 that since 2002, the dialogue seminars have been disconnected from the China–EU dialogue (FIDH 2004: 15).

Predicting the future direction of the dialogue lies beyond the scope of this work. It would not be doing too much violence to reality if we were to assume that China is satisfied with the status quo. Facing it are the EU and human rights NGOs, whose views diverge sharply. The European Commission [COM (2003) 533: 12] insists that dialogue and cooperation must continue to be the main EU approach, though dialogue should not prevent the EU from expressing its comments and observations at the UN. NGOs object that dialogue has become an end in itself or a substitute for action. While giving the appearance of being interested in dialogue, China has used the dialogue to shield itself from EU criticism at the UN and to channel criticism to a private forum. Dialogue has given China a powerful weapon to be used against the EU: if the EU threatened to criticize China at the UN, China could retaliate by threatening to break off the dialogue, depriving the EU of even a simulacrum of a policy. Convincing China to change its policies would require a greater EU willingness to criticize China at the UN (Baker 2002: 59). EU and NGO proposals for improving the dialogue converge on some points, notably on the need to involve Chinese and European NGOs in the dialogue and to brief the press on the dialogue. They differ over the possibility of suspending the dialogue and criticizing China at the UN (FIDH 2000: 3).

The experience of the China–EU human rights dialogue sets the context for an evaluation of ASEM's capacity to provide an additional forum for human rights dialogue between Asia and the EU.

ASEM: the limits of dialogue

The chances that a human rights dialogue will acquire greater prominence, complement bilateral dialogues and perhaps even circumvent, if not remove, the obstacles to progress in bilateral dialogues are rather slim. The main reason for this rather gloomy assessment is that most of the Asian participants in ASEM are not genuinely interested in a dialogue on human rights. The very format of ASEM makes it more likely that all the Asian states will adopt a common stand against discussion of human rights in ASEM. As for the EU, it once more faces the dilemma of pursuing the cause of human rights at the risk of jeopardizing its economic interests: launching of a new WTO round and modification of Asian states' domestic laws. ASEM's existence does little to help the EU to resolve this dilemma. NGOs, the only actors that consistently plead the cause of human rights, are excluded from ASEM. Last but not least, the recent priority attached to the fight on terrorism may lead the EU to make concessions to the Asian participants as regards the protection of human rights.

Taking China as the exemplar of the authoritarian state, we must ask to what extent it is more disposed to engage in a dialogue in a multilateral forum, like ASEM, than in a bilateral forum. One indicator of this willingness is supplied by China's actions with respect to human rights conventions at the UN. Hopeful signs of greater openness toward discussions there may be found in China's ratification of the ICESCR and the Conventions against torture, on the elimination of racial discrimination, on the elimination of discrimination against women and on the rights of the child; its signature of the ICCPR and its compliance with the reporting obligations under each Convention (Kent 2002: 353–4; Möller 2003). Optimism diminishes somewhat once it is noticed that ratification has rarely been accompanied by a willingness to implement most recommendations addressed to China by UN human rights bodies, in particular those supervising the convention against torture and on the elimination of racial discrimination. Perhaps the perceived constraint associated with reporting to the human rights bodies is responsible for China's poor record of compliance? This seems improbable, as the absence of any reporting obligations at the UN Human Rights Commission in Geneva does not prevent China from opposing discussion of its human rights record. China's attitude is hardly a promising sign for the prospects of human rights dialogue in ASEM.

Enlarging the circle of participants in dialogue to include other Asian states will not necessarily alter the interest of China or the EU in a dialogue. The very organization of ASEM will probably encourage all Asian states to adopt a position closely aligned with that of China. Seven out of ASEAN's ten members are authoritarian, albeit to varying degrees. The three democratic states – Indonesia, the Philippines and Thailand – are unlikely to break ranks with the others and are certainly not about to join the EU in public criticism of China in ASEM. The presence of South Korea and Japan adds very little to the weight of an Asian group that could exert pressure in favor of a human rights dialogue within ASEM. It is well known that the promotion of human rights has not been a major feature of either country's foreign policy. No consensus exists between them on the response to the human rights situation in China. At the UN Commission on Human Rights, South Korea abstained every time a resolution critical of China was presented to the body (Johnston 2004: 68–9). For Japan, which is simultaneously Asian and developed, the human rights situation in China has undoubtedly presented serious challenges. Its approach toward China has been described as "non-confrontational" and "pragmatic," stressing positive steps (incentives) rather than (negative) sanctions. Japan did suspend a loan program after Tiananmen but took pains to avoid making the step appear as a sanction. At the UN, Japan attempted a balancing act, seeking to prevent the isolation of China without dissociating itself from the West. In 1997, Japan joined France and Germany in opposing the draft resolution on China submitted by Denmark to the UN Human Rights Commission. Like the EU, Japan started to lift sanctions a year after Tiananmen (Watanabe 2001). Japan's troubled political relationship with China makes it even more improbable that Japan will risk raising the level of bilateral tensions by associating itself in the ASEM context with calls for a human rights dialogue between Asia and Europe.

As for the EU, creating an additional forum for dialogue does little to ease the dilemma that the EU faces in its bilateral dialogue with China between the pursuit of economic interests and the defense of human rights. On the contrary, the existence of this new forum only replicates, if not aggravates, the dilemma. If the EU criticized China's human rights record at ASEM, it would jeopardize the goals of consensus at the WTO and modification of Asian laws. It comes as no great surprise that the EU has not systematically attempted to implement within ASEM its 2001 strategy to promote human rights and democratization in third countries, involving joint establishment of goals between the EU and the latter. To be sure, the EU had left open the possibility of not establishing such indicators if the other participant in the dialogue objected to them. Anticipating such an objection, the EU has not taken the trouble to put the question of indicators on ASEM's agenda, nor has it translated into practice the principle of civil society participation in the dialogue. Perhaps the time has come for the EU to admit that the Asian ASEM participants have no genuine commitment to dialogue, in which case sanctions may be appropriate [European Commission COM (2001) 265 final].

Further evidence of the priority of the EU's economic goals over human rights can be found in the European approach to the two issues. In the Senior Officials' and Economic Ministers' Meetings that followed ASEM 1, the EU vigorously lobbied with the Asians for the formulation and approval of the TFAP and IPAP. Once economic ministers had approved the two plans, a follow-up mechanism was created through a reporting process. There is no publicly available or accessible evidence that the EU has ever envisaged similar mechanisms for any of the issues considered in political dialogue, let alone for human rights issues. The almost certain opposition of the Asian states to any such proposals could be plausibly cited as the reason for this failure, but this merely reinforces the conclusion that the EU would have been reluctant to risk Asian refusal to cooperate on TFAP, IPAP and the WTO issues by proposing a reporting process on human rights similar to that organized for TFAP and IPAP.

The NGOs grouped in AEPF are the only actors who have insisted that improvement in the human rights situation in Asia should be at the center of ASEM, but they are excluded from the official process. Consequently, they are not in a position to bring the pressure to bear either on the Asian participants or on the EU, or for that matter to form coalitions with individual Asian or European states that might be sympathetic to their demands, against the authoritarian states.

In one sense, ASEM may have taken a leaf from the China–EU dialogue on human rights, with the limitations inherent in the latter being replicated. Since 1997, unofficial human rights seminars have become the main ASEM activities in this area, of which six had been held by 2004:

1   1997 (Lund): access to justice; regional and national particularities in the promotion of justice; monitoring the administration of justice;
2   1999 (Beijing): differences in Asian and European values; rights to education; rights of minorities;
3   2000 (Paris): freedom of expression and right to information; humanitarian intervention and the sovereignty of states; right to a healthy environment;
4   2001 (Bali): freedom of conscience and religion; democratization, conflict resolution and human rights; rights and obligations in the promotion of social welfare;
5   2003 (Lund): economic rights (human rights and multinational companies; human rights and FDI);
6   2004 (Suzhou, China): international migration and human rights.

As in the case of the China–EU dialogue, some skepticism is justified as regards the effectiveness of these seminars. Civil society organizations question the composition of participants, the transparency of the proceedings and the follow-up to the seminars. Bersick (2004c: 104) sees a positive sign in the fact that representatives from government, academe and NGOs are systematically invited to the seminars. Statistics are available for the first, third and fourth seminars (see Table 5.2.).

State representatives from Asia as well as Europe obviously dominate the seminars. The larger numbers of academics who participate, as compared to civil society representatives (except in the European cases in 1999 and 2001) is cause for concern, given that the independence of academics from government cannot be lightly presumed in many Asian countries. When academics outnumber civil society representatives, this tilts the balance even more in favor of states.

Access to seminar proceedings is extraordinarily difficult, a circumstance that indirectly answers civil society's questions over the transparency of the human rights seminars. Available records tend to show that Chinese interventions do not depart from the pattern observed in the China–EU human rights seminars: they consist of mere presentations of laws and policies that studiously avoid references to actual practice or explanation of reasons for violations. For instance, during the fourth seminar, China reported that it promotes employment as a matter of national policy; that it has set in place labor and social security

Table 5.2 Participation by sectors in ASEM Informal Human Rights Seminars

Participants from	First seminar (1997)		Second seminar (1999)		Fourth seminar (2001)	
	Asia	Europe	Asia	Europe	Asia	Europe
Government	12	23	15	24	19	15
Academe	9	10	10	4	8	7
Civil society	3	6	5	9	4	8

systems that suit its conditions; and that it has ratified ILO Convention No. 12 on employment policy (Asia–Europe Foundation 2002: 131–3). In other exchanges between Asian and European countries, the tendency of participants is to repeat well-worn arguments. At the same seminar, the arguments for and against a social clause were rehashed. No new information that could convince one or the other to change its position was put forward. The developing (Asian) countries contended that cheap labor was their natural advantage, and the developed (European) countries depicted cheap labor as a distortion of labor markets. They then agreed that the ILO was the proper forum to take up labor issues (ASEF 2002: 138). In other words, it was a mistake to bring up the social clause for dialogue at ASEM in the first place (see also the discussions in Raoul Wallenberg Institute of Human Rights and Humanitarian Law 1998). As for the follow-up in the proceedings, no systematic evaluation of the seminars' impact on actual practice has been undertaken. As in the case of the China–EU dialogue, one cannot help but speculate that the holding of the seminars is a way for the Asian states to preempt criticism against themselves for their unwillingness to engage in a human rights dialogue.

That ASEM may be an even less appropriate forum for a human rights dialogue is confirmed by the way that the controversy over Myanmar's participation was resolved. This is not the place to rehearse the notorious human rights record of that country (see Robles 2004: 156–61). Suffice it to say that in the ASEAN–EU relationship, Myanmar's admission to ASEAN provoked the cancellation of a number of ministerial and Joint Cooperation Committee meetings. In the ASEM framework, ASEAN membership of Myanmar should have automatically made it eligible to participate in ASEM, in much the same way that EU enlargement in 2004 should also have automatically entailed the new member states' participation. EU objections to Myanmar's presence in ASEM raised the specter that the Asian states would in retaliation object to the new EU member states' participation. In July and September 2004, the EU decided to boycott meetings of finance and economic ministers, respectively, in protest against the lack of progress in the human rights situation in Myanmar. The EU position that Myanmar's participation should be conditional on a commitment to such progress was supported by human rights NGOs (FIDH 2004). Predictably, ASEAN insisted that Myanmar should be eligible to join without reservation. In the end, all new members of both organizations were allowed to join the original ASEM participants at ASEM 5 (2004). The EU's objection to Myanmar's participation was transformed into a condition that Myanmar be represented at a lower level (Pareira 2003). The operation of Asian solidarity in ASEM to the detriment of human rights is graphically illustrated by the attitude of Japan, which felt obliged to support the Asian position regarding Myanmar's participation (Reiterer 2004: 262). Even at the AEPF held in Hanoi a month before ASEM 5, the Vietnamese organizations supposedly representing civil society prevented condemnation of Myanmar from being inserted into the final statement (Schmidt and Herberg 2004). These two events constitute further proof that enlarging the circle of participants in a human rights dialogue hardly guarantees progress in the dialogue.

Pessimism deepens once it is realized that the priority given to the fight against terrorism may compel the EU to make compromises undermining its commitment to human rights. In this new context, several Asian states used anti-terrorism as a "pretext for limiting the freedoms of citizens and suppressing their legitimate civil and political activity," as the AEPF had warned. China continued its repression of ethnic Uighurs in Xinjiang, while European states adopted restrictive laws on refugees, asylum-seekers, migrants and other foreigners (Human Rights Watch 2004). In spite of the AEPF's demand that "undemocratic forms of security legislation" be repealed (AEPF 4 2002), the EU yielded at ASEM 4 to Asian insistence that a reference to "domestic laws" be inserted into the following phrase of the Copenhagen Declaration on Cooperation against International Terrorism: "a comprehensive approach by the international community comprising political, economic, diplomatic, military and legal means, in accordance with our respective domestic laws" (ASEM 4 2002c: para. §2). Among the "domestic laws" in question is the Internal Security Act (ISA) inherited from British colonial rule. The Singaporean version allows detention without charges for up to two years, a period that may be renewed without limitation. In Malaysia, the ISA allows the police to detain, without judicial review or the filing of formal charges, people "who may act in a manner prejudicial to the security of Malaysia," for a period of up to sixty days (renewable for further periods of up to two years). As Lim (2004: 18) points out, this is an "about face" for the EU, which in the past would have condemned the ISA as a violation of human rights. Satisfaction at this evidence of willingness to change one's views, one of Todorov's and Habermas's conditions, is mitigated by the negative impact of the change of European views on the promotion of human rights in Asia.

Unlike the human rights dialogue, cultural dialogue, originally conceptualized as a complement to trade facilitation and investment promotion, seems to have moved closer to center stage in ASEM since 9/11.

ASEM and cultural dialogue

A survey of the nature, problems and prospects of cultural dialogue cannot possibly be undertaken here. We shall limit ourselves to recalling some important dilemmas confronting participants in cultural dialogue, as recently analyzed by a Japanese scholar (Tsutsumibayashi 2005). First of all, values are inextricably embedded in a broader cultural context so that it would make little sense to extrapolate and evaluate just the segments that appear to be common to two cultures. The "commonalities" discovered in this manner might turn out to be so general and abstract as to be devoid of content. This outcome would contradict Habermas's condition that it should be possible to express the consensus in specific propositions. Second, mutual understanding is only truly achieved if the values of participants in a dialogue are transformed and expanded to incorporate part of each other's values. It is not enough for the participants to assert that they recognize and understand each other's points of view. "By creating together and sharing a common ethos, A and B may come to internalize some jointly articulated moral values, recognizing them as ours, belonging neither to A nor to B exclusively, but to both" (Tsutsumibayashi 2005: 105).

The emergence of a synthesis is precisely the outcome along the axiological dimension of dialogue that Todorov required. Treating partners as equals, one requirement on which all three authors agree, presupposes mutual respect and trust. One difficulty of dialogue highlighted by Tsutsumibayashi is that this mutual trust is simultaneously a precondition for and an outcome of dialogue. One condition that was identified by Tsustumibayashi (2005: 111–12) but not Todorov or Habermas is that dialogue should have some distance from politics, without being totally divorced from it.

The European Commission addressed the need for cultural dialogue only indirectly in its New Asia Strategy, when it identified raising the EU's profile in Asia as a priority. The strategy would involve an enhanced visitors' program, strengthening of higher education links, town twinning and decentralized cooperation [European Commission COM (94) 314 final: 19]. ASEM 1 (1996: para. 17; see also ASEM 2 1998a: para. 19) appeared to give cultural dialogue a higher priority by asserting that cultural links and people-to-people contacts would help overcome misperceptions. Still, cultural dialogue was not perceived as an end in itself. As Lim (2000: 109) has explained, it was business groups that put culture on the European agenda, in the belief that understanding Asian business culture was crucial to success in Asia. In this perspective, cultural dialogue would be one means, among others, of strengthening trade and investment relations between Asia and Europe. For example, the EU's Asia-Invest Program (1999–2002) provided some funds for cultural familiarization programs for European firms. In the wake of 9/11, the European Commission [SEC (2002) 874: 3] reconceptualized (inter)cultural dialogue as a means of alleviating tension between Muslims and non-Muslims.

The new orientation does not necessarily obviate the need to understand the relationship between economic interests and cultural perceptions, which appears to be particularly close in Japan–EU relations. Once the relationship has been understood, the capacity of ASEM to enhance Asia–Europe cultural dialogue can be properly assessed.

Cultural dialogue as a complement to trade and investment promotion in Japan–EU relations

The rationale for Japan–EU cultural dialogue has its roots in history. In the second half of the nineteenth century, Japanese elites embarked on a policy of modernization that channeled Japan–European economic, political and cultural relations into directions markedly different from those taken by China–European relations. Since then, Japan and Europe have developed a range of positive and negative images and perceptions of each other that they continue to draw upon, depending on the current state of economic and political relations. The interaction between economic and political frictions and cultural (mis)perceptions is the object of a fascinating book, entitled *Japan versus the West: Image and Reality*, published in 1990 by Endymion Wilkinson, who combined academic training on China and Japan with a dozen years' experience as EC representative in Japan and in Southeast Asia. This book deserves more attention from ASEM observers, to the extent that Asian countries that seek to emulate (or are perceived to be emulating) the Japanese growth model may well expect to generate similar images and perceptions in Europe, assuming that these have not already taken root. Furthermore, the steps that Japan and European state and non-state actors have taken with a view to modifying their perceptions of each other may yield lessons for other Asian and European actors interested in cultural dialogue.

As an independent state, Japan has had a much longer experience of trade with and investment in Europe than almost all Asian countries. In the nineteenth century, Europe was not only the model to be emulated by Japan; it was also Japan's main source of technology and main export market. The presence of Japanese firms in Europe goes back to the nineteenth century. In 1878, Mitsui, engaged in the silk trade, set up its first European office in Paris, following Japanese participation in the *Exposition universelle*; a year later, it opened an office in London. The Paris office, closed in 1888, was replaced by a new headquarters in Lyons in 1923. The Bank of Tokyo started to operate in London in the 1880s. On the eve of World War II, all major Japanese commercial institutions had established branches in London (Conte-Helm 1996: 68, 77–8). At this time, Japan was not yet a very attractive market for Europeans. In the twentieth century, Japanese victory over Russia in 1905 produced grudging acknowledgment in the West of Japan's status as a great power. During the Great Depression, Western resentment reached its peak over the fact that Japan alone of the major powers continued to increase its exports.

After World War II, Japanese firms and banks returned to Europe. Mitsui reopened its French office in 1947. Mitsubishi set up sales subsidiaries in West Germany in 1955, and by 1960, its example had been followed by all Japanese trading companies. In 1954, the Bank of Tokyo established a branch in Hamburg; in 1968, it became the first Japanese bank to open a branch in Paris. Japanese firms began to invest in Europe in the 1960s. In 1966, Yoshida Kogyo KK established YKK Fasteners in Cheshire, in the UK, followed a year later by a factory at Mainhausen in West Germany. The pace of Japanese FDI in Europe accelerated in the 1970s and 1980s (Conte-Helm 1996: 69, 77–8, 90).

In the last three decades, disagreements over trade and investment have dominated Japan–EU relations. During this period, economic interests have been influenced, at least in part, and sometimes aggravated, by cultural images and perceptions. Wilkinson argues persuasively that since the Meiji restoration (1867), there has formed in the collective European (and American) mind "a limited stock of images, both positive and negative, about Japan and the Japanese from which, depending on the mood of the day, the relevant image can be recalled any number of times" (Wilkinson 1990: 30–1). Similar remarks may be made about Japanese images of the West. The main difference between the two sets of images is that Japanese images of the West have tended to be more positive and closer to reality than Western images of Japan, simply because it was in Japan's interest to learn from the West and thus to have accurate images of it. It is crucial to understand the content of these images, which persist despite fundamental transformations that have occurred in Japan–EU relations.

Among the Japanese, Europe continues to be seen as the source of high culture. This image, inherited from the Meiji period, goes some way toward explaining why very low volumes of European consumer goods sold at very high prices account for a very high proportion of European exports to Japan. At the other extreme, a negative image of Europe underlies Japan's reaction to European criticism of Japan's trade surpluses and/or practices. The Japanese, who sometimes feel that they are being made scapegoats for the failings of Europeans, see themselves as frugal, hardworking and disciplined. They attribute their trade surpluses to the Europeans' lack of discipline and their inability to work hard. This image echoes Japanese reactions in the 1930s to Western criticism of Japan's dumping abroad of cheap exports and its expansionist foreign policy in Asia (Wilkinson 1990: 85, 201, 218).

On the European side, Japan has been seen as a country of extreme contrasts: an esthetic, and even erotic, paradise, the land of imitators of the West, a monolithic corporation and the source of the Yellow Peril. Until fairly recently, the dominant European attitude was one of superiority vis-a-vis Japan: Europeans were the teachers, and Japanese were the learners or imitators. Consequently, Europeans constantly underestimated Japan and were unable to perceive transformations occurring there. Japan's successes, whether in military conflict or in exporting to Europe, usually caught Europeans by surprise. As an excuse for ignorance, Europeans then blamed Japanese unpredictability and irrationality (Wilkinson 1990: 113, 125, 139, 149, 150).

In the post-World War II period, earlier European images of Japan were drawn upon to provide explanations for Japanese behavior. Japanese trade surpluses in the 1960s and 1970s were explained as the result of dumping of cheap exports. Most Europeans who held this view were unaware that it had its origins in the early twentieth century and ignored the role of industrial planning and R&D in Japanese success since 1945. Practically throughout the entire post-war period, the essentially different nature of the Japanese was held to be the explanation for their economic success. That Japanese lived in little more than rabbit hutches, reported by a 1978 EC Commission Study, captures nicely this impression of difference: the Japanese worked too hard, spent too little on social overheads and saved too much. One widespread fear was voiced by the chairman of I.G. Metall, West Germany's most powerful trade union: "To work like the Japanese ... with their labour conditions and social practices, would be to revert to the Stone Age" (Wilkinson 1990: 208, 215–7). Only Japanese management science found favor among some Western business groups in the 1970s and 1980s.

In this context, bargaining over economic interests had to be supplemented by a dialogue that would combat ignorance and prejudice. States are obviously the main actors when the aim is to modify legislation to promote market access. Are they also the main actors in cultural dialogue? Who are the other actors and what form should cultural dialogue take?

States that wish to project a favorable image of themselves do not need to engage in dialogue with other states or actors: they can always resort to public relations or propaganda. Unfortunately, for states, if Japan's experience in the 1930s is anything to go by, the impact of campaigns of this type on entrenched images is at best uncertain. Japan resorted to radio broadcasts, pamphlets, books, goodwill missions overseas and tours of Japan for foreign visitors and teachers of the Japanese language to defend its foreign policy. Yet their impact on negative Western perceptions of Japan did not seem to be appreciable. In the post-war period, the campaign that sought to capitalize on the holding of the Olympic Games in Tokyo in 1964 and project the image of a technologically advanced country of great scenic beauty did not entirely neutralize the "polluted monster image" of Japan. Official public relations campaigns tend to preach to the converted and are at their most effective when presenting objective information about the country (Wilkinson 1990: 246–8).

A different approach to modifying cultural images comes to mind when we recall that many European images of Japan in the nineteenth century originated from popular literary works and the memoirs of travelers and diplomats. Japan's images of Europe were initially obtained through book learning and, later, through traveling to the West. This being the case, it is logical to suppose that forming new images requires not just inter-state cooperation but also dialogue among those who help to form and disseminate the images, e.g. artists, journalists, scholars and intellectuals. Since Japanese knowledge of Europe is more extensive and more accurate than European knowledge of Japan, a dialogue will probably require more efforts on the European side. Wilkinson argues convincingly that dialogue must attempt to overcome the understandable tendency of European specialists of Japan, who concentrate on history, language and culture, to neglect the present and to highlight the exotic, the untypical and the marginal in Japanese culture. To counteract this tendency, the circle of participants in cultural dialogue must be broadened to non-specialists of Japanese history and culture who happen to be interested in the Japanese experience in their fields. Training of European journalists in the Japanese language would also improve reporting on Japan (Wilkinson 1990: 249–53). In this conception of cultural dialogue, the primary role of states would consist in giving an impetus, through organization and funding, to activities of different types. States themselves would not be the primary actors in the dialogue.

Japanese and EU action plans appear to conform to this conception of cultural dialogue, to which both attach significance and can devote considerable resources. The 1991 Japan–EC Joint Declaration identified the development of academic, cultural and youth exchange programs that would increase knowledge and improve understanding between the peoples of Japan and the EC as one objective of dialogue and cooperation (EU–Japan 1991: 1). The Action Plan for

EU–Japan Cooperation, adopted ten years after the Joint Declaration, declared that mutual understanding would help underpin the wider Japan–EU political and economic relationship. The Plan of action would extend contacts at all levels of academic life; promote training and/or work experience, especially for those early on in their careers; and encourage exchange and contact across civil society (EU–Japan Summit 2001: 21–3). Joint Japanese–EU action sets the context for a cultural dialogue that does seem to fulfil the conditions for dialogue: the participation of all interested parties in the dialogue is sought; state and non-state participants treat each other as equals and are willing to change their perceptions.

The record of Japan–EU relations demonstrates that dialogue between states is not the exclusive means of achieving mutual understanding, far from it. Activities in the private sphere are arguably at the heart of cultural dialogue. In the last three decades, considerable resources have been invested in activities addressed to private citizens, particularly in Europe. These activities included major exhibitions on Japanese arts and styles, which were held in the UK in 1980, in France in 1988, in Belgium in 1989, in Austria in 1990 and in Germany in 1993.

Private actors, particularly those working with Japanese firms in Europe, are in a position to support and reinforce cultural dialogue through a wide range of initiatives broadly aimed at disseminating information and enhancing communication among larger groups of people. These initiatives include exchange of classes between a Japanese school in France and neighboring French schools; donation of a Japanese garden to Düsseldorf in 1975 by a Japanese school in appreciation of the city's donation of land for the school; the construction of a Japanese garden in 1992 in Hasselt, Belgium; the construction of a cultural center in the form of Buddhist temple complex in Niederkassel, Germany, in the same year; and the renovation of Amsterdam's main concert hall by the Japanese Chamber of Commerce and Industry (Conte-Helm 1996: 120–8). Without these diverse initiatives by a multiplicity of actors, cultural dialogue would be confined to a restricted group. These activities have directly contributed, perhaps to a greater extent than official dialogue, to the emergence of a clearly identified Japanese identity among Europeans, who in the past were in the habit of confusing Japan and China (Conte-Helm 1996: 120). The change implies acquisition by Europeans of new knowledge, suggesting that dialogue, reinforced by a host of other activities, has taken place along Todorov's epistemic dimension.

It may be too early to say whether a synthesis of Japanese culture, on the one hand, and the different European cultures, on the other hand, even in limited areas, is emerging. At this point, we can now turn to the question whether bilateral cultural dialogues can be enhanced by a cultural dialogue in ASEM.

ASEM cultural dialogue: toward new synergies?

A dialogue seems to be particularly appropriate for addressing cultural issues. After all, the immediate aim of dialogue is an informed understanding and consensus prior to the adoption of a common strategy or plan of action. Seen in this way, ASEM might appear to be an ideal forum for cultural dialogue. Good reasons can be adduced in support of the view that cultural dialogue among a larger group of participants will create synergies in ways that bilateral dialogue cannot. The work of the ASEF, by its very nature, creates the conditions for dialogue among those who mold and disseminate cultural images. That said, the impact of inter-state cultural dialogue, which has become more prominent with the holding of meetings of culture ministers, is more difficult to assess.

A broader dialogue between Asia and Europe within ASEM might add a qualitative dimension to a Japan–EU dialogue (or China–EU, South Korea–EU dialogues, for that matter) because of the existence of common Asian (mis)perceptions of Europe and/or common European (mis)perceptions of Asia. These commonalities could serve as the foundation of dialogues on crosscutting themes among journalists, artists, scholars and intellectuals. Cost-effectiveness would be the primary advantage of activities organized in this manner: Asian perceptions of Europe and/or European perceptions of Asia in a particular area could be addressed simultaneously by participants from several Asian and European countries. Even a particular European (mis)conception that concerns only Japan at the moment – for instance, the idea that Japanese institutions pose structural impediments to imports – might still be worth discussing in a larger context, if other Asian countries that are encountering trade problems with Europe are likely to be assimilated to the Japanese image. On the other hand, some images and perceptions might be prominent only in Japan–EU relations. Discussion of European fears of the Yellow Peril might have less meaning for the smaller Southeast Asian countries than for China and Japan. Conversely, a dialogue on the consequences of European colonialism in Asia might not be a priority for Japan but may be of great interest to the former colonies of Britain, France and the Netherlands. Defining cultural issues in more or less narrow terms or in ways that render them suitable for discussion by a more or less large group of states should not pose too many challenges. Hence, it is plausible to assume that an ASEM dialogue could enrich bilateral dialogues without necessarily replacing them.

In the ASEM framework, the ASEF, proposed at ASEM 1 by Singapore and now funded by all ASEM participants, was assigned the task of promoting better mutual understanding between Asia and Europe through greater intellectual, cultural and people-to-people exchanges. In the ASEF's conception, intellectual exchange seeks to promote better understanding of the diversity of Asian cultures and civilizations; to assess their ability to face unconventional threats; to mitigate the ecological, social and economic impact of global warming; to promote a fair gender balance, better education and good health; to fight intolerance and distrust; and to reflect on the ways of ensuring a better and safer life for Asia and Europe. Cultural exchange examines issues ranging from security, financial and economic issues to gender, human rights, labor and the environment through roundtables, fora, workshops, conferences and lectures. Cultural exchange aims at nurturing artistic creativity and facilitating encounters among young people for future artistic cooperation and career opportunities; initiating and promoting cultural networks as key structures for the development of sustainable links; supporting the Asia–Europe dimension in international festivals and cultural events; channeling information and acting as interface between cultural policy makers and artists and facilitating exchange through cultural information platforms. ASEF organizes fora for young photographers; art and music camps; a dance forum; a museum network and film development meetings. People-to-people exchange programs strengthen networks among the next generation of leaders from Asia and Europe through exchanges and cooperation in education; contacts, dialogue and cooperation among youth and youth organizations as well as among leaders in key sectors. Activities include the two-week ASEF-University; youth dialogue; young volunteers exchange; youth camp; training program for youth leaders; young parliamentarians' meeting; young entrepreneurs' forum; young leaders' symposia and program for emerging public sector leaders (Asia–Europe Foundation 2005).

As the enumeration demonstrates, ASEF's activities, which are said to have totaled over 300 in ten years, involve the participation of very diverse groups of people who contribute to the molding and dissemination of images in different cultural areas. Thus, they may contribute to the emergence of new images and, in the very long term, new values. Of course, an accurate assessment of the concrete impact of ASEF's activities requires knowledge of the particular area and Asia–Europe relations in that area, a task that is beyond the scope of the present work. Let us simply note some major differences between Japan–EU and ASEM cultural dialogues.

The cofinancing schemes off ASEF, under which most activities are organized, require that funding be obtained from other sources. Unlike in the case of the Japan–EU dialogue, the link between economic interests and cultural dialogue is less evident, if not less immediate. Second, the concrete impact of ASEF activities on particular bilateral relations (e.g. UK–Malaysia or Sweden–Thailand) or on images of particular countries is less easy to ascertain. Third, one cannot avoid the impression that the degree of involvement of states in ASEF's activities seems to be higher. Funding is provided by ASEM participants (states and the EU), and ASEM is governed by a Board of Governors that represents states. The Board determines ASEF's policies, programs and priorities and approves its budget. Although individual governors may not necessarily be civil servants or officials, they do represent states.

Some scholars believe that ASEF must meet the challenge of expanding into other areas, particularly those that may not normally receive financial assistance (European Institute of Asian Studies 2003: 7). This challenge amounts to a demand to include all parties interested in cultural dialogue in ASEF's activities. Civil society groups have complained that their participation in ASEF's work has not been institutionalized. At the Barcelona consultation (2004), they expressed their frustration with ASEF, whom they accused of catering to the elite section of civil society. In their view, ASEF's network was not broad enough to represent civil society, excluding the marginalized sectors of society, such as indigenous peoples and peasants. ASEF, they argued, should provide financial support for the activities of NGOs that are critical of ASEM (ASEF *et al.* 2004).

The complaints expressed at Barcelona raise the question of the relationship between cultural dialogue and political dialogue. As we saw in the previous section, in Japan–EU cultural relations, non-state actors, particularly firms, played roles that at times were as important, if not more important, than those of states. This relationship between state and civil society cannot be easily replicated within ASEF for at least two reasons. First, differences in levels of economic development translate into differential capacities of individuals to participate in activities. To take the example of the ASEF University, a two-week activity bringing together undergraduates from Asia and Europe for a series of lectures around a theme, ASEF provides for boarding and lodging in the host institution. However, each participant receives only a partial subsidy (approximately a third) for travel costs. For Europeans, funding for travel to Asia is costly but not prohibitive. The same cannot be said for students coming from the least developed countries in Asia. The second reason is the composition of ASEM's board. In the Japan–EU dialogue, all partners to dialogue are democratic states, whereas in ASEM, the diversity in political systems, notably within the Asian group, is plain for all to see. It is to be expected that the authoritarian states will be reluctant, to say the least, to envisage participation in their midst of non-state actors critical of states.

The difference in degree of participation of state actors between the Japan–EU dialogue and ASEM cultural dialogue manifests itself in the forms of state participation: an informal retreat at ASEM 4 (2002) and meetings of culture ministers. In the ASEM context, a retreat is informal if there is fixed agenda; exchanges among participants are spontaneous; participants are seated in alphabetical order rather than by regional grouping; simultaneous interpretation in all languages is dispensed with in favor of consecutive interpretation; and no records are kept (Bersick 2004c). The informal character of dialogue makes it extremely difficult to assess the extent to which dialogue has actually taken place. There is no gainsaying that it is useful to convince ministers to change their images and perceptions of other countries/cultures. However, a focus on the perceptions of leaders can hardly be a primary goal of cultural dialogue. It is only in authoritarian systems that a leader who has experienced a change of heart can impose the new orientation on the bureaucracy and on the population and mobilize them on this basis. A scenario of this kind is the complete antithesis of any type of dialogue.

Since ASEM 4, the trend toward institutionalization of the state role in the cultural dialogue is perceptible. A year after the retreat, ASEM ministers of culture met for the first time at Beijing (December 2003). The main follow-up action decided was to organize a second ministerial conference on cultures and civilizations, which duly took place in France in June 2005. According to the Action Plan adopted by the ministers, henceforth cultural ministers would meet regularly, and permanent cultural points of contact would be designated within each ASEM participant. One wonders if the functions of one or the other or both will not overlap with those of ASEF's governors, all of whom are state representatives. The only new contribution to the substance of cultural dialogue was a suggestion to expand its scope to cover sustainable and responsible tourism. Officially, the demands of civil society for institutionalized representation within ASEF or funding for civil society organizations critical of ASEM as a whole were not taken into account.

Having in mind the results of Asia–Europe dialogue in ASEM's different pillars, we can now draw conclusions and suggest possible ways forward.

Summary

The political and cultural issues that could constitute areas of common interest for Asia and Europe are very numerous. In theory, regional security in Asia is one such area. In practice, divisions among Asian states; the balance of power in Asia, characterized by US dominance; and the European and Asian inability to define European security interests in Asia have posed considerable obstacles in the way of such a dialogue. Two crises in Asia in the late 1990s justify the tentative conclusion that for the EU to play a role in Asian security, dialogue with Asia in ASEM was not really indispensable. On East Timor, the EU provided financial assistance to the territory and imposed sanctions on Indonesia without taking into consideration regional views. As regards the Korean Peninsula, the EU made much more substantial contributions to the KEDO than any of the Southeast Asian states or China did, as part of a bargain with Japan.

In the area of international security, ASEM has encountered even more formidable difficulties in defining areas of common interest. ASEM discussions of these issues are the most vulnerable to the criticism of ASEM as a talk shop. Recent appeals by foreign ministers for a focus on global challenges are not of such a nature as to inspire confidence in their ability to circumscribe the extremely broad agenda of foreign ministers' and leaders' meetings. Assuming that ASEM participants are able to engage in serious dialogue as a basis for future action, they may well have to admit that civil society organizations are interested parties that should be allowed to participate in dialogue and that they should cooperate with them in undertaking joint action. This is one of the fundamental conditions for dialogue identified by Todorov and Habermas.

In the wake of 9/11, the fight against international terrorism has acquired greater prominence as an area of common interest, in which dialogue will be the prelude to joint action. A unique ASEM approach, to be contrasted with that of the United States, is said to be emerging, although claims of this kind cannot always resist critical examination. The greater risk is that in the name of anti-terrorism, Europeans might make concessions to Asians that infringe human rights and that Europeans themselves might increasingly tend to consider Asians as the objects of the fight against terrorism rather than just participants in the dialogue.

The China–EU human rights dialogue was examined as a possible paradigm for Asia–Europe dialogue on human rights, a priori an unlikely area of common interest. In the bilateral dialogue, the interest of China in dialogue is questionable; the conflict between EU's political and economic aims is never very far from the surface; and a set of interested parties, Chinese and European human rights NGOs, are excluded from the dialogue. The bilateral dialogue has increasingly been restricted to the holding of human rights seminars, whose claims of making progress are not always matched by genuine improvements on the ground, as the EU itself admits. In these circumstances, it is not likely that expanding the circle of participants to other Asian countries will facilitate dialogue: the other Asian countries can hardly be expected to criticize China when facing the EU. On the EU side, pressure on China at ASEM would have jeopardized the EU's aim of achieving a consensus on WTO issues. The controversy over Myanmar provides further illustrations of the contradictions in the EU policy. EU opposition did lead to the cancellation of several ASEM ministerial meetings, without ever really paralyzing the work of TFAP and IPAP working groups and discussion of WTO issues.

Cultural issues, which were originally subordinated to the economic dialogue, acquired greater importance in ASEM following 9/11. In order to assess the prospects of such dialogue, the Japan–EU cultural dialogue was examined as a possible model. In the bilateral relationship, economic tensions were based on and aggravated by cultural images developed for over 150 years. Consequently, reshaping cultural images was identified as a common interest by Japan and the European states. They play a role in the dialogue by identifying priorities and providing funding. That said, it is non-state actors, particularly Japanese firms in Europe, that are actually carrying out a variety of joint actions that can shape cultural images.

ASEM cultural dialogue, through the ASEF, could add a qualitative dimension to bilateral cultural dialogues that address crosscutting themes and involve the participation of a large number of sectors in different countries. In the last few years, ASEF work is being paralleled by meetings of ASEM culture ministers, signaling a greater role for states in cultural dialogue. Possible overlap with ASEF's work and the participation of non-state actors in cultural dialogue are issues that will have to be resolved as the dialogue is pursued.

6 ASEM at the crossroads and the way forward

The Asia–Europe Meeting (ASEM) process is often cited as a manifestation of a new phenomenon in international relations – interregionalism. This book has been skeptical about claims based on realist, liberal and constructivist approaches that ASEM represents the emergence of a new interregional level at which international actors perform specific functions. The existence of a level presupposes the existence of specific opportunities for and constraints on social action that are different from those at existing levels and thus cannot be lightly presumed.

This book has taken as its starting point the oft-repeated declaration by ASEM participants that they are engaged in a dialogue based on equality, mutual respect and mutual benefit. The concept of dialogue was defined with the help of an approach that synthesizes the work of Tzvetan Todorov and of Jürgen Habermas. In a dialogue, all interested parties should participate; should treat each other as equals; should use reasoned arguments to back up their position; refrain from coercion; be willing to change their minds; and express the outcomes of dialogue in differentiated (i.e. specific) propositions. According to Todorov, the outcome might be either acceptance by one participant of the other participant's views, no matter how alien they seem or a synthesis of the participants' views that is demonstrably new. Thomas Risse points out that in an international setting, dialogue may be a preliminary to negotiation or may take place during the negotiation. In Habermas's view, great powers should be willing to adopt a broader view of their national interest. We have argued that any attempts to analyze the ability and willingness of states to engage in dialogue must take into account structural conditions in a particular issue-area at the appropriate level: national, regional or international.

Several general features of ASEM as a dialogue were identified. Its scope as a dialogue between Asia and Europe aroused controversy. Asia and Europe disagreed about which Asian and European states would be admitted to participate in ASEM, as such participation was perceived as challenging economic and political interests that each side held dear. Nevertheless, in 2002 and 2004, the controversy was resolved with the simultaneous admission of Myanmar, widely criticized in Europe and even in Asia for its human rights record, and Asian and European states that the European Union (EU) supported. ASEM's character as a dialogue between equals has been used by the EU primarily to exclude development cooperation as an area of common interest. ASEM's supposed character as a dialogue in the Asian way ignores the structural conditions in which the Asian way is held to have succeeded and may thus not replicate the socialization process among Asian and European elites that the Asian way triggered. A final feature of ASEM is the exclusion of non-state actors. The Asia–Europe People's Forum's (AEPF) criticism of the EU's economic agenda would make it an ally for developing Asian states, were it not for its advocacy of democratization and human rights. Conversely, its critique of the EU's economic agenda is responsible for the EU's reluctance to accept it as a partner, in spite of the fact that its political agenda supports that of the EU.

This book's three chapters on economic issues cast doubt on the widespread assessment that ASEM has made significant progress in economic issues. Given European firms' inability to match Japanese trade and investment activities in East Asia, the EU's goal is to obtain market access there through implementation of Uruguay Round agreements; launching of a new World Trade Organization (WTO) round, with Asian support for EU positions; and modification of East Asian laws. ASEM offered the EU the possibility of lobbying a large group of Asian states at the same time on a wide range of issues. On the Asian side, no economic goals were shared by all states when the ASEM process was started. Singapore and Thailand did agree on market access, with the latter hoping that the benefits of European integration could be extended to non-member states. The Thai demand was incompatible with the very notion of European integration, and for this reason it was not taken up at ASEM 1 or since then.

Since its launching, ASEM has not fulfilled the function of a forum for dialogue in the areas of economic and social development or economic cooperation. Simply put, the EU has little interest in a dialogue on these issues in the ASEM framework. An external shock – the Asian financial crisis – compelled the EU, which was initially unsympathetic to the Asian plight, to heed Asian calls for assistance, leading to the European agreement to establish an ASEM Trust Fund (ATF) at ASEM 2 (1998). While the ATF created a channel for funding social and financial projects in the crisis-affected countries, the EU's insistence that the ATF be administered by the World Bank introduced into the Asia–Europe dialogue a powerful third party pursuing an agenda of deregulation, privatization and liberalization and not disposed to make concessions on this agenda. Whether the Trust Fund is continued in a modified form so as to encompass Asia–Europe development and economic cooperation remains to be seen.

The EU's willingness to let the World Bank administer the ATF contrasts with its reluctance to agree to a social dialogue between Asia and Europe involving the participation of non-state actors. The scope of the Asia–Europe People's Forum (AEPF) demands that a "Social Forum" must discuss is certainly wide-ranging, whether in terms of categories of individuals (women, children, minorities, migrants and workers) or in terms of nature of issues [e.g. reform of the international financial architecture, the International Monetary Fund (IMF) and the World Bank, core labor standards]. However, this is hardly the main reason for the EU refusal to recognize it as partners in the dialogue. The EU attitude is consistent with the goal of seeking access to the markets of Asian countries. A Social Forum might not only antagonize the Asian countries and jeopardize the consensus that the EU seeks on WTO issues; it might also generate demands for EU financial assistance. The meeting of ASEM Ministers of Labor and Employment in 2006 is an indirect response to civil society demands, but the ministers' inability to specify the areas of dialogue may threaten the pursuit of dialogue.

The idea that ASEM can contribute to multilateralism is closely linked to the EU's market access strategy. When ASEM is urged to facilitate progress in other international organizations, in reality, it is primarily the WTO that the EU has in mind. The Asian financial crisis unexpectedly and timidly opened a small window of opportunity for discussing international financial reform. This window has been firmly shut since the ASEM finance ministers' meeting (FinMM) in Kobe in 2001, largely due to the EU's inability and unwillingness to take a broader view of its self-interest and to enter into a dialogue with the crisis-affected countries. The EU's attitude is in turn a product of the constraint imposed on its action by the long-term trend of European integration, which has been toward the liberalization of internal movements of capital (i.e. within the EU) and external movements of capital (involving non-EU members). The efforts of several crisis-affected Asian countries to use ASEM, in the immediate aftermath of the crisis, as a forum to express their views on the reform of the international financial architecture served them little purpose.

As for the ASEM dialogue on WTO issues, it is mainly the EU that is interested in it. The EU's goals are to ensure implementation by the Asian states of the Uruguay Round agreements and to obtain their agreement to a new round on Singapore issues (trade facilitation, competition, investment and transparency in government procurement). Contrary to expectations expressed by European leaders at ASEM 1 and ASEM 2, it is not ASEM that gives an impetus to WTO negotiations. Rather than being a sounding board for new ideas for the WTO, ASEM appears to resemble an echo chamber for positions and disagreements articulated within the WTO. Examination of the actions of Asians and Europeans before and during three WTO Ministerial Conferences (Seattle 1999, Doha 2001 and Cancún 2003) confirms, with very little room for doubt, that ASEM has not contributed to resolving issues on which the developing Asian countries and the EU disagree. The apparent consensus expressed in ASEM statements is so broad and general that it permits each participant to maintain its position while giving the impression to the other participants and to observers that it has modified its position.

The reasons for the failure of attempts at dialogue within ASEM on WTO issues lie in the structure of ASEM and in the unwillingness of the Asian developed countries and the EU to adopt a broader view of their self-interests and to take into account the developing countries' interests. The Asian group reproduces the division at the WTO between developed (Japan, South Korea, Singapore) and developing countries (China, Indonesia, Malaysia, the

Philippines and Thailand), with the developed countries being the objective allies of the EU. The EU's inflexible attitude is in turn a product of the constraints imposed on its action by the weakness of the European position in Asia and of the fact that on practically all issues, it is the EU that is seeking the agreement of other WTO members. The EU, with the tacit support of Asian developed countries, seeks to use ASEM precisely to counteract the resistance of Asian developing countries at the WTO, without showing any signs of understanding for the latter's positions, let alone a willingness to make concessions. At the WTO at least, all interested state parties (including all developing countries) are present, giving the Asian developing countries possibilities of entering into alliances with Asian, African and Latin American countries, reducing power differences between the EU and themselves, and engaging in bargaining across issues that can compel the EU (and the United States) to take their interests into account.

It cannot be excluded that the Asian developing countries, which are on the receiving end of EU requests, agree to general statements on the WTO at ASEM precisely because they are aware that ASEM is not a negotiating forum; that any apparent consensus does not commit them to any specific concession and that bargaining at the WTO can always offer the chance to modify the apparent consensus achieved at ASEM. If the above analysis is accurate, then it is fair to say that dialogue as defined earlier did not take place at ASEM.

The EU and Asian countries seek access to each other's markets for their goods, while in the area of investment it is Asia that wishes to attract EU investment. In this context, trade facilitation and investment promotion would appear to be in the interests of all parties. However, the issues for dialogue within the Investment Promotion Action Plan (IPAP) and Trade Facilitation Action Plan (TFAP) frameworks are nearly identical to those that the EU wishes to see negotiated in a new WTO round. The EU approach in ASEM is similar to its approach in the Regulatory Reform Dialogue with Japan, which is thus a paradigm for Asia–Europe dialogue, with one significant difference: in the Japan–EU relationship, the two sides are more or less equal in bargaining strength. Although Japan is under pressure to reduce its surpluses with the EU, it is aware that European states seek Japanese foreign direct investment (FDI) in Europe. Europe, for its part, has at its disposal the Trade Barriers Regulation (TBR). Even the Japanese and European weaknesses complement each other: Japanese firms still face occasionally tariff barriers in Europe, whereas non-tariff barriers in Japan seem to be the primary obstacles to European firms' activities. For this reason, the Regulatory Reform Dialogue (RRD) comes close to being a negotiation rather than a simple dialogue.

In the ASEM process, the TFAP and IPAP progress reports reveal that the only option available to the Asian countries, in the EU view, is abolition of their practices characterized by the EU as barriers to trade and investment. In spite of the fact that it is the stronger international partner, the EU is unwilling to consider the development rationales advanced by the latter. If only the Asian states are expected to modify their domestic laws and regulations, the implication is that they are not treated as equals by the Europeans; instead, they appear to be the object of EU policy. The Asians' growing realization that they will be unable to obtain a consensus with the EU, much less concessions from the latter, probably accounts for loss of momentum of TFAP and IPAP implementation processes since 2002.

Turning now to political dialogue, it should be kept in mind that it was upon EU insistence that political dialogue was incorporated into the ASEM agenda. Yet, it is the Europeans who are faced with the dilemma of reconciling their economic and political interests. The assessment of political dialogue in ASEM must differentiate between human rights and security issues, which are further subdivided into regional security and international security. In regional security issues, the interest in dialogue is not uniformly shared. The Europeans are more interested in East Asian security than are the Asians in European security. Furthermore, whereas the Europeans have at least devoted some energy to defining a possible role for themselves in Asian security, the Asians do not even have a coherent or unified vision of the role of Europe in Asian security. At the same time, the weakness of Asian institutions, such as the ASEAN Regional Forum (ARF), allowed Europe to perform security tasks in the Korean Peninsula and in East Timor, without the need for dialogue with the Asians. In the international security area, even less progress was made in dialogue, at least until 9/11. The fact that many of the issues that were proposed for ASEM dialogue were already on the agenda of other international organizations, and the absence in ASEM of most or all of the states concerned with these issues, may be cited as the main reasons for the stagnation. The fight against international terrorism has revived political dialogue in that it is capable of bridging the gap between regional and international security. A risk to be avoided is that of identifying Asian states and their citizens with the new security threats.

The new priority accorded to international terrorism naturally leads to a discussion of the ASEM dialogue on human rights. Based on an analysis of the China–EU dialogue, it can be convincingly argued that an expanded forum like ASEM does not offer the required conditions for dialogue. The authoritarian states in Asia are not interested in it; the EU is torn between pursuit of its economic interests and the promotion of human rights, and human rights nongovernmental organizations (NGOs), which can justifiably be considered interested parties, are marginalized. In at least one instance, the EU has proved to be receptive to Asian concerns: the ASEM human rights dialogue has been relegated to unofficial seminars that are now considered under the heading of cultural issues and not under political issues. In the China–EU relationship, these seminars have been successfully used by China to deflect EU criticism of its human rights record. In the wake of 9/11, a further EU concession, in the form of recognition of the need to take into account domestic laws in the fight against terrorism, tacitly accepts internal security laws that the EU would have earlier criticized on human rights grounds.

In ASEM's third pillar, cultural dialogue is intimately linked with economic interests. Stereotypes and misperceptions can aggravate, and be exaggerated by, tensions arising from trade and investment imbalances. As the example of Japan–EU cultural relations illustrates, cultural dialogue is more likely to have an enduring impact if they involve non-state actors who contribute to the formation and dissemination of cultural images in a wide variety of fields. In ASEM, the circle of participants in a dialogue is expanded considerably, making it possible to address crosscutting themes, to reach out to a broader range of actors and to involve a larger number of countries. ASEM's main mechanisms have been the Asia–Europe Foundation (ASEF) and since 9/11, leaders' retreats and ministerial meetings. ASEM is confronted with the challenge of drawing on the full potential of civil society's contribution to dialogue and allowing the entire range of civil society actors, even those critical of the ASEM process, to take part in the activities of the ASEF.

Throughout ASEM's existence, dialogue has been seen as a preliminary to negotiation (e.g. on WTO issues, for the EU, and reform of the international financial architecture, for the Asians) or to joint action (e.g. on poverty alleviation or economic cooperation, for the Asians). The experience confirms a criticism raised against Habermas's theory: the first major obstacle to be overcome is the unwillingness, particularly of powerful actors, to engage in dialogue. As seen in Chapter 2, the EU's attitude has kept poverty alleviation off the ASEM agenda. Moreover, the combined opposition of European and Asian state actors has effectively prevented a dialogue on social issues that involves participation by non-state actors. Neither Todorov nor Habermas provides us with theoretical means of grappling with this practical bottleneck.

One circumstance that weakened European opposition to a dialogue on development issues was an unexpected shock: the Asian financial crisis exerted pressure on the EU that eventually led to the creation of an ATF. Another circumstance – the perseverance of marginalized actors meeting in the AEPF – has not yet generated a sufficient degree of consensus allowing for the establishment of a Social Forum. At least it has compelled state actors to give the impression that they are responding to the concerns expressed by the AEPF.

A second lesson to be drawn from the ASEM experience is that when powerful actors are convinced to enter into a dialogue, or indeed when they initiate a dialogue, weaker actors continue to remain at a disadvantage for all the protestations of equality and mutual respect. Powerful actors, for reasons that we cannot go into here, find it extremely difficult to respect the ideal conditions of dialogue, particularly those that require them to treat other participants as equal partners rather than as the objects of their lobbying or persuasion, and to show a willingness to change their views. Weaker actors can hope to compensate somewhat for the de facto inequality through the formation of partnerships or alliances with other weaker actors, or perhaps with one or two stronger actors. Both possibilities are precluded by ASEM: the former, because no developing countries from other regions participate in ASEM, and the latter, because a divided Asian group faces a more or less united European group, notably in economic issues. In these circumstances, it is premature to speak of "interregional" dialogue, although this would not necessarily entail a breakdown of the process.

In any case, weaker actors may have no choice but to go through the motions of dialogue and to give lip service to the consensus that has been reached, without necessarily modifying their own views or behavior after the dialogue or outside the dialogue forum. The fact that Association of Southeast Asian Nations (ASEAN) members from 2002 onward negotiated free trade agreements with the US and Japan, in parallel to ASEM work on TFAP and IPAP, seems to bear out this analysis. The EU, by deciding in 2006 to launch Free Trade Area (FTA) negotiations with ASEAN and South Korea, apparently has reached a similar conclusion.

Although the EU has adopted a two-year timeframe for the negotiations, their success is by no means guaranteed. That said, it is likely that the EU's 2006 market access strategy will have far-reaching implications for ASEM in the same way that the 1996 market access strategy was crucial for ASEM's launching. The EU's division of the Asian group into subgroups, the creation of separate negotiating fora and the overlap between the negotiations and the TFAP/IPAP – all these circumstances will inevitably raise questions regarding the utility of ASEM as a forum for dialogue between Asia as a group and Europe as a group.

From a theoretical point of view, the conclusion is that ASEM has thus far not been able to create new and relatively enduring opportunities for or constraints on action. Thus, an "interregional" level cannot be said to have emerged as a result of ASEM. From the practical perspective, recent developments would seem to exclude two courses of action that have on various occasions been raised with a view to ensuring that ASEM promotes joint action: institutionalism and interregionalism. ASEM's lack of achievements has sometimes (mis)led academics to believe that the solution lies in institutionalization. Yet, ASEM participants have consistently resisted the recommendation made by the Asia–Europe Vision Group's (AEVG's) recommendation to set up a lean but effective secretariat, and for good reason. On the European side, there was apprehension that Europe would end up funding a new bureaucracy. For Asians, particularly the Asian developing countries, institutionalization would entail the risk of domination by the EU. At present, the European Commission is the only participant that has continuously acted as a coordinator of ASEM activities since the initiation of the ASEM process. Consequently, it possesses a considerable advantage over the other participants. We only have to recall the European Commission's failure to report accurately Malaysian comments on antidumping and Chinese and Japanese comments on international standards to realize how a secretariat can shape members' views and positions. From civil society's perspective, a new institution would almost inevitably embody the EU's neoliberal ideology, since it would be supported by the developed Asian countries. These debates would lose their pertinence if separate negotiating fora were created between the EU and subgroups of Asian states.

The second path that ASEM has been urged to take is interregionalism, understood here as an ideology that compels the production of a consensus based on the artificial assumption that there are two – and only two – positions to be synthesized or reconciled, one Asian and the other European. As we have seen, the Asian group is divided between developed and developing countries on a range of economic and political issues. Consequently, the developing Asian states went through the motions of dialogue precisely because it was not binding and left them free to modify their positions at the WTO and to pursue bargaining strategies with the United States and Japan. Such behavior is the very antithesis of dialogue. Perhaps the time has come to acknowledge the improbability of Asia as a group and European states as a group arriving at consensus, through dialogue, on a number of crucial issues.

A more fruitful approach to Asia–Europe cooperation, understood here as a combination of dialogue and joint action, could be borrowed from the European practices of multilevel governance, variable geometry (*géométrie* variable) and several speeds (*à plusieurs vitesses*). The levels, loosely speaking, would be national (Asian and European), regional (EU), bilateral Asian–European and multilateral Asian–European. In other words, cooperation would not be necessarily confined to the ASEM framework. The nature of the issues (economic, political and cultural) would determine the geometry or composition of the participating states and the speed or extent of cooperation that they wish to undertake. For example, on cultural matters, some initiatives can be taken by individual European and Asian states. The teaching of the languages of Asian immigrants in European schools could help raise awareness of Asia and at the same time facilitate community integration (ASEF *et al.* 2004). At the bilateral level, Asian and European firms could collaborate in sponsoring activities similar to those carried out by Japanese and European firms in Europe in the last three decades. Consideration should be given to civil society and trade union proposals that ASEF contribute to funding their activities and accept civil society/trade union representative(s) on its Board of Governors.

On human rights issues, resistance to dialogue by Asian states to human rights dialogue may be circumvented through action taken by individual European states and by the EU at the UN. In this undertaking, they should cooperate with European human rights NGOs, which in turn should be encouraged to cooperate with Asian human rights NGOs. Together, they can seek funding for human rights projects under the European Initiative on Democracy and Human Rights (EIDHR), which already funds many projects of this kind in individual Asian countries. Two significant challenges would involve conceptualization and implementation of human rights projects in authoritarian states and the need to involve human rights NGOs from the new EU member states. In the area of international security, it appears that Asia–Europe cooperation, whether at bilateral or multilateral levels, will increasingly concentrate on international terrorism. All the more reason, it is essential to involve civil society representatives in any dialogue, so that Asian countries and citizens are not tacitly or unconsciously identified with the adversaries, and human rights issues are not marginalized.

Dialogue on economic and social issues will not necessarily be any less contentious at other levels than within ASEM. European and Asian civil society organizations, which were excluded from dialogue during the ATF's first two phases, should direct more of their lobby work toward national governments. The AEPF's goal should be to avoid exclusion from any future mechanism that some Asian states are proposing in place of the ATF. Greater attention should be paid to the EU's bilateral dialogue with individual Asian states when preparing country strategies and conceptualizing, implementing and evaluating official development assistance (ODA) projects. Particular emphasis should be placed on lobbying in Europe, which after all is the group that is pushing for Asian acceptance of a new WTO agenda and modifications of Asian laws. The difficulties of arriving at an agreement within the EU are such that once a common position is adopted, the chances of the position being modified through civil society pressure in the course of dialogue of ministers or heads of state are uncertain. Within the ASEM framework, the loss of momentum of IPAP and TFAP should be recognized for what it is – a de facto moratorium on discussion of the two plans and of WTO issues. It should also be admitted that the chances that all Asian states will agree to a process focusing on core labor standards and organized along the lines of the TFAP and IPAP processes are slim. Thus, the alternative strategy would be to allow like-minded groups of individual Asian and European states and civil society organizations to form for the purpose of engaging in dialogue and joint action on issues of interest to them.

In the variable geometry and multi-speed approach proposed, the groups of states would be composed of subsets of the Asian and European groups within ASEM. In the last few years, many ASEM proposals have been put forward on this basis, but these have often turned out to be one-off activities (usually conferences), with little or no concrete results. One sometimes gets the impression that several projects were presented primarily for publicity purposes. In an alternative approach proposed by Rüland (2001), as many groups could be organized as there are issues identified by state and non-state actors. Each group would be authorized to recommend appropriate action to states and to other international organizations and perhaps even to carry out concrete cooperation projects. In this manner, it would be possible for subsets of Asian and European actors to discover common interests, rather than having the interests imposed by an "interregional" perspective. The approach advocated here would introduce three significant innovations: it would be extended to crucial economic and social issues (i.e. core labor standards); concrete cooperation would be a goal of dialogue, thus helping to make the relationship sustainable; and non-state actors would be allowed to participate.

The Asian states could very easily accommodate themselves to this kind of reorientation, given the absence of any structures that bind them and oblige them to arrive at common positions. On the other hand, this reorientation would pose challenges to the EU member states, which are increasingly seeking to coordinate their foreign policies. Ironically enough, the EU aspiration for a Common Foreign and Security Policy (CFSP) might be yet turn out to be a major obstacle to a revitalization of Asian–European dialogue and cooperation. The alternative to reorganizing ASEM would be the pursuit of a simulacrum of dialogue.

Dialogue and joint action between Asian and European actors will be long-term processes. They antedated ASEM, but ASEM's merit is to have mobilized state and non-state actors in a wide variety of fields through a new political impetus. Nevertheless, even if states and non-state actors are all inspired by the best intentions, significant areas of disagreement will persist. In addition, the shadow cast by the past on Asian–European relations cannot be ignored. Throughout most of the modern period, Asians have been alternatively persuaded or compelled to learn and to assimilate European values, technology and systems. It should not be too much to expect the Europeans to go beyond merely listening in a dialogue to Asian views. They should be willing to assimilate Asian values, technology and systems. Lest this be taken as a validation of the "Asian values" championed by authoritarian states, it should be emphasized that "Asia" is as diverse, if not even more so, than Europe. Perhaps one major challenge facing a dialogue between Asians and Europeans, coming from different sectors, representing a diversity of views within each sector, and interacting at different levels will be that of developing new sets of values, technology and systems that are truly syntheses – not recognizably Asian or European but nourished by Asian and European sources.

Bibliography

Acharya, A. (1998) "Collective identity and conflict management in Southeast Asia," in E. Adler and M. Barnett (eds) *Security Communities*, Cambridge: Cambridge University Press.

—— (2003) "Regional institutions and Asian security order," in M. Alagappa (ed.) *Asian Security Order. Institutional and Normative Features*, Stanford: Stanford University Press.

Adam, R. (1993) *Attività Normative e di Controllo dell'OIL e Evoluzione della Comunità Internazionale*, Milano: Dott. A. Giuffè Editore.

Agcaoili, L. (2004) "EU puts on hold free-trade deal with ASEAN bloc," ABS–CBN News, 14 September Available online at: www.bilaterals.org/articleprint.php3?id_article=630 (accessed 5 March 2007).

Ahnlid, A. (1996) "Comparing GATT and GATS: regime creation under and after hegemony," *Review of International Political Economy*, 3: 65–94.

Albala, N. (1998) "Un verrou juridique contre les Etats? Les dangers de l'Accord multilatéral sur l'investissement," *Le Monde Diplomatique*, 528: 4–5.

Algieri, F. (2002) "EU economic relations with China: an institutionalist perspective," in R. L. Edmonds (ed.) *China and Europe Since 1978: A European Perspective*, Cambridge: Cambridge University Press.

Arnason, J. P. (1991) "Modernity as project and as field of tensions," in A. Honneth and H. Joas (eds) *Communicative Action. Essays on Jürgen Habermas's "The Theory of Communicative Action,"* trans. J. Gaines and D. L. Jones, Cambridge, MA: The MIT Press.

Ashley, R. (1986) "The poverty of neorealism," in R. O. Keohane (ed.) *Neorealism and Its Critics*, New York: Columbia University Press.

Asia–Europe Business Forum (AEBF) 1 (1996) *Chairman's Statement*, Paris, 14–15 October.

—— 2 (1997) *Chairman's Statement*, Bangkok, 13–14 November.

—— 3 (1998) *Report to Summit Leaders by Sir Martin Laing, Chairman of the British Overseas Trade Board*, London, 3 April.

—— 4 (1999) *Chairman's Statement*, Seoul, 29 September to 1 October.

—— 5 (2000) *Chairman's Statement*, Vienna, 28–30 September.

—— 6 (2001) *Chairman's Statement*, Singapore, 9 October.

—— 7 (2002) *Chairman's Statement*, Copenhagen, 18–20 September.

Asia–Europe Cooperation Framework (AECF), Seoul, 21 October 2000.

Asia–Europe Foundation (2002) *The Fourth Informal ASEM Seminar on Human Rights*, Singapore: Asia–Europe Foundation.

—— (2005) "Intellectual Exchange, People To People Exchange, Cultural Exchange,"

Singapore: Asia–Europe Foundation. Available online at: www.asef.org/# (accessed 20 October 2007).

Asia–Europe Foundation, Casa Asia, International Institute of Asian Studies, Japan Centre for International Exchange (2004) *The Barcelona Report: Recommendations from Civil Society on Asia-Europe Relations addressed to the ASEM Leaders; Connecting Civil Society from Asia and Europe. An informal consultation, 16–18 June 2004 Barcelona, Spain*, Singapore: Asia–Europe Foundation.

Asia–Europe Meeting (ASEM) 1 (1996) *Chairman's Statement*, Bangkok, 2 March.

—— 2 (1998a) *Chairman's Statement*, London, 4 April.

—— 2 (1998b) *The Financial and Economic Situation in Asia*, London, 3 April.

—— 3 (2000) *Chairman's Statement*, Seoul, 21 October .

—— 4 (2002a) *Chairman's Statement*, Copenhagen, 22–24 September.

—— 4 (2002b) *Cooperation Program on Fighting International Terrorism*, Copenhagen, 22–24 September.

—— 4 (2002c) *Declaration on Cooperation against International Terrorism*, Copenhagen, 22–24 September.

—— 5 (2004a) *Chairman's Statement*, Hanoi, 9 October.

—— 5 (2004b) *ASEM Declaration on Dialogue among Cultures and Civilizations*, Hanoi, 9 October.

—— 6 (2006a) *Chairman's Statement of the Sixth Asia-Europe Meeting*, Helsinki, 10–11 September.

—— 6 (2006b) *Helsinki Declaration on the Future of ASEM*, Helsinki, 10–11 September.

ASEM Conference on Cultures and Civilizations 1 (2003) *Chairman's Statement*, Beijing, 4 December.

—— 2 (2005) *Chairman's Statement*, Paris, 7–8 June.

ASEM Seminar on Anti-Terrorism (2003) *Chair's Summary*, Beijing, 22–23 September.

ASEM Task Force for Closer Economic Partnership between Asia and Europe (2004) *Final Report and Recommendations Presented to the ASEM V Summit in Hanoi, October 8–9 2004*.

ASEM Trade Union Conference (2002) *Statement of the ASEM Trade Union Conference to the Prime Minister of Denmark, Host of the ASEM IV Summit, Copenhagen, 22–4 September 2002*, Copenhagen, 19–21 September.

ASEM Trust Fund, 020611, n.d. *Indonesia: Monitoring Regional Implementation of Structural Reforms and Deregulation Programme*, Washington, DC: The World Bank.

—— 022671, n.d. *Indonesia: Water Utility (PDAM) Rescue Program*, Washington, DC: The World Bank.

—— 022672, n.d. *Indonesia: Water Utility (PDAM) Rescue Program*, Washington, DC: The World Bank.

—— 023513, n.d. *Philippine Out-of-School Children and Youth Development (POSCYD) Project*, Washington, DC: The World Bank.

—— 023514, n.d. *Philippine Out-of-School Children and Youth Development (POSCYD) Project*, Washington, DC: The World Bank.

—— (2005a) *ASEM Trust Fund 2: Status and Challenges. Annual Review. April 18, 2005*, Washington, DC: The World Bank.

—— (2005b) *Asia-Europe Meeting Trust Fund 2 Progress Report: October 28, 2005*, Washington, DC: The World Bank.

Asia–Europe People's Forum (AEPF) 1, (1996) *Asia-Europe NGO Network: An Impulse for the 21st Century*, Bangkok, 27–8 February.

—— 2 (1998a) "Action, not gimmicks: Asia-Europe People's Forum rejects proposed Trust Fund," *ASEM Watch*, 32.

—— 2 (1998b) *A People's Vision Towards a More Just, Equal and Sustainable World*, London, 31 March–1 April.

—— 2 (1998c) "Civil society groups demand a real say in ASEM," *ASEM Watch*, 33.

—— 3 (2000) *People's Vision 2000: Towards a Just, Equal and Sustainable World*, Seoul, 17–21 October.

—— 4 (2002) *Human Rights, People's Security, and Sustainable Development under Attack: No to Militarisation and Free Trade*, Copenhagen, 19–22 September.

—— 5 (2004) *People's Actions for Human Security in Asia and Europe*, Hanoi, 6–9 September.

Asia–Europe Vision Group (AEVG) (1999) *For a Better Tomorrow: Asia-Europe Partnership in the 21st Century*.

Asia–Europe Young Leaders' Symposium [AEYLS] (1997a) *Opening Ceremony and Keynote Addresses*, Miyazaki, Japan, 10 March.

—— (1997b) *Provisional Summary of the Brainstorming Session on Economics*, Miyazaki, Japan, 11 March.

—— (1997c) *Workshop IV: Interregional Cooperation; Identifying Modalities for Cooperation among Sovereign States on an Intra- and Interregional Basis*, Miyazaki, Japan, 11 March.

Association of Southeast Asian Nations–EC Ministerial Meeting 1 (1978) *Joint Declaration*, Brussels, 21 November.

Association of Southeast Asian Nations–EU Eminent Persons Group (1996) "A strategy for a new partnership. Report of the ASEAN–European Union Eminent Persons Group," *World Bulletin*, 12: 70–105.

ASEAN–EU Vision Group (2006) *Report of the ASEAN–EU Vision Group: Transregional Partnership for Shared and Sustainable Prosperity*, Hanoi, Vietnam.

Association of Southeast Asian Nations Labour Ministers' Meeting (1992) *Communiqué of the 9th Meeting*, Manila, 26–27 November.

—— (1994) *Communiqué of the 10th Meeting*, Singapore, 16–17 May.

—— (1996) *Communiqué of the 11th Meeting*, Bangkok, 25–2 April.

Baker, P. (2002) "Human rights, Europe and the People's Republic of China," in R. L. Edmonds (ed.) *China and Europe since 1978: A European perspective*, Cambridge: Cambridge University Press.

Bantekas, I. (2003) "The international law of terrorist financing," *American Journal of International Law*, 97: 315–33.

Bello, W. (1998) "East Asia: on the eve of the great transformation?" *Review of International Political Economy*, 5: 424–44.

Benedetti, F. and Washburn, J. L. (1999) "Drafting the International Criminal Court Treaty: two years to Rome and an afterword on the Rome Diplomatic Conference," *Global Governance*, 5: 1–39.

Bergé, B. (2002) "ASEM and social policies: looking back, looking ahead," in K. Fritsche (ed.) *Social Policies and the ASEM Process: International Workshop, Berlin March 4–5 (2002)*, Essen: Asien-Stiftung.

Bersick, S. (1998) *ASEM: Eine neue Qualität der Kooperation zwischen Europa und Asien*, Münster: Lit Verlag.

—— (2004a) "ASEMployment: Asien, Europa und die Zukunft der Beschäftigung," *Asienhaus Rundbrief*, 12: 2.

—— (2004b) "The ASEM regime: structure, interests and processes," paper presented at

176   *Bibliography*

Philippine Forum on the ASEM: Understanding the Process and Potentials and Defining Civil Society Engagements, Pasig City, Philippines, November.

—— (2004c) *Auf dem Weg in eine neue Weltordnung? Zur Politik der interregionalen
Beziehungen am Beispiel des ASEM-Prozesses*, Baden-Baden: Nomos Verlag.

—— (2004d) "China and ASEM: strengthening multilateralism through inter-regionalism,"
in W. Stokhof, P. van der Velde and Yeo Lay Hwee (eds) *The Eurasian Space: Far More
than Two Continents*, Singapore: Institute of Southeast Asian Studies.

Bevacqua, R. (1998) "Whither the Japanese model? The Asian economic crisis and the
continuation of Cold War politics in the Pacific Rim," *Review of International Political
Economy*, 5: 410–23.

Bigo, D. (2000) "When the two become one: internal and external securitisations," in
M. Kelstrup and M. C. Williams (eds) *International Relations Theory and the Politics
of European Integration: Power, Security and Community*, London: Routledge.

Blackhurst, R., Enders, A. and Francois, J. F. (1996) "The Uruguay Round and market
access: opportunities and challenges for developing countries," in W. Martin and L. A.
Winters (eds) *The Uruguay Round and the Developing Countries*, Cambridge: Cambridge University Press.

Blecker, R. A. (1999) *Taming Global Finance: A better architecture for growth and
equity*, Washington, DC: The Economic Policy Institute.

Bobrow, D. B. (1999) "The US and ASEM: why the hegemon didn't bark," *The Pacific
Review*, 12: 103–28.

Boval, B. (1996) "L'Accord sur les droits de propriété intellectuelle qui touchent au commerce (ADPIC ou TRIPS)," in Société Française pour le Droit International, Colloque
de Nice, *La Réorganisation Mondiale des Echanges*, Paris: Editions Pedone.

Bowles, P. (1999) "Regionalism and development after (?) the global financial crisis,"
paper presented at the Third Annual Conference of the Centre for the Study of Globalisation and Regionalisation (CSGR), University of Warwick, September.

Brittan, L. (1994) "Europe's New Asia Strategy," presented at the European Commission
– Financial Times Interactive Forum "Towards a New European Economic Strategy
for Asia," Brussels, October.

—— (1999) "Europe/Asia relations," *The Pacific Review*, 12: 491–8.

Bronckers, M. and McNelis, N. (2001) "The EU Trade Barriers Regulation comes of
age," *Journal of World Trade*, 35: 427–82.

Brown, C. (1994) " 'Turtles all the way down': anti-foundationalism, critical theory and
international relations," *Millennium: Journal of International Studies*, 23: 213–36.

Brown, D. K. (2000) *International Trade and Core Labor Standards: A Survey of the
Recent Literature*, Department of Economics, Tufts University.

Buzan, B. (1995) "The level-of-analysis problem in international relations reconsidered,"
in K. Booth and S. Smith (eds) *International Relations Theory Today*, University Park,
PA: The Pennsylvania State University Press.

Cahin, G. (2000) "L'action internationale au Timor oriental," *Annuaire Français de Droit
International*, 46: 139–75.

Caillaux, D. (1997) "L'action internationale visant à lutter contre l'exploitation des
enfants," paper presented at the European Parliament, Committee on Foreign Affairs,
Security and Defence Policy, Subcommittee on Human Rights, Public Hearing on the
Social Clause. Human Rights Protection or Protectionism? Brussels, June.

Camroux, D. and Park Sunghee (2004) "Korea and ASEM," in W. Stokhof, P. van der
Velde and Yeo Lay Hwee (eds) *The Eurasian Space: Far More than Two Continents*,
Singapore: Institute of Southeast Asian Studies.

Cardwell, P. J. (2004) "The EU–Japan relationship: from mutual ignorance to meaningful partnership," *Journal of European Affairs*, 2: 11–16.

Cassen, B. (1998) "Le bateau ivre de la finance," *Le Monde Diplomatique*, 536: 6.

—— (1999) "Vive la taxe Tobin!" *Le Monde Diplomatique*, 545: 14.

Cassese, A. (1991) "La valeur actuelle des droits de l'homme," in *Humanité et Droit International. Mélanges René-Jean Dupuy*, Paris: Editions Pedone.

Catholic Agency for Overseas Development (2003) "The Cancun WTO Ministerial Meeting, September 2003: What happened? What does it mean for development?" Submission to the International Development Select Committee, September.

Chambers, S. (1995) "Discourse and democratic practices," in S. K. White (ed.) *The Cambridge Companion to Habermas*, Cambridge: Cambridge University Press.

Chang Li Lin and Rajan, R. S. (1999) "Regional responses to the Southeast Asian financial crisis: a case of self-help or no help?" paper presented at the Third Annual Conference of the Centre for the Study of Globalisation and Regionalisation (CSGR), University of Warwick, September.

Chee Peng Lim (1980) "ASEAN–EEC external relations: cooperation in trade and investment," in *ASEAN External Economic Relations: Proceedings of the 5th Conference of ASEAN Economic Association*, Singapore: Chopman Publishers.

Chua Min Hoong (1998a) "ASEM a success, says PM," *The Straits Times*, 6 April.

—— (1998b) "Fuzz and goodwill at ASEM2, but no panacea," *The Straits Times*, 8 April.

Cochran, M. (2002) "A democratic critique of cosmopolitan democracy: pragmatism from the bottom up," *European Journal of International Relations*, 8: 517–48.

Cohen, R. (1991) *Negotiating Across Cultures: Communication Obstacles in International Diplomacy*, Washington, DC: United States Institute of Peace.

Coloma, R. (1998) "ASEM to tackle trade, finance, environment and social issues," *Asian Financial Press*, 3 April.

Conte-Helm, M. (1996) *The Japanese and Europe: Economic and Cultural Encounters*, London: The Athlone Press Ltd.

Cornwell, R. (1998) "No meat for Asian tigers limping West," *Independent on Sunday*, 29 March.

Council for Asia-Europe Cooperation [CAEC] (1996) "Paris Plenary Meeting. Informal summary."

Cox, R. W. (1983) "Gramsci, hegemony and international relations: an essay in method," in R. W. Cox with T. J. Sinclair, *Approaches to World Order*, Cambridge: Cambridge University Press.

—— (1987) *Production, Power and World Order*, New York: Columbia University Press.

—— (1992) "Multilateralism and world order," in R. W. Cox with T. J. Sinclair (1996) *Approaches to World Order*, Cambridge: Cambridge University Press.

Dallmayr, F. (2001) "Conversation across boundaries: political theory and global diversity," *Millennium: Journal of International Studies*, 30: 331–47.

Damodaran, R. (2006) "Decision on ASEAN–EU free trade pact in August," *Business Times* (Kuala Lumpur), 16 March 2006. Available online at: www.bilaterals.org/article-print.php3?id_article=4151 (accessed 5 March 2007).

Das, B. L. (1998) "Restoring balance to services in WTO," *South–North Development Monitor [SUNS]*, 4336.

—— (2001) *Chairman's Text and Developing Countries*, Penang: Third World Network.

—— (2002) *The New Work Programme of the WTO*, Penang: Third World Network.

De Beer, J. (2002) "ASEM in crisis," *Europe Report*, 25, 27 September. Available online at: www.glocom.org/special_tioucs/eu_report/20020927_eureport_s25 (accessed 17 August 2005).

Dent, C. M. (1997–8) "The ASEM: managing the new framework of the EU's economic relations with East Asia," *Pacific Affairs*, 70: 495–516.

—— (1999) *The European Union and East Asia: An Economic Relationship*, London: Routledge.

—— (2003) "From inter-regionalism to trans-regionalism: Challenges for ASEM," *Asia-Europe Journal*, 1: 223–36.

De Paiva Abreu, M. (1996) "Trade in manufactures: the outcome of the Uruguay Round and developing countries," in W. Martin and L. A. Winters (eds) *The Uruguay Round and the Developing Countries*, Cambridge: Cambridge University Press.

Dhommeaux, J. (1989) "De l'universalité du droit international des droits de l'homme," *Annuaire Français de Droit International*, 35: 399–423.

Dosch, J. (1998) "Emerging multilateralization of security cooperation in the Asia–Pacific region – following European experiences and models or driven by an indigenous approach?" in J. Krause and F. Umbach (eds) *Perspectives of Regional Security Cooperation in Asia–Pacific: Learning from Europe or Developing Indigenous Models?* Bonn: Europa Union Verlag.

Dufour, S. (1995) "La libéralisation des echanges mondiaux et le respect des règles fondamentales en matière sociale: un lien controversé," *Études Internationales*, 26: 275–89.

Drake, W. J. and Nicolaidis, K. (1992) "Ideas, interests and institutionalization: 'trade in services' and the Uruguay Round," *International Organization*, 46: 37–100.

Economic Ministers' Meeting [EMM] 1 (1997) *Chairman's Statement*, Makuhari, Japan, 27–28 September.

—— 2 (1999) *Chair's Statement*, Berlin, 8–9 October.

—— 3 (2001) *Chair's Statement*, Hanoi, 10–11 September.

—— 4 (2002) *Chair's Statement*, Copenhagen, 18–19 September.

—— 5 (2003) *Chair's Statement*, Dalian, China, 23–24 July.

—— 6 (2005) *Chairman's Statement*, Tianjin, China, 26 June.

Edgren, G. (1979) "Fair labour standards and trade liberalisation," *International Labour Review*, 118: 523–35.

Eichengreen, B. (1999) *Toward a New International Financial Architecture. a practical post-Asia agenda*, Washington, DC: Institute for International Economics.

Eschborn, N., Gardill, J., and Mols, M. (1992) "Die Beziehungen EG-Asien," in F. Huscheler and O. Schmuck (eds) *Die Süd-Politik der EG: Europas entwicklungspolitische Verantwortung in der veränderten Weltordnung*, Bonn: Europa Union Verlag.

European Commission COM (1994) 314 final, *Communication from the Commission to the Council: Towards a New Asia Strategy.*

—— COM (1995) 279 final, *Communication from the Commission to the Council: A Long-Term Policy for China–Europe Relations.*

—— COM (1996) 53 final, *Communication from the Commission to the Council, the European Parliament, the Economic and Social Committee and the Committee of the Regions: The Global Challenge of International trade: A Market Access Strategy for the European Union.*

—— COM (1996) 314 final, *Communication from the Commission to the Council, the European Parliament and the Economic and Social Committee: Creating a New Dynamic in ASEAN-EU Relations.*

—— COM (1998) 181 final, *Communication from the Commission: Building a Comprehensive Partnership with China.*

—— COM (1999) 0331, *Communication from the Commission to the Council and to the European Parliament. The EU Approach to the Millennium Round.*

—— (1999a) *EU Priority Proposals for Regulatory Reform in Japan*, 29 October.

—— (1999b) *EU Supplementary Proposals for Regulatory Reform in Japan*, 25 October.

—— COM (2000) 241, *Communication from the Commission to the Council and to the European Parliament: Perspectives and Priorities for the ASEM Process into the New Decade.*

—— COM (2000) 552 final, *Report from the Commission to the Council and the European Parliament on the Implementation of the Communication "Building a Comprehensive Partnership with China."*

—— (2000a) *EU Priority Proposals for Regulatory Reform in Japan*, 16 October.

—— (2000b) *EU Supplementary Proposals for Regulatory Reform in Japan*, 26 October.

—— (2001a) *EU Priority Proposals for Regulatory Reform in Japan*, 12 October.

—— (2001b) *EU Priority Proposals for Regulatory Reform in Japan*, 23 October.

—— (2001c) *Vademecum: Modalities for Future ASEM Dialogue; Taking the Process Forward*, 18 July.

—— COM (2001) 265 final, *Communication from the Commission to the Council and the European Parliament: EU Strategy Towards China; Implementation of the 1998 Communication and Future Steps for a More Effective EU Policy.*

—— COM (2001) 469 final, *Communication from the Commission: Europe and Asia; A Strategic Framework for Enhanced Partnerships.*

—— (2002a) *EU Priority Proposals for Regulatory Reform in Japan*, 17 October.

—— (2002b) *EU Supplementary Proposals for Regulatory Reform in Japan. Updated Version*, 18 December.

—— SEC (2002) 874, *Commission Staff Working Paper: Fourth Asia–Europe Meeting in Copenhagen, September 22–24, 2002. ASEM4: Unity and Strength in Diversity.*

—— (2003a) *EU Priority Proposals for Regulatory Reform in Japan*, 16 October.

—— (2003b) *EU Supplementary Proposals for Regulatory Reform in Japan*, 14 November.

—— COM (2003) 533, *Commission Policy Paper for Transmission to the Council and the European Parliament: A Maturing Partnership – Shared Interests and Challenges in EU-China Relations (Updating the Commission's Communications on EU–China Relations of 1998 and 2001).*

—— (2004) *EU Priority Proposals for Regulatory Reform in Japan*, 28 October.

—— SEC (2006) 1230, *Commission Staff Working Document: Annex to the Communication from the Commission to the Council, the European Parliament, the European Economic and Social Committee and the Committee of the Regions; Global Europe. Competing in the World. A Contribution to the EU's Growth and Jobs Strategy {COM (2006) 567 FINAL}{sec (2006) 1228}{sec (2006) 1229}.*

—— ASEM Counsellor (2001) *Consolidated Version of Measures taken by ASEM Partners to Address the Consolidated and Prioritised List of the Major Generic Trade Barriers among ASEM Partners.*

—— External Relations (2000) *File Note: ASEM NGO Visit of the European Commission. Brussels, 5 June 2000.*

—— (2006) *ASEM 6, 10–11 September 2006, Helsinki: 10 Years of ASEM; Global Challenges, Joint Responses.* Luxembourg: Office for Official Publications of the European Communities.

European Institute of Asian Studies (2003) *Consultative Seminar with Civil Society: Brussels, 17–18 November 2003*, Brussels: European Institute for Asian Studies.

European Parliament (1993) *The Economic Impact of Dumping and the Community's Anti-Dumping Policy*, Strasbourg: Directorate General for Research.

—— PE2971377 Final A5–0076/2001 (1999) *Report containing the European Parliament's Recommendations to the Commission on the Negotiations Conducted within the WTO Framework on the Built-In Agenda [2028/2001 (INI)] Committee on Industry, External Trade, Research and Energy. Rapporteur: Konrad Schwaiger*. 28 February.

European Union-Japan (1991) *Joint Declaration on Relations between the European Community and Its Member States and Japan*, The Hague, 18 July.

European Union-Japan Ministerial Meeting (2000) *EU–Japan Joint Statement on the WTO*, 11 January.

European Union-Japan Summit (2001) *Shaping Our Common Future and Action Plan for EU-Japan Cooperation*, Brussels.

"Europe 'doing more now' for Asia," *The Straits Times*, 4 April 1998.

"Europe must match words with deeds," *The Nation* (Bangkok), 6 April 1998.

Fédération Internationale des Ligues de Droits de l'Homme (FIDH) (2004) "Human rights must be at the core of the discussions!" September 6. Available online at: www.fidh.org/article_print.php3?id_article=1873 (accessed 17 August 2005).

—— and Human Rights in China (2000) "Open letter to EU member states: The EU-China Human Rights Dialogue." 27 September Available online at: www.fidh.org/article.php3?id_article=1112 (accessed 23 October 2004).

Finance Ministers Meeting [FinMM] 1 (1997) *Chairman's Statement*, Bangkok, 19 September.

—— 2 (1999) *Chairman's Statement*, Frankfurt, 15–16 January.

—— 3 (2001) *Chairman's Statement*, Kobe, 13–14 January.

—— 4 (2002) *Chairman's Statement*, Copenhagen, 5–6 July.

—— 5 (2003) *Ministerial Statement*, Bali, 5–6 July.

—— 6 (2005) *Chairman's Statement*, Tianjin, China, 26 June.

—— 7 (2006) *Chairman's Statement*, Vienna, 8–9 April.

Foreign Ministers' Meeting [FMM] 1 (1997) *Chairman's Statement*, Singapore, 13–14 February.

—— 2 (1999) *Chairman's Statement*, Frankfurt, 15 January.

—— 3 (2001) *Chairman's Statement*, Beijing, 24–25 May.

—— 4 (2002) *Chair's Statement*, Madrid, 6–7 June.

—— 5 (2003) *Chair's Statement*, Bali, July 22–24 July.

—— 6 (2004) *Chair's Statement*, Kildare, Ireland, 17–18 April.

—— 7 (2005) *Chairman's Statement*, Kyoto, 6–7 May.

Fitzgerald, V. (2000) "La seguridad en las finanzas internacionales," in J. A. Alonso and C. Freres (eds) *Los Organismos Multilaterales y la Ayuda al Desarrollo*, Madrid: Agencia Española de Cooperación Internacional.

Fogarty, D. (2004) "Suu Kyi proves tricky topic for Asia-Europe summit," Reuters, 12 October.

Fouquet, D. (2001) *Whither the ASEM Process? A forum that needs more substance*, Essen: Asienhaus.

Freeman, C. (1998) "The East Asian crisis, technical change and the world economy," *Review of International Political Economy*, 5: 393–409.

Friends of the Earth International (1999) "Seattle and the WTO: A Briefing," 13 December.

Fritsche, K. (2002) "Joint actions by non-governmental organizations and trade unions," in K. Fritsche (ed.) *Social Policies and the ASEM Process.: International workshop, Berlin (March 4–5, 2002)*, Essen: Asien-Stiftung.

Fritz, J. S. (1997) "[Review of] Andreas Hasenclever, Peter Mayer and Volker Rittberger, *Theories of International Regimes*," *Millennium: Journal of International Studies*, 26: 924–7.

"FTA with EU may cut Burma out," *The Nation* (Bangkok), 9 March 2007. Available online at: www.bilaterals.org/article.php3?id_article=7087 (accessed 5 March 2007).

Germany, China, Ireland, Spain (2002) *Concept paper on the future of employment and the quality of labour*, Copenhagen, September.

Ghebali, V. Y. (1987) *L'Organisation Internationale du Travail*, Genève: Georg Editeur.

Gilpin, R. (1981) *War and Change in World Politics*, Cambridge: Cambridge University Press.

Gilson, J. (2000) *Japan and the European Union: A Partnership for the Twenty-First Century?* Houndmills, Basingstoke, Hampshire: Macmillan.

—— (2001) "Europe in Japan: a growing EU identity," in G. D. Hook and H. Hasegawa (eds) *The Political Economy of Japanese Globalization*, London: Routledge.

—— (2002) *Asia meets Europe: Inter-regionalism and the Asia–Europe Meeting*, Cheltenham: Edward Elgar Publishing, Limited.

Godemont, F., Lehmann, J. P., Maull, H. and Segal, G. (1995) "An agenda for Euro–East Asian security," Unpublished manuscript, October.

Godemont, F., Nicolas, F. and Yakushiji Taizo (2004) *Asia and Europe: Cooperating on Energy Security. Summary*, Council on Asia–Europe Cooperation Task Force 2003–04.

Goh Chok Tong (1994/95) "L'Asie et l'Europe: une nouvelle alliance pour le XXIe siècle," *Politique Etrangère*, 59: 1099–1106.

Government of Japan (1998) *Japan's Requests and Comments Regarding EU Regulations and Access to EU Markets*, 2 March.

—— (2000) *Japan–EU High-Level Dialogue on Regulatory Reform*, 1 November.

—— (2001a) *Japan's Priority Proposals for Regulatory Reform in the EU*, January.

—— (2001b) *Japan's (Supplementary) Proposals for Regulatory Reform in the EU and Related Japanese Comments*.

—— (2001c) *Japan's Priority Proposals for Regulatory Reform in the EU and Related Japanese Comments*, 23 October.

—— (2003) *Japan's Priority Proposals for Regulatory Reform in the EU*, 14 November.

—— (2004) *Japan's Proposal* [sic] *for Regulatory Reform Dialogue: Tentative List of Proposals*, November.

Gross, M. (1988) "Entwicklung des europäischen wirtschaftlichen Engagements in ASEAN-Ländern," in B. Dahm and W. Harbrecht (eds) *ASEAN und EG: Partner, Probleme, Perspektiven*, Hamburg: Deutsches Ubersee-Institut.

Group of 77 and China (2001) *Declaration by the Group of 77 and China on the Fourth WTO Ministerial Conference at Doha, Qatar*, Geneva, 22 October.

Guan Jinghe (2001) "Rights and obligations in the promotion of social welfare," in H. Wirajuda and F. Delon (eds) *The Fourth Informal Seminar on Human Rights, Bali, Indonesia, 12–13 July 2001*, Singapore: Asia–Europe Foundation.

Haacke, J. (1996) "Theory and praxis in international relations: Habermas, self-reflection, rational argumentation." *Millennium: Journal of International Studies*, 25: 255–89.

Habermas, J. (1976) "The public sphere," in S. Seidman (ed.) (1989) *Jürgen Habermas on Society and Politics: A Reader*, Boston: Beacon Press.

—— (1984) "Social action and rationality," in S. Seidman (ed.) (1989) *Jürgen Habermas on Society and Politics: A Reader*, Boston: Beacon Press.

—— (1987a) "The concept of the lifeworld and the hermeneutic idealism of interpretive sociology," in S. Seidman (ed.) (1989) *Jürgen Habermas on Society and Politics: A Reader*, Boston, MA: Beacon Press.

—— (1987b) *The Theory of Communicative Action*, vol. II, *Lifeworld and System: A Critique of Functionalist Reason*, Boston: Beacon Press.

—— (1992) "Further reflections on the public sphere," in C. Calhoun (ed.) *Habermas and the Public Sphere*, Cambridge, MA: The MIT Press.

—— (1998) *The Inclusion of the other. Studies in political theory*, Cambridge, MA: The MIT Press.

—— (2000) "Beyond the nation-state? On some consequences of economic globalization," In E. O. Eriksen and J. E. Fossum (eds) *Democracy in the European Union: Integration through Deliberation*, London: Routledge.

—— (2001) *The Postnational Constellation: Political Essays*, Cambridge: Polity Press.

Hadad, N. (2003) "Water resource policy in Indonesia: open doors for privatization," *Jubilee South*, 12 December.

Haggard, S. and Simmons, B. A. (1987) "Theories of international regimes," *International Organization*, 41: 491–517.

Hänggi, H. (2004) "ASEM's security agenda revisited," in W. Stokhof, P. van der Velde, and Yeo Lay Hwee (eds) *The Eurasian Space: Far more than two continents*, Singapore: Institute of Southeast Asian Studies.

Hansen, S. (2000) *ASEM-Gipfel in Seoul*, Essen: Asienhaus Essen.

Haq, M. ul, Kaul, I. and Grunberg, I. (1996) *The Tobin Tax: Coping with Financial Volatility*, New York: Oxford University Press.

Hathaway, D. F. and Ingco, M. D. (1996) "Agricultural liberalization and the Uruguay Round," in W. Martin and L. A. Winters (eds) *The Uruguay Round and the Developing Countries*, Cambridge: Cambridge University Press.

Hauser, H. (2002) "Die Ministererklärung von Doha: Start zu einer kleinen Marktöffnungsrunde oder zu einer umfassenden Entwicklungsrunde?" *Aussenwirtschaft: Schweizerische Zeitschrift für internationale Wirtschaftsbeziehungen*, 57: 127–50.

Henkel, F., Heberg, M. and Schmit, F. (2004) *For a Social Dimension in the Asian–European dialogue: Challenges before the 5th ASEM Summit Meeting in Hanoi*, Hanoi: Friedrich-Ebert-Stiftung.

Hiemenz, U. (1987) "EG-ASEAN Wirtschaftsbeziehungen: Ergebnisse eines Forschungsprojekts," *Internationales Asienforum*, 18: 315–22.

Hiemenz, U., Agarwal, J. P., Gross, M., von Kirchbach, F. and Langhammer, R. J. (1987) *The Competitive Strength of European, Japanese and US Suppliers on ASEAN Markets*, Tübingen: J.C.B. Mohr (P. Siebeck).

Higgott, R. (2000) "ASEM and the evolving global order," in Chong-wha Lee (ed.) *The Seoul (2000) Summit: The Way Ahead for the Asia-Europe Partnership*, Seoul: Korea Institute for International Economic Policy.

Hilpert, H. G. (1998) "Economic interactions," in H. Maull, G. Segal and J. Wanandi (eds) *Europe and the Asia Pacific*, London: Routledge.

Hilpert, H. G. and Wacker, G. (2004) *China und Japan: Kooperation und Rivalität*, Berlin: Stiftung Wissenschaft und Politik. Deutsches Institut für Internationale Politik und Sicherheit.

Hollis, M. and Smith, S. (1991) "Beware of gurus: structure and action in international relations," *Review of International Studies*, 17: 393–410.

Hook, G. D., Gilson, J., Hughes, C. W. and Dobson, H. (2001) *Japan's International Relations: Politics, Economics and Security*, London: Routledge.

Hormeku, T. (1999) *Dirty Tactics in Seattle*, Penang: Third World Network.

—— (2001) "Invasion of WTO by 'green men'," *South–North Development Monitor [SUNS]*, no. 5008.

Hua Xiaofeng (2003) *Malaysia: ASEM Grant for Financial Sector Strengthening*, Washington, DC: The World Bank, 18 March.

Human Rights Watch (2000) "Open letter to European Union foreign Ministers. Re: China-European Union human rights dialogue," Brussels, 14 July Available online at: www.hrw.org/press/(2000)/07/China_EU0728.htm (accessed 23 October 2004).

—— (2002) "Letter to ASEM summit participant countries," 13 September.

International Confederation of Free Trade Unions [ICFTU] (2004) *Creating Social Partnership in ASEM: Background Document to ASEM Trade Union Forum*, Hanoi, 24 April.

—— (2006) *Trade Union Summit: 10 Years of ASEM – Time to Deliver!* Helsinki, 8 September.

—— European Trade Union Federation and Asian and Pacific Regional Organisation of the ICFTU (2000) *Charting a Social Direction to ASEM: Trade Union Statement to the Third Summit of the ASEM, Seoul 20–21 October 2000, Seoul, Korea, 15–16 October.*

"If Asia suffers, so do we, says Kohl," *The Straits Times*, 6 April 1998.

Iklé, F. C. (1964) *How Nations Negotiate*, New York: Harper and Row.

International Monetary Fund (IMF) (1997) *Summary Proceedings Annual Meeting of the Board of Governors 1997*, Washington, DC: IMF.

Investment Experts Group (IEG) 1 (1998) *Conclusions by the Chair*, Evian, 23–24 November 1998.

—— 2 (1999) *Chairman's Statement*, Singapore, 11–12 February.

—— 3 (1999) *Co-Chairs' Statement*, Brussels, 5–6 July.

Investment Promotion Action Plan (IPAP) (1997) *The Asia-Europe Investment Promotion Action Plan.*

—— (1999) *Most Effective Measures to Attract Direct Foreign Investment.*

Japan Ministry of Foreign Affairs, Economic Affairs Bureau (2002) *Japan's Basic Strategy for the WTO New Round Negotiations*, 4 October.

Jenner, R. M. (2001) "Why civil society opposes a new round," *South–North Development Monitor [SUNS]*, no. 4902.

Jin Nyum (2001) *Strengthening the International Financial Architecture: Progress Assessment and Future Direction from the Perspective of an Emerging Market Country in Asia*, presented at the ASEM Finance Ministers' Meeting, Kobe, Japan, 14 January.

Johnston, A. I. (2004) "China's international relations: the political and security dimensions," in S. S. Kim (ed.) *The International Relations of Northeast Asia*, Lanham, MD: Rowman and Littlefield Publishers.

Jomo, K. S. (1998) *Tigers in Trouble: Financial Governance, Liberalisation and Crises in East Asia*, London: Zed Books Ltd.

Juillard, P. (1996) "L'Accord sur les mesures concernant l'Investissement et liées au commerce," in Société Française pour le Droit International, Colloque de Nice, *La Réorganisation Mondiale des Echanges*, Paris: Pedone.

Jung Ku-Hyun and Lehmann, J. P. (1997) "The economic and business dimension," in Council for Asia-Europe Cooperation, *The Rationale and Common Agenda for Asia-Europe Cooperation: CAEC Task Force Reports*, Tokyo: Japan Center for International Exchange.

Kaiser, K. (2004) *Asia and Europe: Necessity for Cooperation. Report on the findings of the Task Forces of the Council for Asia-Europe Cooperation (CAEC) 2003–04.*

Kang Kyung-wha (2001) "Rights and obligations in the promotion of social welfare," in H. Wirajuda and F. Delon (eds) *The Fourth Informal Seminar on Human Rights, Bali, Indonesia, 12–13 July 2001*, Singapore: Asia–Europe Foundation.

Kapoor, I. (2002) "Deliberative democracy and the WTO," *Review of International Political Economy*, 11: 522–41.

Kent, A. (2002) "China's international socialization: the role of international organizations," *Global Governance*, 8: 343–64.

Keohane, R. O. (1984) *After Hegemony: Cooperation and discord in the world political economy*, Princeton, NJ: Princeton University Press.

Kesavapany, K. (1996) "An overview of recent developments in the WTO," in Chia Siow Yue and J. L. H. Tan (eds) *ASEAN in the WTO: Challenges and responses*, Singapore: Institute of Southeast Asian Studies.

Khor, M. (2000) *Globalization and the South: Some Critical Issues*, Geneva: United Nations Conference on Trade and Development, Division on Globalization and Development Strategies, March.

—— (2001a) "Doha meet kicks off to 'democratic' start," *South–North Development Monitor [SUNS]*, no. 5008.

—— (2001b) *Draft Doha Declaration Sseeks to Launch Big New Round, Ignores Ccivil Society Demands: Comment on the WTO Draft Ministerial Declaration*, Penang: Third World Network.

—— (2001c) "Majority of developing countries reject text on new issues," *South–North Development Monitor [SUNS]*, no. 5008.

—— (2003a) "EC and Japan prepare new draft texts on Singapore issues for Cancun," Penang: Third World Network. Available online at: www.twnside.org.sg/title/twe310c.htm (accessed 18 August 2004).

—— (2003b) "Cancun draft text flawed, imbalanced, say developing countries," *South–North Development Monitor [SUNS]*, no. 5405. Available online at: www.twnside.org.sg/title/5405b (accessed 18 August 2004).

—— (2003c) "G21 developing countries prepare for Cancun agricultural battle," *Third World Network Cancun News Update*, 1 (10 September).

—— and Hormeku, T. (2003) "Anti-development in substance and process," *South–North Development Monitor [SUNS]*, no. 5418.

Kim, S. S. (2004) "Northeast Asia in the local–regional global nexus: multiple challenges and contending explanations," in S. S. Kim (ed.) *The International Relations of Northeast Asia*, Lanham, MD: Rowman and Littlefield Publishers.

Kirsch, P. and Holmes, J. T. (1999) "The Rome Conference on the International Criminal Court: the negotiating process," *American Journal of International Law*, 93: 2–12.

Kiuchi Takashi (2003) "The future of ASEAN-Japan financial relations," in *ASEAN-Japan Cooperation: A Foundation for East Asian Community*, Tokyo: Japan Center for International Exchange.

Koh, T. B. (1998) "Europe can be Asia's friend in need," *International Herald Tribune*, 2 April.

Kohl, O., Lee Jun-Genn, Trach Cuong Loi, and Magata, J. (1999) "Marktzugangspolitik," in C. Derichs, T. Goydke, and W. Pascha (eds) *"Task Force": Ein Gutachten zu den deutschen/europäischen Außenwirtschaftsbeziehungen mit Japan*, Duisburg: Institut für Ostasienwissenschaften, Gerhard-Mercator-Universität Duisburg.

Korean Peninsula Energy Development Organization [KEDO] (2001) *Annual Report*.

Krasner, S. D. (1983) "Structural causes and regime consequences: regimes as intervening variables," in S. D. Krasner (ed.) *International Regimes*, Ithaca, NY: Cornell University Press.

Kratochwil, F. (1988) "Regimes, interpretation and the 'science' of politics: A reappraisal," *Millennium: Journal of International Studies*, 17: 263–84.

—— and Ruggie, J.G. (1986) "International organization: a state of the art on an art of the state," *International Organization*, 40: 229–54.

Krause, J. and Umbach, F. (eds) (1998) *Perspectives of Regional Security Cooperation in Asia–Pacific: Learning from Europe or Developing Indigenous Models?* Bonn: Europa Union Verlag.

Labour and Employment Ministers' Conference 1 (2006) *More and Better Jobs: Working Jointly to Strengthen the Social Dimension of Globalisation; Chairman's Conclusions of the First ASEM Labour and Employment Ministers' Conference, Postdam, 3–5 September 2006.*

Langhammer, R. J. (1989) "The link between trade with and investment in ASEAN countries: Lessons for EC suppliers and policymakers," in G. Schiavone (ed.) *Western Europe and South-East Asia: Co-operation or Competition?*, Houndmills, Basingstoke, Hampshire: Macmillan.

Langhammer, R. J. and Hiemenz, U. (1990) *Regional Iintegration among Developing Countries: Opportunities, Obstacles and Options*, Tübingen: J. C. B. Mohr (P. Siebeck).

Lasserre, P. and Schütte, H. (1999) *Strategies for Asia Pacific: Beyond the Crisis*, Houndmills, Basingstoke, Hampshire: Macmillan.

Leary, V. A. (1997) "The WTO and the social clause: post-Singapore," *European Journal of International Law*, 8: 118–22.

Lee Chong-wha (2000a) "Testing the 'subsidiarity question' for ASEM," in Chong-wha Lee (ed.) *The Seoul (2000) Summit: The Way Ahead for the Asia-Europe Partnership*, Seoul: Korea Institute for International Economic Policy.

—— (2000b) "Trade and investment profiles in ASEM process: issues and prospects," in *The Third Seoul ASEM and Asia-Europe Relations, September 29–30, 2000, Seoul*, Seoul: The Korean Society of Contemporary European Studies.

Lefort, J. C. and Page, J. P. (1998) "Double jeu autour de l'AMI," *Le Monde diplomatique*, 535: 23.

Lehmann, J. P. (1998) "The economic setting," in H. Maull, G. Segal and J. Wanandi (eds) *Europe and the Asia–Pacific*, London: Routledge.

—— (2000) "ASEM and trade issues," in *The Third Seoul ASEM and Asia–Europe Relations, September 29–30, 2000, Seoul*, Seoul: The Korean Society of Contemporary European Studies.

Li Jinxiang (1998) *Die Rolle der VR China im Rahmen des Global-Sourcing deutscher Industrie- und Handelsunternehmen*, Hamburg: Institut für Asienkunde.

Lim, P. (1999) *Political Issues in EU–ASEAN Relations*, Brussels: European Institute of Asian Studies.

—— (2000) "Beyond economic cooperation: prospects for mutual social, cultural and educational ties," in *The Third Seoul ASEM and Asia–Europe Relations, September 29–30, 2000, Seoul*, Seoul: The Korean Society of Contemporary European Studies.

—— (2002) "Ideas of a social pillar in ASEM," in K. Fritsche (ed.) *Social Policies and the ASEM Process. International workshop, Berlin (March 4–5, 2002)*, Essen: Asien-Stiftung.

—— (2003) "Analyzing the ASEM process," *Asia–Europe Journal*, 1: 121–41.

—— (2004) "Security co-operation between the European Union and East Asia: what has changed from ASEM I and II to ASEM III in Seoul to ASEM IV in Copenhagen?"

Contemporary European Studies Association of Australia Review, 32: 6–20. Available online at: www.cesaa.org.au (accessed 17 August 2005).

Lindblom, A. K. (2000) "States, NGOs and the multitude: the problem of representation in international fora," paper submitted to the Parliamentary Commission of Inquiry into Swedish Policy for Global Development.

Love, N. S. (1995) "What's left of Marx?" in S. K. White (ed.) *Cambridge Companion to Habermas*, Cambridge: Cambridge University Press.

Low, P. and Subramanian, A. (1996) "Beyond TRIMS: a case for multilateral action on investment rules and competition policy," in W. Martin and L. A. Winters (eds) *The Uruguay Round and Developing Countries*, London: Cambridge University Press.

Lynch, M. (1999) *State Interests and Public Spheres: The International Politics of Jordan's Identity*, New York: Columbia University Press.

—— (2000) "The dialogue of civilisations and the international public sphere," *Millennium: Journal of International Studies*, 29: 307–30.

—— (2002) "Why engage? China and the logic of communicative engagement," *European Journal of International Relations*, 8: 187–230.

MacLean, R. M. (1999) "The European Community's Trade Barriers Regulation takes shape – is it living up to expectations?" *Journal of World Trade*, 33: 69–96.

"MAI Provisions and Proposals: An Analysis of the April 1998 Text," *Public Citizen Global Trade Watch*, May 1998.

Mahncke, D. (1997) "European interest and Southeast Asian security," *Journal of European Studies Chulalongkorn University*, 5: 1–16.

"Malaysia endorses talks, with conditions," *The Korea Herald*, 22 October 2000.

Martin, W. and Winters, L. A. (1996) "The Uruguay Round: A milestone for the developing countries," in W. Martin and L. A. Winters (eds) *The Uruguay Round and the Developing Countries*, Cambridge: Cambridge University Press.

Maull, H. W. and Tanaka, A. (1997) "The geopolitical dimension," in *The Rationale and common agenda for Asia–Europe Cooperation: CAEC Task Force Reports*, Tokyo: Japan Center for International Exchange.

Maupain, F. (1996) "La protection internationale des travailleurs et la libéralisation du commerce mondial: un lien ou un frein?" *Revue Générale de Droit International Public*, 100: 45–100.

Maystadt, P. (2001) "Evolving institutions and transatlantic relations: reforming the global financial architecture," *Seton Hall Journal of Diplomacy and International Relations*, 3: 21–9.

Mitchie, J. and Smith, J.G. (eds) (1999) *Global Instability: The Political Economy of World Economic Governance*, London: Routledge.

Molle, W. (2001) *The Economics of European Integration: Theory, Practice and Policy*, 4th edn, Aldershot, Hants: Ashgate.

Möller, K. (2002) "Diplomatic relations and mutual strategic perceptions: China and the European Union," in R. L. Edmonds (ed.) *China and Europe Since 1978: A European Perspective*, Cambridge: Cambridge University Press.

—— (2003) *Chinas Außenpolitik: Selektive Multilateralität*, Berlin: Stiftung Wissenschaft und Politik/Deutsches Institut für Internationale Politik und Sicherheit.

—— (2004) *Wirtschaftliche Öffnung und politische Blockade in China. Zwei Gegenläufige Entwicklungen als Stabilitätsrisiko*, Berlin: Stiftung Wissenschaft und Politik/Deutsches Institut für Internationale Politik und Sicherheit.

Möllers, W. (2000) "Viele oberflächliche Gemeinsamkeiten: Dritten Asien-Europa-Gipfel in Seoul," *Konrad-Adenauer-Stiftung. Politischer Kurzbericht*, December.

"Myanmar an obstacle as EU pushes for FTA with Southeast Asia," *Today Online*, 15 May 2006. Available online at: www.bilaterals.org/article-print.php3?id_article=4733 (accessed 5 March 2007).

Navarro-Martín, M. and Olalia, M. (2001) *ASEM Trust Fund Implementation Completion Report. Philippines: Social Protection and Social Housing – TF 22095*, Washington, DC: The World Bank.

Nuttall, S. (2000) "ASEM and political dialogue," in Chong-wha Lee (ed.) *The Seoul (2000) Summit: The Way Ahead for the Asia–Europe partnership*, Seoul: Korea Institute for International Economic Policy.

Øhrgaard, J. (1997) " 'Less than supranational, more than intergovernmental': European Political Cooperation and the dynamics of intergovernmental integration," *Millennium: Journal of International Studies*, 26: 1–29.

Onuf, N. (1995) "Levels," *European Journal of International Relations*, 1: 35–58.

Organisation for Economic Cooperation and Development (OECD). Directorate for Financial, Fiscal and Enterprise Affairs. Negotiating Group on the MAI (Multilateral Agreement on Investment). Confidential DAFFE/MAI(97)1/REV2 (1997) *Multilateral Agreement on Investment: Consolidated Texts and Commentary*.

—— (1998) *Informal Consultations on International Investment*, March.

Outhwaite, W. (1995) *Habermas: A Critical Introduction*, Cambridge: The Polity Press.

Palan, R. (2000) "A world of their making: an evaluation of the constructivist critique in international relations," *Review of International Studies*, 26: 275–98.

Pareira, A. (2003) *ASEM (Asia–Europe Meeting) Bestandsaufnahme, Möglichkeiten und Grenzen einer interregionalen Kooperation*, Frankfurt am Main: Peter Lang.

Paribatra, S. (2000) "ASEM political dialogue: now and in the future," in Chong-wha Lee (ed.) *The Seoul (2000) Summit: The Way Ahead for the Asia–Europe Partnership*, Seoul: Korea Institute for International Economic Policy.

Parry, R. L. (1998) "Asia shows its displeasure with Europe," *The Independent*, 3 April.

Payne, R. A. and Samhat, N. F. (2002) "Discourse norms in world politics," paper presented at the 43rd International Studies Association Meeting, New Orleans, LA, March.

Payoyo, P. B. (1999) "The EU's policy response to the financial crisis in Asia," In V. V. M. Aguirre (ed.) *European Studies: Essays by Filipino Scholars*, Quezon City: University of the Philippines Centre for Integrative and Development Studies and the Institute of International Legal Studies.

Porter, T. (1996) "Capital mobility and currency markets: can they be tamed?" *International Journal*, 51: 668–89.

Pou Saradell, V. (1996) *ASEM: Follow-up and New Developments since the Bangkok Summit*, Geneva: Modern Asia Research Centre, University of Geneva.

Primo Braga, C. A. (1996) "Trade-related intellectual property issues: the Uruguay Round Agreement and its economic implications," in W. Martin and L. A. Winters (eds) *The Uruguay Round and the Developing Countries*, Cambridge: Cambridge University Press.

Puchala, D. J. and Hopkins, R. F. (1983) "International regimes: lessons for inductive analysis," in S. D. Krasner (ed.) *International Regimes*, Ithaca, NY: Cornell University Press.

Radelet, S. and Sachs, J. (1998) "The onset of the East Asian financial crisis," paper presented at a USAID Seminar January 29, 1998 and a NBER [National Bureau of Economic Research] Currency Crises Conference, February.

Raghavan, C. (1999) "A theatre of the absurd at Seattle," *South–North Development Monitor [SUNS]*, no. 4567.

—— (2000) "After Seattle, world trade system faces uncertain future," *Review of International Political Economy*, 7: 495–504.

—— (2001a) "Harbinson-Moore implementation package doesn't fly," *South–North Development Monitor [SUNS]*, 2 October.

—— (2001b) "No new round before settling implementation issues, Mahathir," *South–North Development Monitor [SUNS]*, 27 February.

—— (2003a) "Cancun text sheds 'development' from agenda," *South–North Development Monitor [SUNS]*, no. 5404.

—— (2003b) "Civil society hails Cancun failure, some ask Lamy to resign," *South–North Development Monitor [SUNS]*, no. 5419.

—— (2003c) "Process and substance caused failure at Cancun," *South–North Development Monitor [SUNS]*, no. 5420.

Raja, K. (2001) "WTO drafts biassed towards the North, charge NGOs," *South–North Development Monitor [SUNS]*, no. 4999.

Rasmussen, N. (2000) "Third ASEM to confirm effectiveness of summit as framework for partnership," *The Korea Herald*, 19 October, p. 23.

Raoul Wallenberg Institute of Human Rights and Humanitarian Law (1998) *Premier ASEM Séminaire sur Droits de l'Homme et État de Droit: Administration de la justice, les 11–13 décembre 1997*, Lund: Raoul Wallenberg Institute.

Reddy, R. (2001) "False premises for a new round," *The Hindu*, reproduced by the Third World Network, Penang.

Reiterer, M. (2002) "The importance of the enhanced implementation of the ASEM Trade Facilitation Action Plan to the growth in trade between the EU and Asian ASEM partners," in M. Reiterer (ed.) *Asia-Europe: Do They Meet? Reflections on the Asia-Europe Meeting [ASEM]*, Singapore: Asia—Europe Foundation.

—— (2004) *"Asia-Europe: Do they Meet?* revisited," in Z. Mantaha and T. Tanaka (eds) *Enlarging European Union and Asia: 10th ASEF University, 22 May-5 June 2004, Tokyo, Japan*, Singapore: Asia-Europe Foundation.

Ricard, P. (2006) "L'Union européenne veut placer l'Asie au coeur de sa politique commerciale," *Le Monde*, 12 September. Available online at: www.bilaterals.org/article-print.php3?id_article=6022 (accessed 5 March 2007).

Richards, G. A. (1999a) "Challenging Asia-Europe relations from below? Civil society and the politics of inclusion and opposition," *Journal of the Asia–Pacific Economy*, 4: 146–70.

—— (1999b) "Civil society responses to the Asian economic crisis: Revisioning Asia-Europe relations from below," in Chyungly Lee (ed.) *Asia–Europe Cooperation after the 1997–1998 Asian Turbulence*, Aldershot, Hants: Ashgate.

Richardson, J. L. (1997) "Contending liberalisms," *European Journal of International Relations*, 3: 5–33.

Risse, T. (2000) "Let's argue! Communicative action in world politics," *International Organization*, 54: 1–40.

Robles, A. C. Jr. (2001) *ASEM and Asia–Europe Relations between Investment Promotion and the Financial Crisis*, Barcelona: Institut Universitari d'Estudis Europeus, Universitat Autònoma de Barcelona. Available online at: http://selene.uab.es/_cs_iuee/catala/obs/m_working.html (accessed 21 September 2007).

—— (2003a) "The ASEAN Regional Forum and the European Union as a security system and security actor," *Dialogue and Cooperation*, 2: 19–34.

—— (2003b) "On the limits of political dialogue: Interregionalism in the service of multilateralism? ASEM and the WTO," unpublished manuscript, De La Salle University – Manila.

—— (2004) *The Political Economy of Interregional Relations: ASEAN and the EU*, Aldershot, Hants: Ashgate.

Rocamora, J. (1999) "The 1997 financial crisis and Asian progressives," *ASEM Watch*, no. 48.

Rosand, E. (2003) "Security Council Resolution 1373, the Counter-Terrorism Committee and the fight against global terrorism," *American Journal of International Law*, 97: 333–41.

Ruggie, J. G. (1993) "Multilateralism: The anatomy of an institution," in J. G. Ruggie (ed.) *Multilateralism Matters: The Theory and Praxis of an International Institution*, New York: Columbia University Press.

Rüland, J. (1996) *The Asia-Europe Meeting [ASEM]: Towards a New Euro-Asian Relationship?* Rostock: Institut für Politik und Verwaltungswissenschaften, Universität Rostock.

—— (1998a) "ASEAN and the Asian crisis – repercussions on regional cooperation," paper presented at the Second Meeting of the European Association of Southeast Asian Studies (EUROSEAS), Hamburg, September.

—— (1998b) "The future of the ASEM process: Who, how, why and what," in W. Stokhof and P. van der Velde (eds) *ASEM: A Window of Opportunity*, London: Kegan P. International and the International Association of Asian Studies.

—— (2000) "ASEM and political dialogue," in Chong-wha Lee (ed.) *The Seoul 2000 Summit: The Way Ahead for the Asia-Europe Partnership*, Seoul: Korea Institute for International Economic Policy.

—— (2001) "ASEM – transregional forum at the crossroads," in W. Stokhof and P. van der Velde (eds) *Asian-European Perspectives: Developing the ASEM Process*, Richmond, Surrey: Curzon Press.

—— (2002) "The European Union as an international and transregional actor: Lessons for global governance from Europe's relations with Asia," paper presented at a conference on the EU in international affairs, Australian National University, July.

Rustin, C. (1999) "Habermas, discourse ethics and international justice," *Alternatives: Social Transformation and Humane Governance*, 24: 167–92.

Sachs, J. (1997) "IMF is a power unto itself," *The Financial Times*, 11 December.

Sánchez Rydelski, M. and Zonnekeyn, G. A. V. R. (1997) "The EC Trade Barriers Regulation – the EC's move towards a more aggressive market strategy," *Journal of World Trade*, 31: 147–60.

Sandholtz, W. (1999) "Globalization and the evolution of rules," in A. Prakash and J. A. Hart (eds) *Globalization and Governance*, London: Routledge.

Sandschneider, E. (2002) "China's diplomatic relations with the states of Europe," in R. L. Edmonds (ed.) *China and Europe Since 1978: A European Perspective*, Cambridge: Cambridge University Press.

Scherrer, C. and Greven, T. (1999) *Soziale Konditionalisierung des Welthandels: Die Instrumente Sozialklausel, Verhaltenskodex und Gütesiegel in der Diskussion: Gutachten im Auftrag der Friedrich-Ebert Stiftung*, Bonn: Friedrich-Ebert-Stiftung.

Schlesinger, P. and Kevin, D. (2000) "Can the European Union become a sphere of publics?" in E. O. Eriksen and J. E. Fossum (eds) *Democracy in the European Union: Integration Through Deliberation?* London: Routledge.

Schmidt, F. and Herberg, M. (2004) "Das ASEM People's Forum in Hanoi. Ist ein zivilgesellschaftlicher Diskurs in Vietnam möglich?" *Kurzberichte aus der internationalen Zusammenarbeit Asien und Pazifik Friedrich-Ebert-Stiftung*, September.

Seet-Cheng, M. (1994) "How can the obstacles to an improved EU presence be overcome?" presented at the European Commission – Financial Times Interactive Forum Towards a New European Economic Strategy for Asia, Brussels, October.

Segal, G. (1997) "Thinking strategically about ASEM: the subsidiarity question," *The Pacific Review*, 10: 124–34.

Senior Officials' Meeting on Trade and Investment [SOMTI] 1 (1996) *Chairman's Statement*, Brussels, 25 July.

—— 2 (1997) *Chairman's Statement*, Tokyo, 6 June.

—— 3 (1998) *Chairman's Statement*, Brussels, 5–6 February.

—— 4 (1999) *Co-Chairmen's Summary*, Singapore, 11–13 February.

—— 5 (1999) *Co-Chair's Summary*, Brussels, 7–8 July.

—— 6 (2000) *Chairman's Statement*, Seoul, 13 May.

—— 7 (2001) *Co-Chair's Summary*, Brussels, 4–5 July.

—— 8 (2002) *Chair's Statement*, Bali, 17 July.

—— 9 (2003) *Chair's Statement*, Paris, 6 June.

—— 10 (2005) *Chairman's Summary*, Qingdao, China, 18–19 July.

Sideri, S. (1996) "Regional integration in the Asia-Pacific region and its implications for Europe," *Journal of European Studies Chulalongkorn University*, 4: 53–94.

Siroën, J. M. (1996) "Développement économique et développement social: l'incidence d'une clause sociale," in *Les Relations entre le Développement Economique et le Développement Social: Incidences d'un socle de normes sociales minimum*, Paris: Ministère de l'Industrie.

Snitwongse, K. (1998) "Thirty years of ASEAN: achievements through political cooperation," *The Pacific Review*, 11: 183–94.

Société Française pour le Droit International (1999) *Un accord multilatéral sur l'investissement: D'un forum de négociation à l'autre?* Paris: Editions A. Pedone.

Soesastro, H. and Nuttall, S. (1997) "The institutional dimension," in Council for Asia-Europe Cooperation, *The Rationale and Common Agenda for Asia-Europe Cooperation. CAEC Task Force Reports*, Tokyo: Japan Center for International Exchange.

Solidum, E. (1983) "An ASEAN perspective on the decision-making process in the European Economic Community," in P. V. Quisumbing and B. B. Domingo (eds) *EEC and ASEAN: Two Regional Community Experiences*, Manila: Foreign Service Institute and University of the Philippines Law Center.

—— (1997) "Prospects of security in ASEAN," in M. L. Aranal-Sereno and J. S. Santiago (eds) *The ASEAN: Thirty Years and Beyond*, Quezon City: Institute of International Legal Studies, University of the Philippines Law Center.

Strange, S. (1994) "Wake up Krasner! The world *has* changed," *Review of International Political Economy*, 1: 209–20.

Stuart, L. (2003a) "Cancun diary," Christian Aid, 14 September. Available online at: www.christianaid.org.uk/cancun/030914htm (accessed 12 April 2005).

Stuart, L. (2003b) "Cancun diary," Christian Aid, 15 September. Available online at: www.christianaid.org.uk/cancun/030915htm (accessed 12 April 2005).

Stubbs, R. (1998) "Asia-Pacific regionalism versus globalization: competing forms of capitalism," in W. D. Coleman and G. R. D. Underhill (eds) *Regionalism and Global Economic Integration: Europe, Asia and the Americas*, London: Routledge.

Stückelberger, C. (1996) "Sozialklauseln im internationalen Handel: Wirtschaftsethische Kriterien," *Aussenwirtschaft. Schweizerische Zeitschrift für internationale Wirtschaftsbeziehungen*, 51: 75–100.

Sundberg, D. and Vermulst, E. (2001) "The EC Trade Barriers Regulation: obstacle to trade?" *Journal of World Trade*, 35: 989–1014.

Tan Hong (2002) *Implementation Completion Report ASEM Trust Fund 021697 Malaysia: Enhancing Industrial and Export Competitiveness (Bank-executed)*, Washington, DC: The World Bank.

Tang Shaocheng (2003) "The EU's Taiwan policy in the light of its China policy," *Asia-Europe Journal*, 1: 511–25.

Third World Network, Oxfam International, Public Services International, WWF International, The Center for International Environmental Law, Focus on the Global South, The Institute for Agriculture and Trade Policy, The Africa Trade Network, and The International Gender and Trade Network (2003) *Memorandum on the Need to Improve Iinternal Transparency and Participation in the WTO: Submitted to the Director General, WTO; Minister of Trade, Mexico and Chairperson, WTO Fifth Ministerial Conference; Chairman, General Council, WTO; Chairman, Trade Negotiations Committee, WTO; Permanent Representatives of Member States, WTO*, Penang: Third World Network, July.

Tobin, J. (1996) "Prologue," in M. ul Haq, I. Kaul and I. Grunberg (eds) *The Tobin Tax: Coping with Financial Volatility*, New York: Oxford University Press.

Todorov, T. (1982) *La Conquête de l'Amérique. La question de l'autre*, Paris: Editions du Seuil.

Togo Kazuhiko (2004) "Japan and ASEM," in W. Stokhof, P. van der Velde and Yeo Lay Hwee (eds) *The Eurasian Space: Far More than Two Continents*, Singapore: Institute of Southeast Asian Studies.

Tong Gia-Dong (2001) "The European Union and China: the benefits of openness in international economic integration," in P. W. Preston and J. Gilson (eds) *The European Union and East Asia – Interregional Linkages in a Changing Global System*, Cheltenham: Edward Elgar.

Ton Sinh Thanh (1998) "The Asia-Europe Meeting: ASEAN and EU perspectives," unpublished research essay, Carleton University.

Trade Facilitation Action Plan [TFAP] (1998a) *Framework for the Trade Facilitation Action Plan*, Makuhari, Japan, 27–8 September.

—— (1998b) *Consolidated and Prioritised List of Major Generic Trade Barriers Among ASEM Partners*.

—— (1998c) *Consolidated "Deliverables"/Concrete Goals 1998–2000*.

—— (2000) *Evaluation of the ASEM Trade Facilitation Action Plan 1998–2000*, Seoul, May.

—— (2002) *A Synthesis of Reports by Some ASEM Members on Measures Taken to Address the Consolidated and Prioritised List of the Major Generic Trade Barriers among ASEM Partners*.

Trichet, J. C. (2004) "The international financial architecture: where do we stand?" Dinner speech at the Conference "Dollars, Debts and Deficits – 60 Years after Bretton Woods," Madrid, June.

Tsutsumibayashi, K. (2005) "Fusion of horizons or confusion of horizons? Intercultural dialogue and its risks," *Global Governance: A Review of Multilateralism and International Organizations*, 11: 103–14.

van der Geest, W. (2000) "Comments on 'Testing the subsidiarity questions for ASEM,' by Chong-wha Lee," in Chong-wha Lee (ed) *The Seoul (2000) Summit: The Way Ahead for the Asia-Europe Partnership*, Seoul: Korea Institute for International Economic Policy.

Van Haute, P. (2000) "Concluding remarks," presented at the Second EU-ASEAN Think Tank Dialogue, Strasbourg, October.

Von Hauff, M. (2002) "The significance of social protection for the ASEM dialogue," in K. Fritsche (ed.) *Social Policies and the ASEM Process. International Workshop, Berlin (March 4–5, 2002)*, Essen: Asienstiftung.

Waever, O. (2000) "The EU as a security actor: reflections from a pessimistic constructivist on post-sovereign security orders," in M. Kelstrup and M. C. Williams (eds) *International Relations Theory and the Politics of European Integration: Power, Security and Community*, London: Routledge.

Wallace, W. and Soogil Young (2004) *Asia-Europe: Global Governance Challenge to Cooperation: Our Shared Agenda*, Council on Asia-Europe Cooperation Task Force 2003–04.

Wallach, L. M. (1998) "Le nouveau manifeste du capitalisme mondial," *Le Monde diplomatique*, 527: 22.

Walter, A. (2001) "NGOs, business and international investment: the multilateral agreement on investment, Seattle and beyond," *Global Governance*, 7: 51–74.

Warkentin, C. and Mingst, K. (2000) "International institutions, the state and global civil society in the age of the World Wide Web," *Global Governance*, 6: 237–58.

Watanabe, A. (2001) "Japan's position on human rights in Asia," in S. J. Maswood (ed.) *Japan and East Asian Regionalism*, London: Routledge.

Wendt, A. (1987) "The agent–structure problem in international relations theory," *International Organization*, 41: 335–70.

—— (1991) "Bridging the theory/meta-theory gap in international relations," *Review of International Studies*, 17: 382–3.

—— (1992) "Anarchy is what states make of it," *International Organization*, 46: 391–425.

—— (1998) *Social Theory of International Politics*, Cambridge: Cambridge University Press.

Wermasubun, D. S. (2003) *Privatization of the Indonesian Water Sector*, Jakarta: The Business Watch Indonesia.

Wesley, M. (1999) "The Asian crisis and the adequacy of regional institutions," *Contemporary Southeast Asia*, 21: 54–73.

Wilkinson, E. (1990) *Japan Versus the West: Image and Reality*, Harmondsworth, Middlesex: Penguin Books.

Woodman, S. (2002) "Words obscure actions: human rights research in China," *GSC Quarterly*. Available online at: www.ssrc.org/programs/gsc/gsc_quarterly/newsletter6/content/woodman2 (accessed 23 October 2004).

World Bank, n.d. *Implementation Completion Memo: ASEM TF#020611; Monitoring the Regional Implementation of Structural Reforms and Deregulation Program.*

—— (2003) *Asian Financial Crisis Response Fund 1: Completion Report*, Washington, DC: World Bank.

Yahuda, M. (1998) "Europe and China," in H. W. Maull, G. Segal and J. Wanandi (eds) *Europe and the Asia-Pacific*, London: Routledge.

Yano, K. (1999) "Thirty years of being a respondent in anti-dumping proceedings: Abuse of economic relief can have a negative impact on competition policy," *Journal of World Trade*, 33: 31–47.

Yeo Lay Hwee (2002) *ASEM: The Asia-Europe Meeting Process: From Sexy Summit to Strong Partnership?* Copenhagen: Danish Institute of International Affairs.

—— (2003) "ASEM: from summit diplomacy to regime creation," unpublished thesis, National University of Singapore.

—— (2004) "The ASEM story ... so far," *ASEM Research Platform Newsbrief.*

Yoo Choong-Mo (2000) "ASEM can't resolve bilateral trade conflicts, report says," *The Korea Herald*, 19 October, p. 8.

Youngs, R. (2001) *The European Union and the Promotion of Democracy: Europe's Mediterranean and Asian Policies*, Oxford: Oxford University Press.

Zhang Yunling (1998) "Europe and China," in H. W. Maull, G. Segal and J. Wanandi (eds) *Europe and the Asia-Pacific*, London: Routledge.

Zhao Chenggen and McGough, S. (2001) "China: the politics of 'rational authoritarianism,'" in P. W. Preston and J. Gilson (eds) *The European Union and East Asia – Interregional Linkages in a Changing Global System*, Cheltenham: Edward Elgar.

Zhao Gancheng (1999) "Assessing China's impact on Asia-Europe relations," in W. Stokhof and P. van der Velde (eds) *ASEM: A Window of Opportunity*, London: Kegan Paul International.

Index

For Product Safety Concerns and Information please contact our EU
representative GPSR@taylorandfrancis.com
Taylor & Francis Verlag GmbH, Kaufingerstraße 24, 80331 München, Germany

www.ingramcontent.com/pod-product-compliance
Lightning Source LLC
Chambersburg PA
CBHW050438280326
41932CB00013BA/2168

9 780415 540919